Music
and
Miracles

Other books and tapes by Don G. Campbell

Books

The Roar of Silence, Quest Books, 1989
Music, Physician for Times to Come, Quest Books, 1991
100 Ways to Improve Teaching with Your Voice and Music,
Zephyr Press, 1992
Introduction to the Musical Brain, Magna Music, 1983
Master Teacher, Nadia Boulanger, Pastoral Press, 1984
Rhythms of Learning, Zephyr Press, 1991

Sound Cassettes

The Power of Overtone Singing, IMHE, 1992
Accelerating Learning with Your Voice and Music, Zephyr Press, 1992
Healing Yourself With Your Own Voice, Sounds True, 1990
Healing Powers of Tone & Chant, Quest Books, 1990
Cosmic Classics, Spirit Music, 1988
Runes, Spirit Music, 1986
Crystal Rainbows, Spirit Music, 1986
Lightning on the Moon, IMHE, 1985
Angels, IMHE, 1985
Crystal Meditations, Spirit Music, 1985
The Roar of Silence, cassette book, Quest 1993

Video

The Roar of Silence, Quest, 1992

Music
and
Miracles

A companion to *Music: Physician for Times to Come*

Compiled by
DON
CAMPBELL

*This publication made possible with
the assistance of the Kern Foundation*

QUEST BOOKS
The Theosophical Publishing House
Wheaton, Ill. U.S.A.
Madras, India/London, England

The Theosophical Publishing House
P.O. Box 270
Wheaton, IL 60189-0270

A publication of the Theosophical Publishing House,
a department of the Theosophical Society in America.

Library of Congress Cataloging-in-Publication Data

Music and miracles / Don Campbell, editor.
   p. cm.
   Includes index.
   ISBN 0-8356-0683-X (pbk.) : $14.00
   1. Music therapy.   2. Music, Influence of.   I. Campbell, Don G.
ML3920.M876   1992
155.9'115 — dc20   92-50145
                                             CIP
                                             MN

9 8 7 6 5 4 3 2 1 * 92 93 94 95 96 97 98 99

This edition is printed on acid-free paper that meets the
American National Standards Institute Z39.48 Standard

Printed in the United States of America by Bookcrafters

I AM Music

I am Music, most ancient of the arts. I am more than ancient; I am eternal. Even before life began upon this earth, I was here—in the winds and the waves. When the first trees and flowers and grasses appeared, I was among them. And when humanity came, I at once became the most delicate, most subtle and most powerful medium for the expression of emotions.

In all ages I have inspired people with hope, kindled their love, given a voice to their joys, cheered them on to valorous deeds, and soothed them in times of despair. I have played a great part in the drama of life, whose end and purpose is the complete perfection of human nature. Through my influence, humanity has been uplifted, sweetened and refined. With the aid of humanity, I have become a Fine Art. I have a myriad of voices and instruments.

I am in the hearts of all and on their tongues, in all lands among all peoples, the ignorant and unlettered know me, not less than the rich and the learned. For I speak to All, in a language that all can feel. Even the deaf hear me, if they but listen to the voices of their own souls. I am the food of love. I have taught people gentleness and peace; and I have led them onward to heroic deeds. I am comfort for the lonely, and I harmonize the discord of crowds. I am a necessary luxury to all. **I am MUSIC.**

Anonymous

To the memory of Carr P. Collins, Jr., whose foresight and inspiration taught me how to sense the everlasting miracles held in sound

Contents

Foreword:
A World of Tangible Sound
KEN CAREY

Students in physics classes often conduct experiments with pure tones, observing their effects on various media such as sand, oil, and water. Participating in these on occasion, I have seen sand arrange itself in precise geometric formations when the bow of a violin was drawn across the tin plate on which it was resting. I have seen certain tones cause oil floating on the surface of water to coagulate into cell-like configurations that seemed to grow and divide like amoebas as the tone's pitch was slowly raised. I have seen tiny grains of salt stand one upon the other and dance like human figures as they responded to a vibrating surface beneath them.

Physicists, attempting to determine the precise nature of this physical stuff that we call matter, have probed deeper and deeper into the realms of atomic and subatomic behavior, only to find that there is nothing there, at least no "thing" in the sense in which we normally think of matter. They describe the tiniest subatomic particles as "interference patterns of various sound frequencies." They call them "nodes of resonance."

The nucleus of each atom is made up of these nodes of resonance. Each atom is itself vibrating at a phenomenal rate of up to ten to the fourteenth power times per second, emitting a single note about twenty octaves *above* the range of our hearing. Seismographs pick up minor but consistent tremors of the earth, with vibration periods every 53.1 and 54.7 minutes. These mini-earthquakes produce a tone about twenty octaves *below* the range of our hearing. Existing midway between the subatomic sopranos and the planetary basses, human beings inhabit a world of audible sound. Perhaps Pythagoras was on to something twenty-five hundred years ago when he suggested that matter is actually "frozen music."

Even the electrochemical activity of the brain is directed and organized by subtle wave vibrations, so that our five physical senses are each rooted in vibration. Perception of light is a vibratory event. When you glance for a single second at the yellow leaves of an autumnal elm, the dye molecules in the retina of your eye vibrate five hundred trillion times. Vibration is found at the root of every phenomenon; but in our cultural bound perception of the world around us, not all sounds affect us equally.

There are discharged sounds that deplete human energy as well as charged sounds that bring strength and vitality. The power of these charged sounds is illustrated by Benedictine monks who can go for years on no more than three hours sleep per night *provided they chant six to eight hours each day*. When the periods of their chanting are shortened, their need for sleep increases proportionately.

The same mechanism that allows us to hear a portion of the sound spectrum provides us with our sense of balance. The very same ear with which we listen to our world provides us with our alignment to the earth's gravity.

At the fluid point of balance between time and eternity, our mind-brain faces the opportunity of replicating all creation in specified dimensional terms. When resonance occurs, we sense the creative first sound with every breath and feel a timeless purpose with every beat of the heart. Within us, around us, the music of the spheres unfolds in rhythms celestial and melodies terrestrial. More than just the hills are alive with music. Matter and light themselves are secondary aspects of sound. The phenomenal structure inherent in every tone emerges as the first expression of reality formation.

In the beginning was the word, and the word was with God and the Word was God.

John 1:1

In the beginning was the creative sound, the primal tone, that contained within it every sound, symphony, harmony and melody, every pattern and structure ever to be. The Word that *was* with God has not ceased to be. This very moment it holds, suspended within its vibratory magnificence, every atom, molecule, cell and organism. It sings the very earth into being. The sun, the moon and the planets share in a symphony of the heavens that includes every comet, every asteroid and star-system in our galaxy—and in a billion others. In this beginning *is* the Word. The Word *is* with God. And the Word *is* God.

The Word brings each of us into dimensional expression. *Music and Miracles* brings to mind this dimensional and transformational expression of sound and music. Here are the stories, dreams and possibilities for music in the future. Miracles, mysteries of the music of the spheres, are everywhere. Listen, listen!

Acknowledgments

The compiler wishes to thank Shirley Nicholson and John White of Quest Books for their support, clarity and vision. The authors are gratefully acknowledged for their devotion and skills in bringing music into a new focus for the future.

Special thanks to the staff of the Institute for Music, Health and Education and the students of Naropa Institute in Boulder, Colorado, for their commentaries and insight on how to present these new paradigms of music and sound.

And ultimately, appreciation to the nurses, doctors, psychologists and their patients who have experienced the transformational uses of sound. Without their questions, doubts, encouragement and transformations, there would be no anticipation of greater miracles.

Contributing Authors

JEANNE ACHTERBERG, PH.D., has received international recognition for her research in medicine and psychology. A faculty member for eleven years at Southwestern Medical School, University of Texas Health Science Center, she is currently a Professor of Psychology at the Institute of Transpersonal Psychology and on the Executive Faculty at Saybrook Institute. She also serves as a research consultant and advisor to foundations and government agencies and is a director of the Bear Foundation for Research in Multicultural Healing Practices. She has authored over one hundred papers and five books, including *Imagery in Healing: Shamanism and Modern Medicine, Woman as Healer,* and *Rituals of Healing.*

JUDITH B. BELK is a certified speech-language pathologist and audiologist who also holds credentials in developmental psychology and special education. Her clinical and research work encompasses acoustic therapy programs and the enhancement of listening in academic, personal, social, and vocational settings. She provides therapy programs and workshops on the mainland and in Hawaii, working collaboratively with multidisciplinary colleagues.

LANCE W. BRUNNER is Associate Professor of Music History at the University of Kentucky, where he has taught since 1976. He held a Kellogg National Fellowship from 1985–88, during which time he investigated the links between music and health. He cofounded with Arthur Harvey the Music for Health Services Foundation in 1986. He has published extensively on medieval and twentieth-century music topics.

KENNETH BRUSCIA is Professor of Music Therapy at Temple University where he has taught for the last fifteen years. He has had extensive clinical experience and has authored articles and books, including *Improvisational Models of Music Therapy, Defining Music Therapy,* and *Case Studies in Music Therapy.* He is a certified music therapist and a fellow in Guided Imagery and Music.

DON G. CAMPBELL is a teacher, trainer, and musician, who travels throughout the world. He is founder and director of the Institute for Music, Health, and Education in Boulder, Colorado. He also serves on the faculty of the Naropa Institute and is a leader in the emerging field of sonic healing, a therapeutic mode gaining increasing recognition in traditional medicine. *Music: Physician for Times to Come, The Roar of Silence, Rhythms of Learning, Introduction to the Musical Brain, 100 Ways to Improve Teaching with your Voice and Music,* and *Master Teacher, Nadia Boulanger* are books Campbell has written. His extensive discography as an artist and composer includes *Cosmic Classics, Crystal Meditations, Crystal Rainbows, Runes, Lightning on the Moon, Angels, Heal Yourself with Your Own Voice,* and *Healing with Tone and Chant.* His educational background includes studies with Nadia Boulanger and Robert Casadesus at the Fontainebleau Conservatory of Music. He taught music and humanities for seven years at St. Mary's International School in Tokyo. He was appointed to the Guggenheim Education Project in Chicago, which is developing an innovative curriculum for inner-city schools.

KEN CAREY is founder and administrator of Greenwood School. He is the author of *Starseed: The Third Millennium* and *Return of the Bird Tribes* and is known internationally for his lectures and workshops.

PAT MOFFITT COOK is an award-winning film and television composer. She has traveled worldwide, collecting primitive and ethnic instruments and recording and taking part in musical celebrations and rituals. She holds the M.A. in Music Composition from Southern Methodist University and is currently a doctoral candidate in Music at the University of Washington. She is director and editor of *Open Ear,* a publication dedicated to sound and music in health and education, a candidate for Fellow of the Helen Bonny method of Guided Imagery and Music (GIM), and a mentor at the Institute for Music, Health and Education in Boulder, Colorado.

DAVID DARLING is a cellist, teacher, composer, and recording artist. A former member of the Paul Winter Consort, he has performed with such diverse artists as Bobby McFerrin, Jan Garbarek, Terje Rypdal, Ralph Towner, Peter, Paul and Mary, The Western Wind, Spyro Gyra, Pilobolus, and Chungliang Al Huang. Recently, he collaborated as solo cellist and improvising artist on Wim Wenders' *Until the End of the World,* starring William Hurt. His most recent recording is a solo, produced by E.C.M. records.

LARRY DOSSEY, M.D., is a physician of internal medicine affiliated with the Dallas Diagnostic Association and former Chief of Staff of Medical City Dallas Hospital. He lectures widely in the United States and abroad. In 1988 he delivered the annual Mahatma Gandhi Memorial Lecture in New Delhi, India, the only physician ever invited to do so. He is author of *Space, Time & Medicine, Beyond Illness, Recovering the Soul,* and *Meaning & Medicine.*

DONALD M. EPSTEIN, D.C., graduated from New York Chiropractic College in 1977. He established two practices in New York, in which he was actively involved until late 1991. After thousands of clinical experiences, Dr. Epstein began writing articles and giving seminars on what became known as Network Chiropractic. He serves on the Board of Regents and Extension Faculty of Sherman College of Straight Chiropractic and is president of the Association for Network Chiropractic.

REV. VIRGIL C. FUNK is a Roman Catholic priest of the Diocese of Richmond, Virginia, and is the founder and president of The National Association of Pastoral Musicians.

RUTH-INGE HEINZE is Research Associate at the Center for Southeast Asia Studies, University of California, Berkeley. For over thirty-two years, she has conducted fieldwork on shamanism, alternate states of consciousness, and healing in Europe, the

United States, and Asia. She holds licenses in Reiki I and II, acupuncture, and Chinese herbal medicine. Her books include *Shamans of the Twentieth Century, Trance and Healing in Southeast Asia Today,* and *Tham Khwan—How to Contain the Essence of Life.*

LORIN HOLLANDER was a child prodigy and has been a professional concert pianist for most of his life. He has lectured worldwide on the creative process, arts in education, and music and its relationship to human knowledge and wisdom. He has performed all over the world with major orchestras, and has been in residence at many colleges and universities.

JEAN HOUSTON, PH.D., is internationally known as a seminar leader and consultant on human development. A philosopher and cultural historian, Dr. Houston and her husband Dr. Robert Masters are co-directors of the Foundation for Mind Research in Pomona, New York. A past president of the American Association for Humanistic Psychology, she has written or coauthored twelve books, including *The Possible Human, The Search for the Beloved, Godseed,* and *Life Force.* She guides two schools in spiritual studies based on the ancient mystery schools.

BARBARA MARX HUBBARD is a futurist and a "social architect." She is the cofounder of the New World Design Center based in Boulder, Colorado. She conducts seminars in high-synergy processes for businesses and communities. She has written five books, chaired Soviet-American Citizens Summits in Washington, D.C. and Moscow, and is a founding member of the World Future Society.

BONNIE INSULL is cofounder with David Darling of *Music for People,* a national network dedicated to the joy of making music. For ten years, she was flutist with the classical chamber music ensemble, The Apple Hill Chamber Players, and on the music faculty of Dartmouth College. She presently performs, composes, and teaches music and improvisation at Keene State College and is editor of *Music for People's* quarterly newsletter *Connections.*

KHEN RINPOCHE, THE VENERABLE LUNGRI NAMGYAL, was Abbot of the Gyuto Tantric College during the 1970s. He has traveled to the West several times with the Gyuto Tantric Choir.

KITARO is a Japanese master of heart melodies. Originally a pop-rock musician, he gradually developed intuitive music for expressing the simplicity of nature, emotions, and awareness. He has composed music for dozens of albums, including *Silk Road*. He plays ancient Japanese ritual drums and each year leads musical meditations on Mt. Fuji for world peace.

ARDEN MAHLBERG, PH.D., is a psychologist in private practice in Madison, Wisconsin, where he is also the director of the Integral Psychology Center. He has published in the areas of archetypes and morphic resonance, Jungian personality type theory, and the resolution of somatic conflicts. A strong emphasis of his work is therapeutic methodology for evoking specific archetypes as well as methods for reducing archetypal influence.

MELINDA C. MAXFIELD, PH.D., specializes in crosscultural health care methodologies and research on the physical and psychological effects of percussion. She is executive director of The Bear Foundation, which supports interdisciplinary approaches to research in applied medicine and is vice president of the Maxfield Foundation, which supports cancer research. She is on the board of the Association for Transpersonal Psychology and the Foundation for Shamanic Studies.

RON MINSON, M.D., is a board certified psychiatrist and a graduate of UCLA Medical School. He has directed psychiatric and behavioral science activities for major medical institutions, including Mercy Hospital and Presbyterian Medical Center in Denver, Colorado. He has also served as a psychiatric consultant to various mental health organizations in Denver and Arizona, as well as maintaining a private psychiatric practice. In 1991, he established the Denver Tomatis Centre.

SHIRLEY NICHOLSON is Senior Editor of Quest Books. She has lectured around the world on theosophical ideas and is the author of *Ancient Wisdom, Modern Insight.* She is also compiler of two anthologies, *The Goddess Reawakening,* and *Shamanism,* and is the co-compiler of *Karma: Rhythmic Return to Harmony,* and *Gaia's Hidden Life.*

LAURIE RUGENSTEIN, M.M.T., R.M.T.-B.C., is the Associate Director of the Institute for Music, Health and Education in Boulder, Colorado, where she has served as mentor to over two hundred toning students. She holds the M.A. in Music Therapy from Southern Methodist University and maintains a private practice in music therapy, specializing in life-challenging illnesses. She also facilitates women's drumming-chanting circles and sweat lodges.

THERESE SCHROEDER-SHEKER is Associate Professor of Music and Program Chair at Regis University in Denver, Colorado. A harpist, singer, and performer on various early instruments, she founded and is director of the Chalice of Repose Project, which uses music to support the spirituality of a conscious death. An international concert and recording artist, she has released five solo recordings, including *The Luminous Wound* (1992), and has twelve television and film scores, and numerous guest-artist performances in the United States and Europe to her credit. She has won an Emmy and other awards. She publishes frequently on eleventh and twelfth-century music manuscripts and on themes of medieval medicine, women mystics, and musicology.

SARA JANE STOKES, PH.D., R.M.T., is co-director of Mid-Atlantic GIM Training Institute in Virginia Beach, Virginia. She is a fellow of the Association for Music and Imagery and a certified GIM trainer. She is past Director of Music Therapy at Saint-Mary-of-the-Woods College and is presently adjunct professor at Duquesne University in Pittsburgh. Her specializations in GIM include leadership development, addictions and recovery, and pain management. In her doctoral work, she explored a creative approach to music and healing called music synergy.

PATRICIA WARMING is a Jungian analyst in private practice in Seattle, Washington. She received her graduate degrees from Princeton Theological Seminary and the C. G. Jung Institute in Zurich, Switzerland. She is a member of the Association of Graduate Analytical Psychologists of the Zurich Institute, Jungian Analysts/North Pacific, and the International Association for Analytical Psychology. She is a founding member and past president of the C. G. Jung Institute in Denver, Colorado.

DON WRIGHT, M.A., is a staff psychotherapist with New Life Therapies, clinical associate of the Milton Erickson Institute, and a member of the board of directors and faculty of The Institute of Human Vitality in Albuquerque, New Mexico. He has published articles in *Univercolian, Southwest Source,* and *The Sacred Earth News.*

Prelude:
Music and Miracles

Music has a long reputation of invoking religious states, healing the diseased, comforting the sorrowful, energizing the weak, soothing the stressed and even raising the dead. Drumming, harmonic singing, chanting, lyric harp playing and rapturous organ music all create altered states of perception and evoke awakenings. Spontaneous remission of physical disorders and moments of spiritual insight and bliss are important parts of our natural abilities and instinct, though foreign to the overly logical twentieth century mind.

Ten years ago today I underwent a powerful physical, mental and spiritual transformation that altered my outlook on my musical profession. Coming from a spontaneous and joyous musical background in south Texas, at age thirteen I entered the most rigorous and disciplined music study in France with the renowned teachers Nadia Boulanger and Robert Casadesus. After university study in conducting and organ performance, for nearly a decade I lived in Haiti and Japan where my traditional training was greatly expanded. I saw the drumming, singing and dancing of Haiti induce states of deep trance and transformation. I saw hundreds of people enter into altered states of consciousness. Sometimes bleeding would cease, physical diseases would instantly heal and endless psychological dilemmas would balance. These experiences did not fit into my previous perception of music and life, so I had to put them into a separate envelope of consciousness.

In Japan, I began to hear completely new forms of music. *Gagaku,* the ancient court music of the emperor, is clearly the oldest form of written music in the world, but it sounded new, fresh and potent. I

1

heard stories about how people were "refined" and cured when they heard these sounds. I knew I was experiencing strong sensations in my body through this music.

I had a very strong reaction to the smog in Tokyo in 1971. Western doctors said I had a type of photochemical poisoning that created life-threatening asthmatic attacks, that my only choice was to leave Japan. I knew a Japanese woman, a member of the Theosophical Society, who sent me to a Manchurian doctor who treated allergies. When I saw him he asked me simply to place the palms of my hands on top of his for two minutes. I experienced warm energy and electricity in my hands, and instantly my breathing became deep and free. He said he could help me if I would come to him twice a week for two months while he "put the missing tones" back into my body. During each visit to his office I soaked my feet in hot water for five minutes and then lay on my back while he electrically burned herbs in a "sound lamp" for ten minutes. I left with a slight fever each day. Within two months the attacks stopped, never to return, and I stayed in Japan six more years. I did not question the doctor about the electric herbal sounds, but this experience went into that separate envelope of consciousness that I had created in Haiti.

After the years in Asia and Europe, I returned to Texas to work in traditional education and in religious music. Performance standards were high and teaching techniques were finely developed. But the mystical power of sound was never considered, spoken of, or experienced openly.

Gradually I became ill and developed a degenerative bone condition as well as a lump in my left lung. By New Year's Eve ten years ago, I was depressed, outraged and in a state where music, sound and art were no longer my most intimate friends. While writing my New Year's resolutions, I remembered the power of transformation of the sounds of Haiti and Japan. I began to chant, tone and pound my hand upon the desk. I kept on and on, knowing that many unsounded pains and emotions were being released. After nearly an hour of the improvised soundings and movement, I entered deeply into tone. I felt the power of one tone, one sound, so full, so complete, so deeply, that I lost track of time. Nearly twelve hours passed as I held a tone all night and into the morning. The sound was like an open mouthed hum, powerfully vibrating my body, massaging me from the inside out.

I continued this toning for the next twenty-four hours while I listened to Bach's *St. Matthew Passion,* the music of Terry Riley, sacred Indian ragas and Gregorian Chant. My body and mind became one vibrating wave, and a strange sense of completion and fullness began to emerge. No trace of the lump in my lung or the pain in my bones ever recurred. Tone and sound opened my body and mind to the importance of that "separate envelope of consciousness" that could be called miracle.

In these past ten years, tone has become highly significant in my work at the Institute for Music, Health and Education in Boulder. Music has become a far more poetic and elegant envelope to carry the energy that is inside sound, and the voice has proven to be the secret self-healer.

In preparing this anthology, I became aware that many of my colleagues from the medical, musical, religious and therapeutic worlds became professionally uncomfortable when the word "miracle" was mentioned. If "miracle" had not been in the title, they would have gladly contributed and, I believe, described healing and curative experiences through logical, interesting and sometimes amusing anecdotes. False hopes, quick cures, quackery and lack of professional education do haunt history. Overtly emotional exaggerations of personal experiences are natural for many people, and even personal memories are often altered by subjective recollection. Yet, while it is important to be cautious and grounded, there is little need to block out the miraculous significance of music's role in healing and transformation.

Because of the tremendous knowledge gained in the past century, some events that seemed miraculous to our ancestors are now commonly understood. What appear to our Western technological society to be folk medicines, primitive ritual and romantic "new age" exaggerations may be as clear and prescriptive to second and third world nations as our present medical therapies are to us. No doubt, the use of x-ray and antibiotics would seem miraculous, perhaps ridiculous, to ancient healers.

Miracles are special events that cannot be explained. C. S. Lewis defined "miracle" as an interference with nature by a supernatural power. Saint Augustine's comments about such events are wise and appropriate to contemporary thought: "Miracles happen, not in opposition to nature, but in opposition to what we know of nature." These uncommon events defy the natural logic of the senses and impose a rare juxtaposition of awareness on the modern mind. Such

3

moments of great astonishment, wonder and marvel are common to
the arts.

Once the mystery of a miracle is explained, it is no longer "miraculous." Once the process, the formula and the results of a spontaneous shift in reality are explained, miracle becomes science, religion, a method or a reference. But the basic quest of science,
medicine and religious art is for transformation. If we negate the
miraculous, thus blinding our awareness to spontaneous shifts in
reality, we have greatly limited the scope of scientific process.

All of the saints are credited with miracles. Without an extraordinary circumstance, no canonization could have taken place. But
certified miracles are rare today, though anecdotes of unexplainable
curations are numerous. To call them miracles in a contemporary
context creates doubt, dilemma, cynicism and fear. The Catholic
Church has been the most meticulous recorder of seemingly miraculous events. Usually, by the time the Church investigates a miraculous cure or mystical happening, all its witnesses have died. Somehow, it is easier to analyze written and historical evaluations than it is
to appraise the account of a witness to an exceptional event. The
Church's careful observation of cures and miracles has given medicine and other forms of contemporary therapy new components to
hasten the restoration of mental and physical health.

It is rare to find the word "miracle" in the New Testament. "Marvel" (*thaumasion*) is rare, but "power" (*dunamis*) and "sign" (*semeion*) are more common. In ancient and medieval times, miracles
were common and a primary part of the socio-religious experience.
In Asian as well as Western cultures, the miraculous is often connected with holy springs, caves, trees, shrines and special mountains. Repetitive prayers, mantras, tones, chants and songs are often
the invocation of healing. After a holy event roaring sounds, hymns,
loud trumpets and "angelic" chords were often experienced. The
healing place, the holy priest or "healer" and the pilgrimage to that
physical and psychological place of surrender are a natural part of the
archetypal pattern of empowerment and curation.

With the exception of the Mormons and the Native Americans,
miracle places generally have not been a part of the North American
psyche. We travel to special places where miracles happen: Jerusalem, Lourdes, Mount Athos, Mexico and the Philippines.

Miracles defy the law of logic, professionalism and our "com-
monsense" modern insight. We seldom stand in awe of an event.

When phenomenal events occurred in Fatima, Lourdes, or Medjugorje a magnitude of questions arose. We respond to miracles with a full spectrum of interpretations, intercessions, assumptions, beliefs and projections. Our education insists that we doubt before we believe, that we pacify the left brain before we feel. Yet as we look more closely into the worlds of vibration, pattern, coding and energy pulsation in light and sound, we see mysteries that insist that we bypass much of our local, simple-logic, left-brain manner of inquiry. We are beginning to understand that intelligence is everywhere in the body, everywhere in nature and perhaps even everywhere in the universe.

Music, before the time of radio, television and home stereo systems, had quite a powerful effect on the nervous system and the physical body. But currently we are so habituated to sounds that it is miraculous to have even a few days a year to be in a natural sound environment. The earth as well as the physical body is noisy. When sounds of automobiles, appliances, computers and air vents are removed from our habitats, the physical body relaxes and responds to sound differently. Rather than taking in sounds, the ear's natural function may be to filter out sounds, to discriminate sounds and to charge the brain. What we hear has profound effects on us at many levels.

I have seen many unexplained events associated with music. After half an hour of singing "Bajans" with Satya Sai Baba in Madras a few years ago, I saw the miraculous *vibhuti* (sacred ash) appear in his hand. He made this magic powder, as well as rings, talismans, and gems, appear thousands of times during the past thirty years. I have seen eight-year-old girls in Bali miraculously move and dance to sounds in perfect unison with no preparation. I have witnessed Alzheimer patients who could not be reached in any other way respond clearly to questions asked through song. I have seen comatose patients regain awareness through response to music. Dyslexic and autistic children have learned languages, new ways to spell, new physical movement patterns through the innovative sound stimulation of Dr. Alfred Tomatis' invention, the electronic ear. I have seen that music can produce seeming miracles.

In my first anthology, *Music: Physician for Times to Come* (Quest, 1991), dozens of researchers, musicians, physicians and therapists defined what we know about the properties of music in the healing process. The purpose of this book is to explore the unexplained

5

mysteries of curation, healing and transformation caused by organized or spontaneously improvised rhythmic sounds. The writings of some of the most visionary listeners, researchers, healers and musicians have been brought together. The maturity of the ideas and techniques in this book brings a new awareness of the miracles of sound and the miracles of science. The miracle of music opens us to the joyous miracle of life that is transcendent, perpetual and ever present in the midst of the disharmonies and challenges of our twenty-first century global community.

Don G. Campbell
January 1, 1992
Boulder, Colorado

I

The Miracle of Sound

*Music is the answer to the mystery of life;
it is the most profound of all the arts;
it expresses the deepest thoughts of life and being
in simple language which nonetheless
cannot be translated.*

Arthur Schopenhauer

Schopenhauer says music cannot be translated. Yet music is being translated, reinterpreted and reorchestrated for the coming century. We now realize that the seemingly simple language of music and sound is an energy coded with patterns, an energy that involves more of the conscious and unconscious aspects of life than we ever dreamed. The power of sound is miraculous. But what is miracle?

In this section, Jean Houston discusses with me the extraordinary connections of miracles to expanded consciousness and awareness, not only for ourselves, but for each other and the planet. Her brilliant ability to stand back from centuries of Eastern and Western thought and sense the creation of new textures and weavings of sound places Music and Miracles *in a universal arena where we can gain new understandings.*

From universal thought and awareness to the personal task of facing death with dignity and fullness, music is a perfect metaphor. Therese Schroeder-Sheker describes with the elegance of language the profound depth of healing that can take place during the bridge time between life and death. Her descriptions penetrate all aspects of life: harmony, dissonance, timing, themes, counterpoint, orchestration, composition, performance. Prof. Schroeder-Sheker's medieval voice and resplendent harp-playing are captured on her five albums, including Rosa Mystica *and* The Luminous Wound. *Her mission is profound and refined. It reminds us of the choices we have in orchestrating the miraculous experience of life even in the face of death.*

Miracles evoke theological questions as well as medical and scientific ones. Rev. Virgil Funk surveys Roman Catholic thought on miracles and its place in twentieth century usage. He clearly conveys his personal beliefs and acknowledges the emerging challenges of miracles in other belief systems. As director of the National Association of Pastoral Musicians, he writes with the integrity of a theologian and the heart of a sacred musician.

Shirley Nicholson, senior editor for Quest, then reminds us of the esoteric systems that use sound. What was hidden can now be seen as the unfoldment of facts and truths in modern science.

1

Sound and the Miraculous
An Interview by Don G. Campbell
JEAN HOUSTON

Jean Houston is a profound thinker and visionary. Whether she speaks on quantum physics, education, psychology or world myths, she evokes a deep awareness and perception in listeners. In this interview she speaks of music's essential role in social, mental and physical health.

Don Campbell: Jean, can you recall two or three instances where music and sound was just so right that the dancing of the cells and the resonance of the spirit-body relationship produced a miracle?

Jean Houston: I see this all of the time in my work, so it's hard to talk about any specific miracle story. I often work with groups of minimally a hundred and fifty people and often many more. Using music in an exercise, we will have people self-orchestrate body energies and communicate with their own brain-mind systems so as to bring up the plenum of human potential—on the sensory, psychological, mythic and spiritual levels. As we move through the dimensions of body, mind and spirit, we often see a substantial number of the participants brought to the place where suddenly there are no longer any aches and pains. People are healed, and breakthroughs of various kinds happen. They believe that they have turned a corner and that they are no longer the same. I see this regularly, so to me it is not a singular miraculous event. It is the order of the day. That which was considered extraordinary has become ordinary.

Don: In this world of transformation and paradigm shifts, the word "miracle" comes in and out of favorable usage. It can imply both physical and spiritual transformations and change, rather than just the "unexplained." What do you think a miracle is, and what do you think miracles in the future will become?

Jean: I think that miracles are the conscious utilization of more patterns of reality than are normally seen by the usual encapsulated point of view. Miracles are very natural and they are a part of the Divine Nature. They are simply multiple levels and dimensions of experience being woven simultaneously into reality as we understand it.

Don: How has the sense of miracle changed in society over the last few hundreds of years?

Jean: Miracles were events that were taken quite naturally. The natural and the supernatural were on a continuum with each other. The formal definition is: the manifestation of supernatural power of a Divine Being that fulfills His or Her or Its purpose in history. But individuals that had certain access to depth reality—whether they were shamans, charismatics, saints or mystics—could orchestrate their consciousness to tap into the nature of miracles in their diverse forms. On a neurological level, these "miracle-makers" were able evidently to activate an extraordinary degree of resonance and cross-exchange of their own neurological systems, driving their mind-brain systems to a new level of awareness and capacity. In these instances, the brain would seem to be a different instrument, one that can do different things, and perhaps obey different laws. In "miracle-making" the enhanced and activated brain system is used to its fullest.

In the past, miracles were always seen as social phenomena. There was need for "miracles," and "miracle-workers" were there to help. They were people who were essentially sensitives and who were not only utilizing much more of the mind-brain-psyche energy systems, but were also using the music of the innate system of the body, mind and spirit, whose ecology was more expansive and inclusive of other possibilities. They were part of a larger universe, so naturally they could do remarkable things outside the usual because they were living beyond the boundaries of ordinary space and time. The miracle workers were living in hyper-dimensions as well as the usual kind of dimensionality.

With the emergence of the scientific point of view in the West, attitudes changed. By the way, one of the things we have to watch out for in these kinds of discussions is to say, "—and then it changed." It changed for whom? There was a major change for only a very tiny portion of humanity that we call the Western world. The rest of the world just continues to do miracles. I have found this to be so in my travels all over the planet. With the scientific point of view and the fear of meta-rational realities and the power of the sacred, an experience of the larger universe is often felt as miraculous, partly because it is not subject to the bureaucracy and hierarchy of church or state or science. Since miracle workers operated within a pre- or post-political capacity, they were generally regarded with some suspicion, unless they were performing within politically correct shrines, such as Lourdes or other places of orthodox miracle-working.

The fact is, shamans or miracle workers were always on the fringe of society. They were often treated as witches, occultists or aliens and pushed to the edges of their communities. In traditional societies they became the priest-priestesses, shamans and medicine people because of their ability to access and orchestrate energies of body, mind, psyche and nature and put one back into *ab*-original space and time. This was often done with a great deal of singing, clapping, and other accompanying music, because music lifts and shapes consciousness.

I think music actually raises the very molecular structure of body, brain and being to these larger dimensions. With music, you gain a coherence or bridging of one reality with another. Again, this is a pre- or post-political event. That is why the miracle-worker has been regarded with *extreme* caution and, indeed, often seen as demonic.

With the coming of classical science of the Newtonian varieties, where things could be measured and objectified, the objectification of the world was a limiting of that world. It was an exclusion of anything that did not come within a very horizontal approach to natural law. It was not the law of the depths, but only the limited law of probable cause and effect, the law governing the miniscule part of reality, the part that could be measured. As for the rest of reality, it did not exist and until recently, science borrowed the ecclesiastical

11

dictum that "outside of the church there is no truth." This is where church, science and state join together to create a kind of consensual agreement as to a very limited form and framework for reality.

Until recently this viewpoint has dominated the Western mind-set, but not the rest of the world where miracles happen quite naturally and the miracle-workers continue their vocations. Throughout large parts of Asia, Australia, North America, Siberia, and South America, the power of healing, the power to change events, the quickening and deepening of nature (the bringing of rain and nurturing weather, good and plentiful crops) are considered part of the most generally accepted reality. These societies have continued to live in the sacred as providing extended worlds of awareness and possibility. When these extended worlds or realities are ridiculed or trashed by scientific or church driven notions, they tend to shrink because of the closing of doors and gates in people's minds.

Miracles are the conscious activation of more patterns of reality than are usually seen in local, limited, unloving consciousness. Whether a state of resonance is brought in through loving, drumming, music or a state of deep empathy, one experiences the thinning of the membranes between the worlds. When the membranes are thinned, then all kinds of deeper realities are present and present themselves to be lived in and worked with. Then of course, one naturally performs miracles!

What is happening today is the multicultural interweaving of different ways and styles of being and the reexperiencing of the miraculous. We are entering into a reconceptualization of miracle in a very creative and productive way, because the nature of our reality is being stretched by the sheer intensity and complexity of our times.

If we don't perform miracles in our time we are going to lose the world!

Entropic patterns will speed up, as we already see happening. The expansion of desert regions is not just the desertification of the world, but the desertification of the mind and soul, the leaching of the mind or soul of their basic nutriments of archetypal and depth realities. This inner devolution runs as a negative resonance, parallel with the erosion in the outer world of soil and air.

So what are miracles? They are the telling proof that what we call ordinary reality is only one special case in the nature of reality itself. There are not only depth structures as well as many other dimensions to reality, but there are multiple laws governing form and function within these separate realities. Just as different states of consciousness give us access to different capacities, so do the different states of planetary awareness, which we find in the study of the earth's many and varied cultures, give us new planetary capacities, options and opportunities.

We are being asked in our time to partner the planet! We are asked to take responsibility for its biological and evolutionary governance, which for our ancestors would be an incredible miracle. We are becoming the gods that our ancestors spoke of! We can move mountains in seconds, and communicate instantaneously with any part of the globe. By the year 2000, with the new phone systems, we will be a planet of incredible interconnectedness. Everyone will be able to call up anybody. We will look at our luminous picture boxes at night to find out what the other gods are up to.

Unfortunately, we are still archaic in our mythic structure. We still suffer from the disabilities of archaic gods. That is why I think the gods (meaning the psycho-spiritual potencies in ourselves) are trying to be regrown. The doing of miracles is not simply a question of remarkable things. Rather, the God Self, which performs the miracles, has to be regrown and extended. We are, as Nikos Kazantzakis said, becoming "the Saviors of God," regrowing the God force in its *human* dimensionality. We are at a time when the local law of form has become too limited a paradigm, and we sense that there is soon to be a much more complex reality standing in the wings of the present one. We have long suspected that we are citizens in a universe larger than our aspiration and more complex than all our dreams. This larger universe, which our old mind considers miraculous, is about to be woven into the grid of space and time.

Don: If you were to take ten seconds or all the time you need to show how music can build its transformational state into this larger universe, how would you see it being used a hundred years from now?

Jean: That's an interesting question. To begin with, I think that instruments themselves are going to be different. Certainly, we will still have the traditional instruments, yet they will have an absolutely transcendent function. Last night on TV, I watched the life story of Yehudi Menhuin. Did you see it?

Don: Yes, I did.

Jean: It was quite interesting, to watch him playing the Stradivarius and to feel one's very soul being played in a way that a synthesizer simply does not, at least presently. A synthesizer is not made out of the same elemental stuff as we are, as is an instrument made of bone and wood and the innards of animals. A synthesizer is not soil-sprung, vegetable-spun, sun-lured. Thus, its sounding belongs to another kind of physical and psychological order, which doesn't have the same elemental power.

I think what is going to happen is already in its early stages—the gathering of world instruments and music. This is going to create a different ecology of sound. We have the new California cuisine, a new ecology of taste, with Japanese techniques being used in French and Italian dishes. The same thing is happening with our music. It is happening with the experts now, and it has not yet reached the general public. But I think it will, especially in the next twenty years. Together, we will be congruently creating a new world sensibility and with it a planetary music. With the new fiber optic phone lines linking all of us, what we will be able to do sonically is going to be quite extraordinary. The borders of world sound will be crossed as people from all over the world simultaneously play riffs together on their computer-linked keyboards. Can't you hear it, Don, a low dirty blues playing in New Orleans being joined by a Tibetan horn coming out of the Himalayas, tempered by a Chinese stringed instrument from Hunan Province, and the whole piece being lit and made ecstatic by someone playing mad Celtic cascades on an Irish harp in a house on Galway Bay?

This morning I was listening to Nana Mouskouri, who for me, more than any singer I know, has the capacity to incarnate so many different kinds of sound patterns. I heard tone or chord shadings in certain Greek tunes that do something radically different to consciousness—literally take it to another level altogether, such as I have rarely, rarely experienced before. There are also sounds in certain kinds of Japanese music that open the senses and expand the mind's frequencies.

In a sense, this music does for the brain-mind what much of the work of Dr. Alfred Tomatis has been doing to retrain the ear and brain. I think there are chords that create a rebalancing or extension of the mind. With the advancement of this acoustical science, there will be an extraordinary new use put to musical sounds harvested from the many fields of world music. I suspect these sounds are more universal than we think. There will be a kind of universal grammar of music that is going to be able to call people beyond what has been traditionally accomplished. As we bring in things like the Tomatis sound technology and blend it with the ecology and grammar of world music, we are going to know a great deal more about calling human beings into their fuller capacities.

Right now, for example, with hard electronic rock, you get battered consciousness. Some kinds of rock music, at least as I experience it, have a toxic effect on consciousness. The reason I don't join an exercise club is because the music constantly played there is so terrible that I just can't take it. It may drive the adrenalin in the system, but it trashes everything else. This music is recapitulating the holocausts of the wars and the pogroms of the twentieth century, before the birth of an essentially new order of music, based on an expanded vision of what human beings can be.

I think that we will have instruments that you can get inside of and walk through, so that you will play them in a way not unlike the way in which the Kodo drummers perform. Playing these instruments will be a whole dance in itself. We will have a kind of prosthetically extended orchestra where you will be able to play different kinds of things, literally, with your whole body. This one woman band will be a leaping, dancing, breathing, multi-modal kind of artistic endeavor. To be able to play within it, with all its different functions, will require the performer to be in an extraordinary state of consciousness, one prepared for spiritually, as well as physically and musically. This kind of musicianship will be the most honored profession for both the skills it will require and the beauty it will call forth. I can see that development happening in the twenty-first century.

Don: What do you think of the research of the French physician, Dr. Alfred Tomatis? (See Judith Belk's article in this book.)

Jean: I think he is an Einstein of sound. Dr. Tomatis has created a real measurement base that can be duplicated. He has broken through many, many barriers because he is able to get results that nobody else could get. When you read how, not long ago, doctors would put strychnine in the vocal chords of singers like Caruso, you know we

15

have really come out of the Middle Ages. Tomatis has created a whole new knowledge base on the critical use and application of music and frequency upon body and mind. He is creating a Copernican revolution in terms of music, sound and science.

Don: How do you see the world of science and acoustics merging with this psychoacoustical sense to create a marriage of the use of music and sound to affect and heal the body-mind?

Jean: I think that the measurement of sound upon the body is getting to be a very interesting science. Every person has a different tonality and is made up of different sonar frequencies. That is why we prefer different things and are so radically different from and to each other. It is this sonar individuation that is very, very important! We must not impose, as let's say Adolph Hitler did with a Wagnerian derived music, a limitation of mind through a sonar imprisonment of people. This politicizing of brain function through various kinds of sounds and forms is not only what happened in Germany, but also occurs whenever and wherever totalitarian states and dictators prevail. It happens in certain kinds of marching music. Marches are fine, but you have to have a great variety of different kinds of music in order for the mind to discover its freedom and its capacity.

I think that in the future sound will be used for its evocative potential. It will serve to call forth health, feelings, ideas, as well as other potentials and levels of the self that usually remain dormant. Science can assist in this, but it's not going to be science as we understand it. It will have to be a very high art form. And people like yourself, Don, are leading the way in trying to create a new convergence between art and science and spirit, using musical forms and sonar reflections, but it has to be an art form first before it can be a science. The science is there as background, as handmaiden to the art form.

Don: You often mention in your workshops, if your life had taken you in this direction, that you would have wanted to be a musician.

Jean: There is no question in my mind. I heard music in my mother's womb, primarily Italian opera. My cranial nerves grew with *Aida*. My little feet and fingers grew out of being fins through *Traviata*. I stopped being a fish and became a mammal with *La Boheme*. Music is the very substance of my being, and as a child I was known as "the little, little girl with the big, big voice." At five I sang mezzo and used to perform in the old USO shows. I would have had a career in opera. I had the vocal and physical dimensions for it. But one day, in first grade during a spelling bee, Cookie Colozzi coughed in my face. I got whooping cough and whooped out my high vocal chords.

As my father was a comedy writer, we were always on the road and moving so much that I went to twenty-nine schools before I was twelve. I never had much of a chance to take music lessons, but still music remains in every part of me. My personal entelechy was to become a musician and composer. It is almost as if, in another dimension of my consciousness (one world over, as it were), I have an alternative life as someone who has continued the life of a musician and composer. Even now, if I listen, I can often hear what she is working on. I hear symphonies and concertos, and at present she is working on an incredible world music, integrating many, many different kinds of instruments and modalities.

In a sense, she, this depth character whom I imagine in that alternative life, is doing what I am doing on a very different scale. My workshops are seen essentially, for all their speech and drama, as musical orchestrations. I tend to understand everything musically. I try to bring consciousness to the level of a new story through using the structure of a musical sonata. I sense when it should be *andante,* when it should be *allegro,* when it should be *presto.* I follow to some degree, these eighteenth and nineteenth century forms of musical structuring and pacing. Sometimes the entire workshop is musically paced, either by a musician such as yourself or by very judicious use of tapes. These exercises call people into a new potentiation of body, mind and brain.

The processes that we do to activate the deep capacities are almost always accompanied by appropriate music. I have gathered thousands of tapes over many, many years from all different places on the planet. The great sound engineers I have been fortunate to work with, especially my colleague Mickey Houlihan, have phenomenal mastery of musical selection and orchestration. From *Chariots of Fire* to the Kodo drummers of Japan to the reconstruction of a musical chorus from Euripides to a wild zhikr from Saudi Arabia, I work with world music that calls up new worlds of being for many of the participants in our seminars.

Don: Jean, this was a delicious conclave. You continue to inspire me as you do so many others to get on with our own inner orchestration.

2

Musical-Sacramental-Midwifery:
The Use of Music in Death and Dying
THERESE SCHROEDER-SHEKER

There is a place where medical miracles and miracles of the human spirit intersect. For me, the sanctuary there in the middle has been a completely musical, lyrical field. The sixth century statesman Boethius knew that music was related to mortality as well as to genuine knowledge, and identified *pure music* not as repertoire, but as an *all-pervading force* streaming throughout the universe as well as a *principle that actually unites* the integrity of the body, soul, and spirit. The equanimity maintained while imprisoned and awaiting an excruciating death sentence enabled Boethius to experience the harmony of the spheres, the *Being of Music,* even in the face of human suffering. For him, repertoire would have been valued only as a shadowy reminder of the heavenly harmonies; repertoire was more coarse in that it would be burdened by subjective colorings. The fact that music would be, then and now, a primary agent during the rite of passage which commands the dissolution or "unbinding" of the body-soul-spirit unity points somehow to *mystery,* to sacrament,[1] and is worthy of the thoughtful, awe-filled expression: miraculous. It is this pure music that can remind us of our heavenly pre-natal existence, and music that can welcome us into considering our post-mortem life as a return journey home. This article is about the recognition of those quiet miracles of the spirit in the branch of pastoral and palliative medicine identified as music-thanatology.

Long before the modern use of the term, medieval French monastic infirmaries anticipated and extended the notion of *palliative medicine.* Eleventh century Cluniac infirmarians developed a systematic three-dimensional *praxis* specifically aimed at the acceptance of death into the life cycle, the mitigation or resolution of pain, and the possibility of a conscious, blessed death. Intentional communities addressed the potent spirituality inherent in embracing the human dying process. No sentimental movement or denial impulse was operational in this world view; on the contrary, it vigorously acknowledged human resistance, enigma, and paradox in a sophisticated series of infirmary customs. Like the recent obstetric advances in natural childbirth, the *commendatio animae* indications focused particular support for the conscious participation of a patient's entry into and creation of the final personal biographical process. At Cluny, contemplative musicians tended and comforted the dying, essentially anointing the terminally ill with sound and song. They wanted to relieve or reduce the severity of any physical or interior obstacle that might cloud, impede, or separate an individual from the multiple meanings of transformation. The infirmary, during those times, served as a sanctuary for completion, and protected the vulnerable work of the dying. *The Chalice of Repose Project* is the name of the music-thanatology initiative in which home, hospital, and hospice deaths are musically tended by individuals or teams of highly trained workers. Extended archival research, the natural sciences,[2] an anthropological interpretive method, a new medical-scientific non-invasive research model, and nineteen years of bedside application attempt to restore and expand this historical clinical method into a fabric wholly appropriate for the twenty-first century. Specific music is played for conscious patients, other music for those who are comatose, those in physical pain, mental agony, etc. The Chalice workers practice a musical-midwifery with noteworthy effect in cancers, respiratory illnesses, and AIDS-related syndromes. The pain-resolution work employs bedside use of harp and voice, and is particularly attentive to the recovery of dignity, intimacy, reverence, and tenderness within the personal and community experience of death. The Chalice repertoire moves toward the reconciliation of art and science, and holds concrete and practical concerns of social welfare central to the revisioning of a future culture.

The First Vigil

This work is called *musical-sacramental-midwifery*. I first began tending the death-bed vigil when I was a young, naive, undergraduate student, proceeding only from intuition. Today I am a grown woman and have personally and professionally experienced manifold kinds of death. This has involved tending the deaths of men, women, and children of all ages. The processes demanded now in writing, formulating a reflective and accurate language that addresses both matter and spirit, are slow and difficult. It necessarily concerns a distillation of medical observation, practical clinical applications, humanized and warmed by the experiential details, all eventually tempered and purified through the uses of metaphor and image. It is patient, long-term, systematic observation of and response to the needs of the dying that has provided the fertile possibility of insight. These multiple ways of knowing constitute and determine the new field of music-thanatology.

This story begins with two dissimilar figures, a priest and a patient. The priest lived in a near-by town, and knew of my work with the dying elderly. He had taken me aside for a long quiet walk and had said with simple but burning solemnity: ". . . Protect them. . ." He said to memorize special lines from the world's sacred scriptures, from the *Bhagavad Gita,* the *Talmud,* and the *Prologue* to the *Gospel of St. John,* and to pray these internally by each bedside. He challenged me to deepen and expand beyond the limitations of personal religious identity, to hold and carry the *Lord's Prayer* as something that belonged to the world, not to a group. He suggested a compassionate growth process that could be, in time, developed without ever diminishing the mysteries of true spirituality. The second person, a patient, compelled change as well. He was a sinewy man in his eighties who was the terror of a geriatric home that housed elderly Russian emigres, all of whom were Jewish or Orthodox (Christian). He was a mean old buzzard on the days of plainly mischievous pranks, and deteriorated into downright viciousness in the moments most clearly revealing his brokenness. It is true: he was not the favorite of the caregivers. It is ironic that this man who began to die as no-one's beloved, who seemed so brittle and selfish, scoffing at truly human contact, died in a manner that bore fruit. His death (of emphysema) heralded a practical way in which to protect and serve countless others. His passage also initiated me into a delicate and paradoxical spiritual reservoir which one might call *pulsating silence.* It was holy, and concerned a suffused void.

When I entered the room, he was struggling, thrashing, frightened, unable to breathe. No more respirators, dilators, tracheotomies, or surgical procedures were available. No more medicine could resolve his disintegrated lungs. He could take no more in, could swallow no more, and, in his complete weariness, there was almost nothing he could return to the world. Both fear and agony filled the room. There was no-one to call for mediation or assistance. I climbed into his hospital bed and propped myself behind him in midwifery position. With head and heart lined up behind his, and legs folded near his waist, it was possible to bolster his frail diminished body and slightly suspend his weight. At first I held us both in interior prayer, but without knowing what to do, had leaned down into his left ear and had begun to sing gregorian chant in an almost inaudible pianissimo: the *Kyrie* from the *Mass of the Angels*, the *Adoro te devote*, the *Ubi caritas*, the *Salve Regina*.

He *rested* in my arms and began to breathe much more regularly, and we, as a team, breathed together. It was as if the way in which sound anointed him now made up for the ways in which he had never been touched or returned touch while living the life of a man. The chants seemed to bring him balance, dissolving fears, and compensating for those issues still full of sting. How could they do anything less? These chants are the language of love. They carry the flaming power of hundreds of years and thousands of chanters who have sung these prayers before. It seemed that the two of us were not alone in that room. When his heart ceased to beat, I stayed still for long moments. Almost twenty years later, the silence that replaced his struggle and that was present in his room has continued to penetrate the core of my life, birthing stages of hearing that even now flower at unexpected times and places.

What is this holy emptiness, this loss full of presence, this mystery? When you are really peacefully present with someone whose time has come, all that matters is that they are allowed *to shine through the matrix*. I mean this implicitly and explicitly. People ask: isn't the work depressing? Aren't you filled with fear or sorrow? None of that exists if you are really with the dying person: *it is their time*, not yours. Any burden or sorrow, or wounds of your own disappear. You hold the person and keep vigil while they quietly, almost invisibly, shimmer an indescribable membrane of light. If there is no tenderness in the room, this film dissolves unnoticed. If a midwife is practicing inner-emptiness, and is capable of profound stillness, this gossamer film can be guarded for a moment or an hour.

dying person's stillness fills the entire room, you can gently let go and lay them to rest. Then you thank them for affirming what is so bright.

The Laboratory of the Soul

". . . Clay is molded into vessels, and because of the space where there is nothing, you can carry water. Space is carved out from a wall, and because of the place where there is nothing, you can receive light. Be empty, and you will remain full. . ."

Lao-Tsu (Tao Te Ching)

The mandatory practice of silence and inner emptiness creates a reservoir of intuition for the contemplative musician that defies words. Hildegard of Bingen suggests that "hearing is receiving," and as such, the reception of some rare experiences (one hears both sounds and souls) can cause the hardness of your heart to be shattered. When that kind of hearing has penetrated your center with a seemingly luminous wound, the place where you've been pierced can only be filled with an entirely new kind of love. This new radiance must be returned and sung continually, or you burn. This burning is a kind of grace, and it is a kind of singing that anoints the dying person: *it is audible warmth,* and has the silver sound. This warmth helps someone slip from a body of pain into a birth canal. This is the turning point when you see that you must die to things every moment so that you can continually warm to life and living, and experience the Resurrection, or the Midnight Sun. This burning transfigures your body, soul, and spirit, and also becomes unbearable unless you give your voice away.

Sometimes you literally sing for those who can turn around and receive, but sometimes this burning voice must be content in silence, and must shine out through your eyes. Sometimes the one person in the whole world whom you've heard, received and loved with the most startling purity cannot trust it. You wait for him to turn. But you can never turn back, so you must turn *in* and listen to the way that Spirit sings in circling flames. In letting that reception cauterize the bleeding loss of the loved one, you come full circle, receiving God.

The new midwife is a chalice, and sings with bright longing for the simultaneous reception of spirit and matter, humanity and divinity.

Cartesian dualism suggested that we had to polarize and choose one at the cost of the other. The music-thanatology paradigm has come full circle, returning to the time-honored mystery of the hypostatic union. This effort in becoming more fully human involves the longing, the gesture towards hearing, receiving, and responding to the Divine while being fully engaged in the practical work of the world. Nothing less!

It is clear that the contemplative musician, the new music-thanatolgist, in working with death and dying in this way, is attentive to the reception of spirit into matter and the dissolution of matter into spirit. A conscious, blessed death changes everyone involved. The one who is singing vigil breathes in light, but the one who has just crossed the threshold becomes a source of luminosity. These transformative moments weave shining vestments for our living: we wear them when we celebrate. Together, the living and the dying form choirs of celebrants who bridge the two worlds by dissolving and creating themselves in the mystical body of Christ or the Rainbow body of Buddhism: in either case, the activity is a source of light for the entire community.

The Jesuit theologian Karl Rahner, writing like a metaphysical poet, taught that death is a central and definitive event which *each person performs interiorly*. Rightly understood, this is a royal invitation to personal responsibility and self-realization. The phone rings: it is the spouse of a woman in an oncology unit, or parents torn with grief over the impending loss of their first-born child. Every *transitus* is exceptional, and, on one level, it is the ability to hear and draw inspiration from the burning reservoir of silence that allows you to sing vigil for any person who asks you to come. The contemplative musician was born to give service within the context of reverence, an intimate gesture with tender proportions. In the Orthodox tradition, *philokalia* is understood as the love of beauty, the good, and the exalted. One can tend the death-bed vigil in a philokalic spirit, *singing radiance,* so that what is truly beautiful is an audible shining forth, an epiphany, something witnessing the intimate relationship between the body and the spirit. At its best, *this* kind of quiet beauty might re-introduce God into the soul like a burning bush, mediating elevation and expansion. *Sung prayer, love brought to life, re-arranges interior organization.* You bow your head for a moment before entering the room of the patient approaching death. Can I put aside any excess baggage today? Can I make room to receive? Can I be still? Can I hear what they need? You enter the room, and in the end, thank them, again and again, for transforming you fully into the life of sung prayer.

Clinical Narratives: Miracles of the Human Spirit

> ". . . Friendship is vowing toward immortality
> And does not know the passing away of beauty
> (Though take care!)
> Many years ago through loss I learned
> That love is wrung from our inmost heart
> Until only the loved one is and we are not. . ."
> The Epic of Gilgamesh

Many years have passed since that first vigil. Two quiet hours with an "old man" required a complete re-examination of my life and future. Recent years have challenged me to examine and comprehend a different kind of vigil for which none of us could prepare. There is simply no question that the non-religious agnostic patient welcomes comfort, respect, beauty, and caring intention as deeply as a dying monk or nun: some parts of our humanity are woven and bound together in similar substances, even if we name them differently. One group rightly calls it "sung prayer," another understands and receives it as *love*, another constituency prefers the tender nursing term "human caring". It remains our commitment to respect each language that is appropriate, secular and sacred, and *to serve* each and every person with full attention. The ecumenical issues are simple, straight-forward, and, historically, old as the hills.

One of the kinds of death that concerns and teaches me most deeply now revolves around the abandoned death. The entire epidemic population of young homosexual males diagnosed with AIDS often involves excruciating loneliness. Anyone can contract this terminal disease, but the gay struggle is made more complex since it is so often burdened by family, church, and governmental rejection or at least denial. It would be insulting to everyone to be less than truthful about these stories, and about what I have witnessed. This may at first sound too strong, but my experiences as a thanatologist clarify that no other current chapter of medicine or social justice requires so much depth and integrity from the health-care-providers.

Entire teams and individuals alike *must practice self knowledge* as they face multi-layered ethical questions, bump up against personal and media-influenced fears and myths, and swallow shameful organizational failures. The opposite is also true. Many of these gleaming narratives will eventually be gathered, honored, and returned to the world as profound new models of towering bravery and transfiguration. No other group has taught me more about the Crucifixion and the Resurrection than the AIDS patients, perhaps because of the ways some patients deal with long-suffering. No other group has asked me to open my eyes and heart and "walk that talk" about Christian love and compassion. Their faces alone show how the world could be rewritten, if only we would learn to love selflessly. Every drop of each (internal) journey home is somehow externalized around their eyes and cheek-bones. Those who actually support and care for them never forget this look. Their faces have become members of shining choral ensembles that I hear even in my sleep, so deeply do they ask us to *be present*. Some kinds of suffering etch the soul, and burn out brightly through the eyes as an ineffable, unforgettable beauty begotten from complete transformation and transfiguration. This is the song that wakens the sluggish conscience and pierces the hardened heart. Like everything worthy that has garnered fuller meaning in life, these case histories evade categorization. They are troubling, uneven, spotty, painfully bright.

One young man dying of AIDS came to me through an anonymous phone call left on a home answering machine with an unpublished number! This in itself was slightly troubling. Driving to the designated address, I was full of hesitation. It was a frightening neighborhood, there was no physician referral, and I would have to unload a harp, carry it alone up several flights of garbage-laden stairs in a building with a broken-hinged front door. I would have never let one of our interns respond to this call. It was a moment of truth. Everything from Boethius to El Salvador to Dachau crossed my mind, because in essence, I am part nun, part boring middle-class working-girl idealist, and part chicken. Every person has confused layers of fear and pride that can disguise motivations and support unwise decisions. It was because I could recollect the tone of voice on the answering machine that I could listen to a *quality of truth* that I needed to hear in order to feel safe about getting out of the car. Upon quiet recollection, a decision was made. It was right to hold this vigil.

I am grateful for the ability to remember and discern qualities of sound; it seems to me like a grace. I wouldn't have had the courage to respond to his death had it not been for that suspension of linear activity and reliance instead on the intuitive. Tim was a young inner-city college student who had been a member of the work force for such a short time that his insurance coverage had become depleted. He had somehow fallen through the cracks of our legal-social systems. His room was wretched, without windows or ventilation. The smells accompanying human disintegration became magnified in the summer heat. It is true that his demise had indeed begun with the virus, but came to completion through an agonizing lack of sleep and a broken heart. He was completely alone, and only once mentioned family and religious background. Accordingly, I chose to let the historical infirmary methods rest. Putting aside the hymns and chants, even the antiphon for the "unbinding of pain," I sang lullabies instead, the true anointing that he had lost and needed, the selfless *protection* of motherly love. (*The Gartan Mother's Lullaby*) Usually after my lectures at the university were over, I would come home and find a different address anonymously left on my machine. This lasted ten days, but this mere boy was transferred from place to place sometimes daily because of poverty. I often arrived just hoping that my presence would elicit enough shame to warrant a change of sheets. It was the only time I had ever met wholesale corruption.

In the end, on the night of a full moon, he was even removed from this filthy corner. I played for him *to bring sleep* while he died of exhaustion on the loading dock of a "private-home-facility." The fork-lifts clanged, engines roared, and the truckers cursed me for sitting with a "queer." That time it was actually about physical protection; I was afraid to leave, fearing he would be dumped in an alley. There was no morphine, there were only Irish and Rumanian lullabies. I don't know where or when or if he was buried; I am only certain that his much longed-for release involved expansion into the blessed quiet of a silvery night. It took time to recover from that, but I detail his story to rekindle all of us. Had I known in the first days of AIDS what (and whom) I know now, this story would never have happened, and that dubious facility would have been closed or at least penalized with criminal investigation. Today, any nurse or physician could make one single emergency phone call to free an abandoned person from the scandalous deprivation that characterized this narrative, but then, we are speaking about *advocacy*. So many die alone, and for those who are forgotten, advocacy is a moot point.

Our world has become so very small and accordingly the threads of the miracles are picked up ever-so quietly. Much later while on a concert tour, I stopped at a well-known record store, found titles I wanted, and went to the register. I was happy and excited with my purchases, but I noticed that the fellow waiting on me was peering at me very intensely. Was he sick? Had he just had a riff with the manager? Was my face ugly? Still, no words. As he returned the change, he averted his gaze, turning away so I couldn't see tears welling up. "Thanks for taking care of Tim," he choked. "I had read about your work, and I was the one who called. . ."

It would be unconscionable to detail only our failures. Although there are difficult and blessed deaths in every milieu and illness, there is another special constituency within the diagnosed AIDS community that will puzzle and challenge theologians and historians of spirituality well into the next century. These are the well-organized, *spiritually mature*, creative gay males who, being older, meet and carry their diagnosis with rare preparation, nobility and compassion. I have come to define this spiritual maturity as separate from spiritual identity. I now see this maturity as the ability and commitment to continue growing by learning from everything and everyone: digesting, discerning, and integrating progressively more complex human issues into the dimensional fabric of our lives. This concept of spiritual maturity has enabled me to *get. to work* rather than avoid work, and is foundational to genuine community-building values.

At this point, there is a need to compress eight case histories in order to maintain privacy. These stories summon facilities in me that previous work in oncology, geriatric or even pediatric medicine did not demand. Sensitive readers are asked to shift into an alternative mode of presentation.

Thoughtful, articulate spokesmen within gay communities have observed a recurring theme in their first and second waves of high visibility. In conversations with me, they have addressed the disproportionate centrality that youth and beauty once held in the emergence of their urban aesthetic and identity.[3] The passage of time has now produced the first generation of these men who are visible, active, successful members of the arts, sciences, academic and business worlds, and invaluable contributors to community and cultural affairs. Diagnosed HIV-positive, they are, for the first time, *ageing* while they are simultaneously being disfigured by the skin cancers and other symptoms. This loss focusses deep concern and commitment to interior growth and cultural, even religious expressions that can wisely teach the younger brothers and sisters who will soon follow. The former presence and necessity of aesthetic beauty must now be extracted and clarified from an outside world, and distilled into a tincture for the heart, soul, and spirit. What is demanded of any person who has been stripped of a former personal identity in which the surface exterior expression (youthful beauty) was more important than the *integration of beauty into the fullness of human life?* Heterosexual women especially understand this aspect of middle-age crisis and its cruel amplification in media fantasy. Often but not always, they prepare for the loss of simple, surface girlhood beauty, but it requires real fortitude. Again, other people suffer agony over loss of beauty too, for example, when they have been critically burned in a fire or automobile crash. One big difference is that these patients benefit from the care of medical teams who are not frightened, and generally receive extraordinary familial, community, and/or church support.

Eventually everyone faces this challenge who enters into the ageing process truthfully, but I see clearly that this *wound* is, for many, a central *point of departure* in the interior transformation that occurs in the extended AIDS death. What is really involved when one loses physical beauty and simultaneously gains the chains of contagion, isolation, and rejection welded to cultural fear? The element, presence, and passage of time impresses itself like a branding iron into the conscious act of witnessing. A person stands all alone at a very dark abyss and wonders if anyone could ever possibly love them again. No matter what fame, financial security, or success one's past accomplishments might have brought, self-worth and lovability are central to our humanity. Relationship with God can be developed, hindered, severed, maintained, distorted, liberated, revitalized or matured all through our experiences of love, loving and lovability.

Playing and singing within their ranks, I have witnessed new expressions that differ from work in other wards. I have seen the amplification of dimensionality flourish as a conscious preparation for death (and this we see in some other kinds of cancers as well, though the struggle is different). For each of us, attentiveness to layers of details mends and repairs the long-term *fragmentation* of body-soul-and-spirit, thinking-feeling-willing. Thus, the original meaning of integrity involves enormous individual responsibility and accountability, and cannot depend on someone else's values and meanings. The values and meanings perpetuated by the dominant structures may be strong, but are not necessarily eternal values. Individual meaning is brought to birth in the depths of the soul. Paradoxical meanings are recognized which ask great strength. Permeability and sensitivity assume double meanings in the acknowledged gifts gay men bring. The very sensitivity that enables them to develop such meaningful friendships is also a permeability. This is clearly a two-edged sword, separating the essential from the nonessential.

For the dying AIDS patient, the disintegration of the immune system is another way of describing literal loss of boundaries and permeability. One of their primary internal beauties, *permeability,* becomes in fact the vernacular of their dying. A taxi-cab driver coughing in a face may deliver the final message, unwittingly and certainly, unintentionally infecting and invading the weakened host. Some AIDS patients live with and master fear by taking care of details, looking details right in the eye. Without protection, many begin to be less and less active in the outside world. When I have been ill with even a small respiratory bug, I would call a patient first, just to let them know I did not forget them, but I would already know their response. "Therese, please, I need the music, and I am getting close, but not fully ready to die yet. Stay away till you are certain there is no trace of the cold left. . ." They know themselves.

There is some burning attention, an ignition process, going on here that is closely allied to the spirituality of individuation. In the distinct movement towards self-ordained home-bound discussion groups, many of the dying facilitate each other with startling depth and honesty. These circles tend each other, they do not displace this movement by deferring to an exterior authority figure, a minister, a psychologist, a social worker. It reminds me so much of the original, radical response of the early Christians, who through forced necessity and social departure from established norms, met at night to sing and pray in the catacombs. Because there is so little time remaining in which to face crisis, I have observed more demand and more support for the urgent re-examination of personal details and community-building values *as a group,* than in many other illnesses. This is the first class of "terminal" patients that has ever asked me to come to attend group sessions. Every other kind of vigil has been devoted to single patients.

When one contemplative musician is playing and singing for one dying patient, it entails profound stillness and concentration. With your entire heart and soul, you are paying attention to their special signs, and responding musically according to their needs. I was never prepared to be *surrounded* by a circle of these brave pilgrims. In no other expression of this music-thanatology ministry have I been more aware of faces, time, suffering, the immeasurable ability of the human spirit to turn, to change, to forgive, to love, for beauty to shine through the eyes like streams of commanding light. I know there are still people in the world who want to say that this or that disease is a curse, but I will say without hesitation, in no other circles have I ever been so humbled, asked to be a better person, asked to follow the *Gospels* of *Matthew* and *John* so deeply. In special individual cases, as the patients become utterly transparent, they also unveil every superficiality, thoughtlessness, double-standard and lack of refinement in me as well. I might walk out feeling like a failure, if they did not forgive my limits too, and teach me about unconditional love.

Courage, strength, struggle and *forgiveness* characterize the political and spiritual awarenesses freed in this particular terminal illness. When I watch them, sometimes covered with lesions, greet each other with a quiet but calm and conscious holy kiss, I think: they are the lepers of our day. They are Franciscans all, in spirit, holding and comforting each other as brethren despite or perhaps because of the purpled horrors. I remember the priest Damian de Veuster and his deeply personal and moving response to disfigurement on the island of Molokai. He embraced the leper, not the disease of leprosy, although he eventually died as one of them.

I have listened to some in awe as they solemnly divest and free themselves of the multiple betrayals they have suffered, slowly forgiving the individuals and systems, even the hospital worker who fearfully leaves the tray of food on the floor when no-one is looking. It is no metaphor to suggest that they hover in complete vulnerability, unintentionally rechristianizing our responses as they require that we stand for something eternal, that we mean what we say and say what we mean.

The elements of time and urgency are present in each exchange, and compel alarming levels of honesty in group work. Once, after playing and singing with real purity and simplicity, the group was as if *lifted* in a blessed certainty. We all felt it. There is always a challenge, and one man also addressed his frustrated truth.

Joe: "I don't know a God! I don't have a God! I wish I did, but I don't get it. I see how much comfort it brings everyone and I want it too. . . ."

Therese: Gulping, "but . . . surely, you know *love*, you can die safely surrounded *in love*. . ."

Joe: Painfully, "I don't love or trust anybody, and I am all alone."

Again, I am not a chaplain, what could I possibly say? With alarming nerve and disarming impatience, one member of the group spoke with inner-city candor, almost growling. "Get real, Joe. You gotta give love to get love. You want God for selfish reasons. You wanna learn how to love real quick? Go down to the children's ward at . . . . and volunteer for a week. Guarantee you'll meet God in every kid's face. . ."

We can never underestimate the awareness of any patient, and his or her own relationship to conscious multi-layered enactments of piety, ritual gesture, and liturgical symbolism. During a very intimate and unexpected conversation, an esteemed eye surgeon described to me how he had come to translate each act of surgical preparation and procedure as if he were a priest celebrating the Holy Eucharist. With every movement, the washing, holding, touching, making of incisions and sutures, the use of laser beam technology, the reading of vital signs, he quietly approached patients on the operating table as if they were on a consecrated altar, and the art of surgical medicine literalized or at least paralleled transformation and spiritual transubstantiation. He never discussed the spirituality of his practice with his colleagues, but, following recovery, his patients often shyly related profound stories involving new levels of seeing, not just with the eyes, but seeing with the heart. This surgeon is a young Catholic physician who, in his forties, has retired from practice because he is HIV-positive and dying of AIDS. Singing and music have also become central expressions in his own personal preparation for *transitus*. He might leave us soon, but not without having promoted spiritual healing as well as physical healing. This quiet model of integrity continues to grace the community with serenity and compassion. He has made his time count before it has run out. I suspect there are many of these stories, but unless the dying have kept journals, historians will not be privy to the depths of internal meaning lived and ritualized by those so capable of multi-dimensionality.

Ordinarily, I play for any individual who calls, and often a patient drifts in and out of consciousness. For those who are comatose, the music anoints and assists in the unbinding process. There are patients who remain conscious and have wakened the desire to cross the Threshold as consciously and as peacefully as possible. They can often listen to the music with such concentration and *appreciation* that they seem to be breathing in bread. How deeply I am humbled. They sigh in relief, forget the past, and request the chants and hymns of timeless beauty. Some of them are able to die in peace, forgiving those who feared and psychologically scourged them while they were alive. With a shining and spiritually mature internal beauty that is woven of equal parts of truth and goodness, these exceptional souls respond to the living truths of sacramentals, not the limitations of religious polemic, theory, and abstraction.

I have tended many kinds of death. It has taken a long time to witness a dying group who so fully participates in the creation of biography, the witness of bodily dissolution, transfiguration, epiphany and transition, that *they want to sing themselves out,* like Thomas Aquinas and his swan song, *Adoro te devote.* The first small group will set an example for others. This is not a hidden gesture towards euthanasia; this is a cultural re-enactment of a valuable, classical western monastic model, despite the lack of named religious identity. Here, in the perfect freedom won from plumbing life's complex teachings fully, it is the dying person's *holy intention* to cross the threshold as consciously as possible, the most quiet act of dignity and faith in any age. These struggles have mothered my eyes, heart, fingers, voice, and intentions. I want to continue singing with and for them. They have taught me much about the increasing presence of God in our lives. I thank them, over and over, for giving new meaning to the life of music, song, and sung prayer.

Concluding Remarks

When exploring enigma, language can be used transformationally rather than informationally. These narratives revolve first around the personal experiences of the dying, second, the memories and observations of a second party seeing, honoring, questioning, integrating. It is my belief that the minute personal details of these experiences would not, at this point, be dignified by the effort to conceptualize or categorize. The work of dying is vulnerable, and every death signals the need for quiet protection. Regarding AIDS, this is only one part of my commitment. I am clearly an outsider: I am not a gay man and I do not have a diagnosed terminal disease. I am an insider, in that I am present through critical moments, through the fight and loss, struggle, spiritual healing, and resolution. I do face the nit-grit of emotional fear and physical fears. I have assisted with bed-pans and catheters, and also heard details of their last bright dreams. I am not trying to paint a picture of saints or martyrs, although some of them are. This piece is also not meant to represent an entire spectrum of death, but a significant cluster of stories.

Being trained in the classics, I do think in historical terms, and see profoundly authentic and organic parallels to historic patterns of spirituality and the flowering of spiritual life. This *is* about advocacy, meeting public fear and ignorance, public and private tendencies to emotional and judgmental moral-reductionism. Once, after a long hard concert-lecture-clinical run in another city, I received a serious letter in the mail written from a deeply concerned, and surprisingly educated woman. She was utterly disappointed in my work, and in fact, concerned for the well-being of my soul. "You have the most important opportunity to bring Christ into this work, and yet you don't make it central enough," she said. Sometimes, actions do speak louder than words, and many concepts and people (from physicians to theologians) really do become known by their fruits. The original Cluniac infirmary methods are deeply rooted in the mysteries of Christian sacramental love, but it is not and has never been and never will be the purpose of music-thanatology to make converts. I strongly believe that each person finds a way to the spiritual life in their own time and way. If a patient chooses to dismiss spirituality, that right to individual choice is also sacred. The presence of God occurs in the human heart and within the horrors of human suffering repeatedly, and the Christian tradition has offered me a rich model of understanding death, dying, Transfiguration, and new life. I have not begun to exhaust its well-springs.

Some people want to stop the train and nail down a "moral decision." From reading historical documents, we see that understanding and discerning movements or groups takes time. Premature observations can often eliminate perspective and reflect old or inappropriate assumptions, mainly resulting in hostility and reductionism. When

Joe Patient is rushed into Hospital-Anywhere with a cardiac or bullet wound, the emergency medical team wouldn't dream of attempting to judge his acceptability before the Divine, in order to begin work. We won't either. It has always been my hope to reconcile aspects of art and science through the marriage of the medical and musical models. Future detailed articles will begin to describe the scientific aspects of this field. This chapter is about comfort. Music can easily be described as luminosity and proportion made audible; it can ensoul the hospital, humanize medicine, and bring comfort to individuals. This lifetime work is a *vocation* and has only just begun. These new partnerships put us all on hot-seats. Good medicine, authentic art, and true spirituality each require the ability to continue formulating burning questions while we simultaneously maintain devoted practice and systematic attention to detail. As my mother used to say, the age of miracles will never cease.

Author's Postscript: Today an international team of experts is forming a clinical, educative, and developmental consortium to implement music-thanatology practices in home, hospice, and hospital settings. Symbiotic partnerships and co-operative alliances support the complex needs for this musical-medical model. In the summer of 1992, the entire Chalice of Repose Project will relocate to Missoula, Montana. There an historic constituency is being gathered to re-align under this vision: concerned physicians of diverse expertise, administrators, historians, paleographers, translators, physiologists, medievalists, chaplains, musicians, social workers, fund-raisers, nurses, and nuns. At that time, the Chalice of Repose Project will be housed at St. Patrick Hospital, and will benefit from combined support from St. Pat's, The Institute of Medicine and the Humanities, the Sisters of Providence, the University of Montana, Community Hospital, and Mountain West Hospice. The new Chalice faculty will be greatly expanded; the new curriculum will be in place, music-thanatologists will begin training for certification, and internships and residencies will also be conducted there under the supervision of the founding team. Readers may contact St. Patrick Hospital Chalice office at: 554 West Broadway, Missoula, Montana 59806. Telephone 406-542-0001 ext. 2810.

Endnotes

1. *Sacrament* is Latin for the Greek *mysterion*, and has an honorable history prior to its rich and specifically Christian meaning. In the Greek rites, the mysteries insured new birth after death, and to the philosophers, it referred to symbols of heavenly reality and teachings that bring wisdom. To

the Christians, this refers to seven central liturgical rites through which the faithful participate in the presence and grace of the Divine. Theologically, *sacramentals* include a variety of signs, objects, and prayers.

2. The disciplines involved include physics, biology, geometry, cymatics, sentics, physiology, neurophysiology, and pharmacology.

3. It is essential to refrain from double standards. For thousands of "straight" college students, those same standards are found vividly expressed during spring break on Florida beaches every year.

3
It's a Miracle

REV. VIRGIL C. FUNK

"It's a miracle" is not a statement for a Roman Catholic priest to make lightly. The fact may surprise people who think that Christian ministers are in the business of miracles, especially since their sacred stories are laced with miraculous events. Televangelists are constantly trumpeting their own roles as God's vessels of healing; some Christian television shows even end with a segment on reports of miracles sent in by listeners.

So why do I have so much trouble talking about miracles? Perhaps it comes from my introduction to biblical miracles in a class taught by Fr. Raymond Brown, SS. We were studying the Gospel according to Mark, and Father Brown led us carefully through the theological mine-field of Mark 4:35–5:43, sometimes innocuously referred to in commentaries as "a group of miracle stories."

A Journey into Miracles

Father Brown's first task was to get us to understand what the gospels took a "miracle" to be. He started with a little history. The Latin word *miraculum* meant "something to be wondered at"—an oddity of one kind or another. For example, a two-headed cow born on the emperor's farm would be a *miraculum*. This word does not appear in the Latin translations of the Bible; it entered "church talk" from the culture and began to be used to describe all sorts of wonders. Thus, Christian teachers had to distinguish between two-headed calves and the wondrous doings described in the gospels. They first drew a distinction between *sports* like the aforementioned calf, which, though unusual, were within the realm of natural happenings, and *true miracles* that went beyond the rules of nature as then understood.

Thomas Aquinas (1225–1274) made a further distinction. To Aquinas, a true miracle was something that was only within the power of God to effect. Then Benedict XV (who was Pope from 1914 to 1922) narrowed things a bit more. His concern at the time was the rules for canonization—the process by which someone becomes a saint. His definition of true miracle brings us fairly close to the biblical meaning. Benedict XV decided that the church would accept as a miracle only something that was done in a religious context; the context provided the supernatural meaning for the event.

The *wonders* in the Bible are described in a variety of ways, though the Hebrew and Greek words are frequently translated into English as *miracle*. Sometimes these events are a *mopet*—a "symbolic act"—or an *'ot*—a "sign," though neither of these "need refer to anything marvelous." When a marvel is intended, a modifying clause is added.[1] Translation of the Hebrew Scriptures into Greek (the Septuagint translation) increased the element of the extraordinary in such happenings, for the translators turned a *symbolic act* into a *wonder* by using the Greek word *teras*.

In describing the doings of Jesus and his followers, the Christian writers kept to the biblical understanding of miracles as signs pointing to God. They used terms like *dynamis,* "act of power," or *semeion,* "sign." The word *teras* as applied to the works of Jesus occurs in the New Testament only once (Acts 2:22), and there it is used in concert with the other words normally applied to these acts.[2]

So while our cultural tendency might be to think of miracles as something done to dazzle or impress, the fact is that the originating stories speak about signs that reveal God's presence—means of teaching in which the point of the teaching is made evident in the act itself.

Still, the Christian narratives were not immune to influence from the surrounding Hellenistic culture. The telling of Jesus' miracle stories, especially in the Synoptic Gospels, reflects a narrative pattern used for stories about Greek wonder-workers. In the Greek stories, the *setting* describes a sick person with special difficulty, and the *mode* of involving the wonder-worker is a request for a cure made in faith—not faith as creedal affirmation, but faith in the power of the healer. The *action* consists of the effective healing, and the *reaction* comes from the crowd: they respond in wonder and walk away. What is interesting in such narratives is that, after the cure, we never find out more about the faith of the person who has been cured.

But while Hellenistic wonder-workers performed their feats in order to appropriate power to themselves, the biblical authors point out again and again that Jesus deliberately refused to respond to the request, "Show us some trick as a sign of your power, so that we may believe in you." Jesus would not work wonders for the devil as tempter (Matt 4:1–11), nor for Herod (see Luke 23:8), nor even for people in his own religious party, the Pharisees (Matt 12:38–42), or to save himself on the cross (Matt 27:38–44). Jesus deliberately disassociated himself from the wonder-workers who were rampant in his day. In fact, some of his miracles were done in secret (Mark 7:30). At other times, Jesus ordered people who had been healed and any witnesses to the healing not to tell anyone about it (Mark 7:36; 8:26), partly at least because people were coming to look for him in order to witness such wonders (Mark 8:11–12).

Jesus' harshest judgment, in fact, was reserved for those who failed to understand the meaning of his miracles, especially if one interpreted these events as signs of transformation, because he was chiefly interested in personal transformation—the reform of one's life. Here was no Hellenistic wonder-worker; Jesus worked miracles as part of his role as teacher or *rabboni* to show the power of God to forgive sins (Mark 2:1–12) or to show that this new teacher had the power to interpret (and change the observance of) the Sabbath (Luke 6:6–11; 13:10–17; 14:1–6). Jesus used signs to invite the audience to have faith in him (Luke 7:1–10; 8:40–48) or to show that even Gentiles were invited into God's reign (Mark 7:24–30). Jesus' miracles attested to God's power to work in him to conquer Satan (Matt 12:22–28) or to bring to people the mercy of God.

The reaction of the crowds to Jesus' miracles was mixed. It was not a logical response to a syllogism like this: Only God has the power to do this action; Jesus is performing this action; therefore, Jesus is God. Rather, the miracles were teachings with the purpose of inviting a response from the crowd (usually a small crowd) of conversion and faith. They invited personal transformation, but they did not require it: "So that *you* may know that the Son of Man has authority on earth to forgive sins. . . ."

Whatever Jesus' purpose, however, human beings being what they are, it didn't take long for his followers to begin embellishing the narrative. There are early signs of this in Mark, which is probably the earliest gospel text, but Matthew and Luke added the really impressive and dramatic details, as in the narrative of the woman with a hemorrhage (Matt 9:20–22; Luke 8:42b–48). In an earlier version of one "nature miracle," Jesus cursed a fig tree, and when he passed by the next day, it had withered (Mark 11:12–14, 20–21). In a later version, the fig tree withered "at once" (Matt 21:19). In various gospel narratives, there are about twenty-five healing stories told in different versions, and ten nature or cosmic miracles.[3] These stories have served Christians well for two thousand years. They are worth rereading, but they demand interpretation.

No doubt many of the miracle stories have a certain apologetic intent in that they wish to affirm the extraordinary power and mission of Jesus. But Jesus' miracles were not only or primarily external manifestations of his message; rather, the miracle was the vehicle of the message. These accounts are really revelation stories. Side by side, word and miraculous deed gave expression to the advent of God's redemptive power.[4]

This view of miracles in the Christian Scriptures and the rest of the Bible began in me a complete revision of my understanding of God and what religion is. The magical elements of religion are often stressed by television faith healers, but they are completely outside the mainline Christian understanding of miracles, certainly of the miracles of Jesus. For the believing Christian, Jesus' miracles are first of all signs that contain teaching. They were deliberately and consciously chosen not to dazzle, impress, or create awe and wonder at the raw power of God to manipulate events at will. Rather, they reveal "the advent of God's redemptive power" at work in ordinary circumstances and daily life.

There Are Miracles, and Then There Are Miracles

The contrast between miracles as manipulative acts and as redemptive revelations suggests that it is not too bold to say, "Tell me what you believe about miracles, and I will tell you what kind of God you believe in." If you hold, for instance, that God is essentially outside the normal (or human) universe and has to insert a divine influence on us from outside, then you hold to a God compatible with a pre-Copernican, earth-centered worldview. On the other hand, if you hold that a miracle is an awesome deed, then you have to define what *awesome* means in your worldview. In the ancient world, for instance, anything that could not be accounted for in the normal course of events (a great tragedy, a sudden victory in battle, the explosion of a volcano) was in the hands of God and was regarded as an "act of God."

People respond to the view that everything is in the hands of God in different ways. Religious types might give thanks to God, or offer sacrifices, or atone for their sins. In one religious form, then, in a world that views God as being in direct and manipulative charge of odd weather, you might respond to a drought by singing and dancing, entreating God to enter your world and bring rain for the crops. In the same worldview, unscrupulous people might wrap themselves in a divine mantle and claim responsibility for the rain, naming themselves as God's representatives on earth. Christopher Columbus deliberately fooled the Arawak people on the island now called Jamaica by interpreting a lunar eclipse of the sun (which in his world was a normal event) as a "divine sign" of God's anger. Since such an event was abnormal and unexplainable in the Arawak world, the people believed his interpretation.

Thus there are two views of miracles. In one view, a miracle is a mental, physical, or spiritual transformation—a specific instance in which divine power enters and changes the world. A healing, for example, is such a transformation. In a second view, on the other hand, a miracle is a demonstration of God's redemptive power. There is one area, however, in which these two understandings of the miraculous come together—music, as a tool of transformation and healing. It is the premise of many essays in this book that making music by humming, toning, and chanting has the power to heal in surprising or unexpected ways. While I, as a Roman Catholic priest, do not believe that a healing by music is necessarily miraculous, I do believe that there is a fundamental relationship between miracle and music. I pursue this link in what follows.

Cosmology and Music

In early Greek thought there was a clear connection between music (tone) and mathematics (number). Over the entrance to Plato's Academy at Athens there was an inscription that could be translated: "No one may enter who does not know earth's rhythm."[5] The harmonic scale and the certainty of mathematical formulas were seen to reflect one another, and both were seen as primary subjects whose study would develop the *arete,* the "ideal person." The Greek invention of system and logic in mathematics and harmonics was thought to be a discovery of the underlying structures of the universe. This connection was projected into the cosmos in the belief that what held all things together was music.

Contemporary cosmology is not quite as ready to project human harmonics onto the universe. We have discovered that we live on a secondary planet in a small corner of a secondary galaxy. Earth is not essential to the functioning of the cosmos. It is even more certain that we human beings play no essential role in the workings of the cosmos. Despite all of that, there seems to be some relationship, after all, between the vibration that is at the heart of music, and even of mathematics, and the universe as we are coming to understand it. Mickey Hart, musicologist and drummer for the Grateful Dead, offers an interesting spin on the big bang theory of origins that describes what I mean:

> The conventional wisdom maintains that fifteen or twenty billion years ago the blank page of the universe exploded and our story began. We call this fortunate event the big bang, which is a bit misleading as a name since the conditions for sound didn't arise until almost a billion years later, and the conditions for ears some time after that.
>
> A better way of beginning might be to say that fifteen or twenty billion years ago the blank page of the universe exploded and the beat began, since what emerged from that thick soup of neutrinos and photons were rhythmic pulses vibrating through empty space, keying the formation of galaxies, solar systems, planets, us.
>
> It is possible, however, that in the metaphorical and mathematical concept of the big bang we are unwittingly brushing against a larger truth. Hindus believe there is a seed sound at the heart of creation, the Nada; a passage in the Tibetan Book of the Dead describes the essence of reality as "reverberating like a thousand distant thunders."
>
> In the beginning was noise. And noise begat rhythm. And rhythm begat everything else.
>
> This is the kind of cosmology a drummer can live with.[6]

New Genesis

In this view, vibration is the beginning of light, motion, interaction, sound, and indeed, of music. If we place this master image of the cosmos as vibration together with an appropriate master image of human beings' place in the cosmos, we have to revise our understanding of the first version of the creation story in the Hebrew Scriptures, the Bible's first miracle story.[7]

Darwinian evolutionists long ago collapsed the supposed historical accuracy of the seven-day creation sequence, but our new understandings of cosmology offer a direct attack on the supposedly sacrosanct teaching contained in the poetic narrative. Genesis teaches that God created everything, that creation is good, and that man and woman are equal, made in God's image and likeness, with control over the rest of creation.

The worldview that established the logic of this story is, of course, one that existed 3,600 years ago: the earth is flat, with a blue dome above it and a vast sea below it, and outside or beyond the dome is where God dwells. That worldview expressed the best science of the time, and without modern science telling us otherwise, it is probably what we would still experience as our reality.

But science tells us that we sail on a secondary planet in a secondary galaxy, one small unit among many. The master image of God described in Genesis will no longer fit into (or even outside or beyond) the master view of the cosmos that we have learned from science in the last eighty years. Neither will the old master image of humanity. The idea that the man and the woman might "have dominion" over all creation (at least over "every living thing that moves upon the earth"—Gen 1:28) worked in the domed, flat world, but it makes little sense when we grasp that creation was in existence for fifteen billion years before the human species emerged into consciousness.

The belief that God created man and woman "in the divine image" made some sense in the domed world. It meant that human beings resonated with God because they were able to know and love—knowing and loving being essential constituents of God in the biblical view. Today, however, our image needs a new focus. Any idea that the human characteristics of knowing and loving provide us with a ready access to the source of creation, given our secondary position in the cosmos, is almost too ludicrous to entertain. Any creation story that places human beings at the center of the universe or makes the human experiment the apple of God's eye means that we have not so much been made in the divine image as that we have made God in our own image. And current cosmology cannot tolerate such a limitation of God.

A Christian interpretation of the new cosmology is still in formation. Perhaps its first phase is a negative one: stripping away past beliefs that are found to be inadequate in the new worldview. One such older belief is the claim that knowing and loving are central to the cosmos. These qualities are certainly central to human well-being and our reproduction as a race, but the cosmos has been able to function for billions of years and in millions of universes seemingly without knowing and loving. This suggests a theorem: the God of the cosmos holds knowing and loving in the divine self in the same proportion as the cosmos is dependent on knowing and loving. This is not to say that these emotions/feelings are not important to human identity, but that they do not seem to be *the* essential constituents in the functioning universe.

Does the new cosmology offer any alternative for the essential constituents of the cosmos consistent with a belief in God? That question brings us back to music. After twenty years of examining the function and effect of music in different cultures, I am convinced that the Greeks were right. There is something cosmically essential in vibration. Everything, so far as we know, vibrates. I say so far as we know, for we must rely on the information provided by our senses and interpreted by the vibration in our minds, and our senses are geared to respond to vibration. Light is visible vibration; sound is audible vibration. Cells vibrate; so do quanta. The human process seems designed to echo this vibration, to accept it, receive it, and then to mold and shape it into a new thing. We fracture light into its component parts to create color; we shape the vibrations we hear, and we make music.

The miracle of music is that it transforms human beings from solitary units into active components in the cosmic process. It allows us to become one with that process and then, off in our little corner, to shape and mold it into a new thing—the creative event that Mickey Hart described: "In the beginning was noise. And noise begat rhythm. And rhythm begat everything else."

Somehow music appeals to a function of the human species that we have yet to name, but our involvement in music begins to help us reshape our vision (or our hearing, perhaps) of ourselves. For that reshaping begins with a new insight into hearing: the ear and its functions affect (shape) the whole person. (The work of Alfred Tomatis and others is key here.) Our hearing is woven with our other responses to vibration, especially to touch, sight, and even our magnetic orientation to the planet. Music unifies human receptors and therefore begins to structure the mind, body, emotions, spirit, and person in new ways. Music, miraculously, as sign and act of power, is the beginning of a new creation, a new link to the cosmos and a new experience of the God of the cosmos. Understood this way, I can truly say: "Music, it's a miracle."

Endnotes

1. See Donald Senior, C.P., et al., "Aspects of New Testament Thought" in Raymond E. Brown, S.S., Joseph A. Fitzmyer, S.J., and Roland E. Murphy, O. Carm., eds., *The New Jerusalem Biblical Commentary* (Englewood Cliffs, NJ: Prentice Hall, 1990), 81:94 (page 1369).
2. Ibid.
3. The twenty-five healing stories include those of the curing of a blind man (Matt 20:30 and parallels); two blind men (Matt 9:27); a demoniac (Mark 1:23 and Matt 8:28 and parallels); the helpless man at the pool of Bethsaida (John 5:2); the man with a withered hand (Matt 12:10); the woman with a crippled spirit (Luke 13:11); the mute demoniac (Matt 9:32); a deaf and mute demoniac (Mark 7:31); a deaf and blind demoniac (Matt 12:22; Luke 11:14); one leper (Matt 8:2 and parallels); ten lepers (Luke 17:11); the centurion's paralyzed servant (Matt 8:5; Luke 7:1); the fevered son of an official (John 4:46); the daughter of the Syrophoenician woman (Mark 7:24; Matt 15:21); a paralytic (Matt 9:2 and parallels); a blind man (Mark 8:22); a man born blind (John 9:1); a man with dropsy (Luke 14:1); a woman with a fever (Matt 8:14 and parallels); a woman with a hemorrhage (Matt 9:20 and parallels); an epileptic boy (Matt 17:14 and parallels); Malchus's severed ear (Luke 22:50); and three restorations from the dead—Jairus's daughter (Matt 9:18 and parallels), the widow's son at Naim (Luke 7:11), and Lazarus (John 11:38).

   The nature or cosmic miracles include stories of Jesus changing water to wine (John 2:1); stilling a storm (Matt 8:23 and parallels); walking on the sea (Matt 14:25 and parallels); feeding four thousand people (Matt 15:32; Mark 8:1); feeding five thousand people (Matt 14:15 and parallels); cursing the fig tree (Matt 21:19; Mark 11:14); one or more great catches of fish (Luke 5:1; John 21:1); finding a coin in a fish's mouth (Matt 17:24); passing invisibly through a crowd (John 8:59); and Jesus' resurrection (Matt 28:1–10 and parallels).
4. Senior, "Aspects of New Testament Thought" 81:111 (page 1372).
5. The Greek phrase is normally translated: "Let no one enter who does not know geometry." The word geometry is normally taken to refer to mathematics, but in its root form it can mean "the earth's measured beat" and therefore "the earth's music." The mention of this inscription is found in Elias Philosophus, *In Aristotelis Categorias Commentaria* 118:18.

6. Mickey Hart with Jay Stevens, *Drumming at the Edge of Magic: A Journey into the Spirit of Percussion* (San Francisco: Harper, 1990) 11.
7. The Bible actually begins with two different creation stories, set side by side. The first version contains the familiar six days of creation plus one day of rest (Gen 1:1—2:4). The second story gives a radically different account of creation, but it contains the familiar story of the garden set among four rivers, the temptation of the first humans, and the fall (Gen 2:5—3:24).

4

The Miraculous Potency of Sound

SHIRLEY NICHOLSON

According to esoteric philosophy there is no such thing as a miracle, only events we do not understand. What a miracle television would have been in the Middle Ages! Yet, in spite of all we have come to understand about nature, an aura of mystery still surrounds such things as sudden healing and life circumstances that unexpectedly come right. We have hardly begun to explore all the factors involved in such occurrences. How powerful are the effects of mind and thought? What unseen energies are at work?

Perhaps one day we will better understand the enormous power of sound, tone, and music and the "miraculous" results they can produce. But according to esotericists such as H. P. Blavatsky, Rudolf Steiner, and George Gurdjieff, we will have to acknowledge and explore unseen realms and energies that surround and interpenetrate the physical world. Studies by researchers like Hiroshi Motoyama and Valerie Hunt of U.C.L.A. are beginning to corroborate the existence of these subtler levels. For example, Hunt attached electrodes usually used to measure the electric potential of muscles over areas of subjects' bodies where the chakras are said to be situated. She found radiations of far higher frequency than what is typical of the human body (Sherman 1988, 133–4). Motoyama, too, detected unusual energies in the vicinity of the chakras. According to yoga philosophy, chakras channel superphysical energies. These studies suggest that the energies described in esoteric and yogic philosophy are real.

Esoteric philosophy holds that a sound on the physical plane reverberates through superphysical levels to produce vibrations, energies, even forms. According to H. P. Blavatsky, "Esoteric science teaches that every sound in the visible world awakens its corresponding sound in the invisible realms, and arouses to action some force or other on the occult side of nature" (Blavatsky 1980, 12:535). Furthermore, the subtle effects of sound linger after the audible sound has died out, so that the any results are long-lasting.

Joscelyn Godwin, author and professor of music, explains: "Although to the outward eye . . . music seems to be over as soon as the last chord has sounded and the celebrants have dispersed, this is not the case. It has also been created on a subtle plane and remains like an exquisite flower hovering over the sanctuary. . . . No musical vibrations are ever lost: even though they are dispersed, they will go on vibrating through the cosmos for eternity" (McClellan 1991, 84).

Clairvoyants such as C. W. Leadbeater and Geoffrey Hodson have described the moving patterns and colored forms produced by music in the subtle worlds around us. An artist painted Hodson's impressions of "music forms," such as a brilliant, dynamic plume Hodson saw as being produced by Beethoven's "Coriolan Overture" (Hodson 1984). The vibrations and energy of these music forms, according to Hodson and others, influence people in the vicinity in a beneficial way. In addition to the mental and emotional impact of music, the quality of the music forms themselves is infectious.

Rudolph Steiner held that music comes from a spiritual source, and that its harmonies have an uplifting effect that puts us in touch with our true essence. "Man's original home is in the Devachan [heaven world], and the echoes from this homeland, this spiritual world, resound in him in the harmonies and melodies of the physical world. . . . [These echoes] throng through his innermost being and thrill it with vibrations of purest joy, of sublimest spirituality, which this lower world cannot provide" (Godwin 1987, 82). Gurdjieff, like Plato and the ancient Greeks, related music to the cosmos, thus linking humans with universal order. "The seven-tone scale is the formula of a cosmic law which was worked out by ancient schools and applied to music" (Godwin 1987, 180).

Indian philosophy offers the most explicit explanation of how human music relates to the cosmos. It holds that vibration is at the root of all creation and that music mirrors this cosmic music. Thus, total immersion in music can put us in touch with the sound of the universe, and therefore with our basic Self. Much of the music of India is composed for this purpose.

The effect of music forms in the invisible worlds around us is automatic and without deliberate intent. However, if a knowledgeable person consciously and deliberately uses the potency of sound, seemingly miraculous effects can result. This is not so surprising if we consider the awesome power of nuclear energy which exists at an immaterial level that cannot be perceived by our senses. Like nuclear power, sound has an effect out of all proportion to the initial impulse. As Blavatsky put it, "Sound is a tremendous occult power; it is a stupendous force of which the electricity generated by a million of Niagaras could never counteract the smallest potentiality when directed with occult knowledge" (Blavatsky 1978, 1:555). There are those who have wondered, in the light of this information, whether the biblical account of Jericho being destroyed by sound might be true.

Blavatsky tells us that sound is "the most potent and effectual magic agent" (Blavatsky 1978, 1:464). The ancient practice of reciting mantras is an example of a spiritual technology based on the properties of sound. Lama Govinda, authority on Tibetan Buddhism, acknowledged that the physical world rests on a cosmic, primal vibration, and explained that its power can be focused for various purposes through the use of mantras. He said that "all mantras are held to be modifications of an original underlying vibration which sustains the whole energy pattern of the world . . . the energies concentrated by mantras can be directed to specific magical purposes, including healing" (McClellan 1991, 61).

Unlike most music, seed tones and seed syllables, which are single-syllable mantras, produce effects due to the vibration of the sound itself, not to psychological associations with the sound. They "create vibrational sound patterns in space" (McClellan 1991, 61). Music forms and mantras using meaningful language do this, too, but their effects are compounded by subjective emotional responses.

Perhaps within the framework of Eastern philosophy and the light it throws on sound, we can begin to understand the healing effects that come from music and elongated tones. Seen from this view, beneficial changes from working with music and sound are due, at least in part, to vibrational changes on inner levels. As musician and music therapist Randall McClellan points out: "If we are willing to accept the Tantric philosophical principle that sound creates form . . . then we might also be able to conclude that the power of mantra lies in its ability to create new vibrational patterns that through resonance can stabilize our mental attitudes and physical energies" (McClellan 1991, 65).

Physician Richard Gerber also considers the nonmaterial source of the material world, but from a Western point of view. He considers that the vibration that underlies all creation is the energy that Einstein equated with matter, and he goes on to apply this perspective to healing. To him humans are networks of energy fields that interface with the body and its cells. Dr. Gerber holds that a new breed of physicians and healers is arising, people who work with energy to affect human energy systems. He calls this method of healing "vibrational medicine." It includes such practices as herbology, electrotherapy, homeopathy, acupuncture, and therapeutic touch.

Though Dr. Gerber does not specifically address healing with tone and sound, he offers a framework and worldview that easily accommodate such techniques. He shows how healing now and in antiquity has been successful using energy as the only therapeutic tool. Dr. Gerber predicts that future scientists will be trained to probe the energetic structure of the human body.

Furthermore, Dr. Gerber sees vibrational medicine as leading the way to the integration of science and religion: "The recognition of our relation to these higher frequency energy systems will ultimately lead to a fusion of religion and science as scientists begin to recognize the spiritual dimension of human beings . . ." (Gerber 1988, 66). As we come to understand more and more of the energy structures in ourselves and in nature, we come closer to understanding the ways of God. Thus eventually, through developing paraphysics and knowledge of subtle dimensions, what appears as miracle today will be understood as perfectly natural.

We can even now come to sense something of the "miraculous" dimensions within ourselves. Don Campbell, writing about toning, says, "Exploring the inner world through vibration is an easily available and grounded way to learn of the spirit. . . . It is simple. We need only to have the courage to see God within ourselves . . ." (Campbell 1988, 13).

References

Blavatsky, H. P. (1978). *The Secret Doctrine.* Adyar, Madras, India: Theosophical Publishing House.

————, (1980). *Collected Writings*, Vol. 12. Wheaton, IL: Theosophical Publishing House.

Campbell, Don G. (1988). *The Roar of Silence*. Wheaton, IL: Theosophical Publishing House, Quest Books.

Gerber, Richard, M.D. (1988). *Vibrational Medicine*. Santa Fe: Bear & Co.

Godwin, Joscelyn (1987). *Harmonies of Heaven and Earth*. Rochester, VT: Inner Traditions, Ltd.

Hodson, Geoffrey (1984). *Clairvoyant Investigations*. Wheaton, IL: Theosophical Publishing House.

McClellan, Randall (1991). *The Healing Forces of Music*. Rockport, MA: Element.

II

The Body of Sound

*As is well known, sound has great power over inorganic matter.
By means of sound it is possible to cause geometric figures to
form on sand and also to cause objects to be shattered. How
much more powerful, then, must be the impact of this force on the
vibrating, living substance of our sensitive bodies.*

 Roberto Assagioli, M.D.

Dr. Oliver Sacks in his fine books, Awakenings, Seeing Voices *and* The Man Who Mistook His Wife for a Hat, *has brought to public attention the awesome role of sound and music in psychotherapy. Auditory hallucinations, musical epilepsy and interesting forms of communication possible only through music are now more commonly recognized. In a report to the Senate Committee on Aging Dr. Sachs sited instances of music allowing patients with Parkinson's Disease to sing even though they could not speak. He also noted that some patients in the middle and late stages of Alzheimer's disease were able to use music and song to connect with lost memories and emotions.*

In this section four doctors give significant insight into the nature of sound and music in healing, curation and spontaneous remission. Philosopher-physician Larry Dossey devoted a full chapter on the "Body as Music" in his book Meaning and Medicine. *He recognizes the need for new integration between the mystical, philosophical and medical worlds.*

Dr. Donald Epstein recounts how, through chiropractic practices, tone, wave form and sound emerge into the physical body. His awareness of sounds coming from the breath suggests fascinating possibilities for all practitioners working with the structural and nervous system of the body.

Lance Brunner, musicologist and cofounder of the Music and Health Services Foundation, relates his research into spontaneous remission and music. In his lectures at national conferences on music and health he recounts being ear-witness of transformation through sound.

Dr. Alfred Tomatis, as Jean Houston described him in the previous section, is an Einstein of sound. The Tomatis Method greatly influenced the personal and family life of psychiatrist Ronald Minson. Here he gives us his daughter's personal story of transformation with the insight of a father-physician.

Composer-teacher Pat Cook relates her personal challenges in health and shares the ways music, toning, imagery and Tomatis assisted her.

5

The Body as Music

LARRY DOSSEY, M.D.

There will come a time when a diseased condition of the soul life will not be described as it is today by the psychologists, but it will be spoken of in musical terms, as one would speak, for instance, of a piano that was out of tune.

Rudolph Steiner

Sound and the continuation of life, go hand-in-hand. Many living organisms communicate so richly through sound that it is hard to imagine their survival without it. In many species the life-sustaining processes of mating and reproduction rely solidly on systems of calls—birdsong and the songs of whales are examples—that are bewilderingly complex, and some of which are decidedly musical.

In humans, the physical body reflects the sounds we perceive, down to the biochemical level. So sensitive are we to sound that noise pollution has been called the most common modern health hazard. High levels of unpleasant sounds cause blood vessels to constrict; increase the blood pressure, pulse, and respiratory rates; release extra fats into the bloodstream; and cause the blood's magnesium level to fall. Noxious sounds are a particular hazard in the modern hospital, where there can be a steady barrage of sonic unpleasantness. Patients recovering from heart attacks in modern coronary care units are particularly susceptible to unpleasant sounds; noise pollution in these settings can affect survival and recovery.[1]

People are disturbed not only by loud sounds but also by those that are dissonant or inharmonic. They can also be disturbed by silence. If healthy persons are confined to bed and exposed to soft but varied harmonic sounds, they perceive this stimulus as more restful than subjects who are in a completely quiet environment.[2]

But sounds can mean something to us that is not adequately explained by an analysis of the physical changes they cause. Some are tied to levels of reality beyond the physical processes of mating, reproduction, species survival, and bodily chemistry. Larry Ephron of Berkeley, California, has suggested that certain sounds are connected to the recognition of transcendent and spiritual realities. The repetition of these sounds conveys something that can't be analyzed in terms of decibels or cycles per second. As he says,

> It suddenly came to me . . . that the word for the spirit of the universe or whatever you want to call "It" has the sound "aahhh" in many languages. To wit: God, Jah, Ra, Allah, Brahma, Atman, Yahweh, Ram, Baal, Ahura Mazda (I'm using the Thesaurus), Og, Hachiman, Mab, nagual, mana, wakan, huaca. . . . I think it's because the "aahhh" sound is so relaxing of the jaw and throat, letting go, giving in to what is. Makes me reminded of the oneness of all us folks.[3]

For millennia, many great spiritual traditions have prescribed the repetition of certain sounds that are known to promote the experience of transcendent realities. The ritualistic use of specific chants, prayers, incantations, affirmations, and holy words is truly worldwide. Are these sounds affecting our spiritual health, just as other sounds can affect our physical health? Could certain sounds affect *both* our physical and spiritual well-being—a kind of sonic wonder drug that works on all the dimensions of human experience? There is evidence for this possibility. Certain meditation practices that emphasize the repetitious chanting of special sounds, or mantras, are associated with demonstrable health benefits. For example, Transcendental Meditation (TM), which employs mantras, has been helpful in treating serious medical problems such as irregular heart rhythms,[4] and evidence suggests that the prolonged use of TM can reverse many aspects of the aging process. Statistics also show that the rate of hospital admissions and the overall health costs of TM practitioners is lower than that of non-meditators.[5]

Although we ordinarily think silence excludes sound, certain sounds can be helpful, paradoxically, in coming to the Great Silence of which all the major spiritual traditions speak. This is the mystical experience of oneness and unity of all things, that state of emptiness where the recognition of a higher reality can take place.

Cultivation of *silence* has also been shown to have positive health benefits. In one study, when men with high blood cholesterol levels learned to quiet their mental activity for twenty minutes twice a day while simply sitting in a chair, their cholesterol levels fell by one-third.[6]

As we shall now see, sounds—particularly music—can open the possibility for an entirely new meaning of the body, a counter to the mechanical views that have recently dominated our thinking.

Is DNA Musical?—The Body as a Melody

Music is a strange thing. I would almost say it is a miracle. For it stands half way between thought and phenomenon, between spirit and matter, a sort of nebulous mediator, like and unlike each of the things it mediates—spirit that requires manifestation in time and matter that can do without space . . . we do not know what music is.

Heinrich Heine[7]

Why are we moved by music? One reason may be that the body itself is intrinsically musical, right down to the DNA that makes up our genes.

The idea that DNA and music might be connected comes from the work of Dr. Susumu Ohno, a geneticist at the Beckman Research Institute of the City of Hope in Duarte, California.[8] In order to understand Dr. Ohno's insights, recall that every organism's genes are composed of strands of DNA, which in turn are made up of four so-called nucleotides containing the bases adenine, guanine, cytosine, and thymine, arranged in sequences that are unique for each species. In an imaginative leap, Dr. Ohno assigned musical notes to these substances—*do* to cytosine (C), *re* and *mi* to adenine (A), *fa* and *sol* to guanine (G), and *la* and *ti* to thymine (T). Then, having assigned musical notes to each base, Dr. Ohno chose a particular key and timing, as well as the duration of each note. The result was a melodic composition that was finally fleshed out with harmonies by his wife, Midori, a musician. When completely transcribed, the scores were then performed by professional musicians on instruments such as the piano or organ, violin, and viola.

Dr. Ohno has notated over fifteen songs of the DNA of a variety of living organisms during the past two years. He finds that the more evolved an organism is, the more complicated is the music. The

55

DNA of a single-cell protozoan, e.g., translates into a simple four-note repetition. But the music transcribed from human DNA—e.g., from the body's receptor site for insulin—is much more complex. To listeners knowledgeable about classical music, these DNA-based compositions have been taken variously for the music of Bach, Brahms, Chopin, and other great composers. These melodies are majestic and inspiring. Many persons hearing them for the first time are moved to tears; they cannot believe their bodies, which they believed to be mere collections of chemicals, contain such uplifting, inspiring harmonies—that they are *musical.*

Not only is it possible to make music starting with DNA, one can do the reverse: one can start with great pieces of music, assign nucleotides to the notes, and end up with a particular type of DNA. When he transcribed a Chopin piece into a chemical notation, sections of the resulting formula were the DNA of a human cancer gene. It seems that even cancers have their own music![9]

Many great artists, writers, and musicians have heard messages in nature, some of them musical. When Mozart heard a complex, lengthy piece of music fully formed, where is it coming from? When Hesse said in the prologue to *Demian* that he had learned to listen to the messages his blood whispers to him, what was he actually hearing? How do we explain synesthetes, those individuals in whom multiple instead of single senses operate simultaneously, people who smell sounds and see musical tones? Where is this information coming from? Are they in touch with some music encoded in their bodies?

Concert pianist Lorin Hollander has described the rich visual imagery he has experienced all his life on playing the works of the great composers. These images, he states, often take the form of highly complex geometric designs. (His experience affirms Pythagoras's assertion in the fifth century B.C.: "There is geometry in the humming of the strings. There is music in the spacings of the spheres.") Hollander was astonished when he later discovered that these forms, which he had visualized since childhood, were practically identical to many of the beautiful tile designs on Islamic mosques scattered throughout the Middle East. The pentagonal and hexagonal shapes that are repeated in these designs show striking similarity to the way DNA is represented in two-dimensional chemical notation. In the body the nucleotides that make up DNA are not, of course, two-dimensional figures; that is only the way we draw them "on paper."

But that may be the way they display themselves to the imagination—whether to Hollander, whose music calls them forth, to molecular biologists, or to the great artists who embellished the mosques of Islam with these images.

If connecting DNA and music seems fanciful, we should recall that there is no reason in principle why DNA has to be described in the familiar alphabetical symbols of organic chemistry—C for carbon, N for nitrogen, O for oxygen, H for hydrogen, etc. It could be described using many symbols, even musical notes. If we were imaginative enough to think musically as well as alphabetically, this just might permit us to hear the music of the body. This experience could provide us with nobler visions of the body, and might allow us at long last to escape the tyranny of machine thinking.

Recognizing the music latent in DNA suggests a new way of looking at evolution. Rather than a method of passing *genes* from one generation to another, the evolutionary process could be a way of passing the *music* along, each generation "making music" for the next. Mutations would be ways of tinkering with the melody, of creating new, more complex tunes. "Survival of the fittest" might mean "staying in key," "playing with the orchestra," or "maintaining the harmony." The natural world would not be "nature red in tooth and claw," it would be a gigantic symphony instead, composed of innumerable instruments. Since the composition of some structures in distant species such as protozoa, mice, and humans is identical—the chemical receptors for insulin and endorphins are examples—we might conceive of ourselves as "in the same section of the orchestra" with these species, or that these species are "playing the same instrument." Instead of sitting imperiously atop the evolutionary chain, we might see ourselves as simply occupying the "first chair," dependent on our "colleagues" to flesh out the score and enrich the performance. We might even begin to think of the Absolute not as a blind watchmaker who fashioned a mindless machine, but as the Maestro who wrote the melody and interwove all the harmonies.

But the material world is more than just the DNA of living creatures, it is nonliving things such as rocks, stars and galaxies as well. One could conceivably notate *any* of these things musically. When Pythagoras spoke in the sixth century B.C. of "the music of the spheres," was he comprehending this sort of notation in the heavens? Could the music in our genes reflect the music of the Universe? After all, the stuff of which our bodies are made was spawned in remote galaxies, and the atomic components of our DNA have been processed through the lifetimes of several stars. Is the distant Universe, then, the source of the primordial melodies that eventually precipitated in our protoplasm? Is the cosmos an immense music bank from which the music of our DNA is on loan? Was Plotinus correct?—

All music, based upon melody and rhythm, is the earthly representative of heavenly music.

Many of the scientists who have pondered the nature of the Universe have responded deeply to music. Pythagoras measured harmonies on a lyre string; Nobel physicist Richard Feynman beat salsa rhythms on his bongos; and Nobelist in physical chemistry, Ilya Prigogine, is a gifted pianist.

Psychologist Lawrence LeShan has noted that at the famous Copenhagen Conference of 1932, which was attended by the greatest physicists of the day, at which a major view of reality was worked out, there was enough musical talent and training for a first-rate orchestra.[10] The thoughts of Einstein, who was famous for his affection for the violin, come tantalizingly close to uniting the scientific and musical visions. He said,

[Music and scientific research] are nourished by the same source of longing, and they complement one another in the release they offer.[11]

Plotinus' suggestion of a music-permeated cosmos echoes through many traditions. The legendary Zen patriarch Lao-tzu spoke of the Great Tone that is "the tone that goes beyond all usual imagination." In the Hindu tradition the Great Tone is *Nada Brahma,* the tone from which God made the world, "which continues to sound at the bottom of creation, and which sounds through everything."[12]

The image is one of music embedded in everything, perhaps in human tissue itself. Could different body parts "have their own music," music that is more differentiated than the DNA music shared by all cells as suggested by Professor Ohno? Could they *respond* to certain music?

Without doubt, body parts can respond to the "wrong" music. The British neurologist Macdonald Critchley mentions a report in 1605 in LeLoirier's *Treatise of Spectres* in which an individual would develop urinary incontinence on hearing the music of the lyre; and that Shakespeare in *The Merchant of Venice* spoke of "some that are mad if they behold a cat, and others when the bagpipe sing i'th'nose cannot contain their urine." Critchley relates a famous case dating to 1913 in St. Petersburg of a rare disease known as musicogenic epilepsy—epilepsy brought on by music. It involved, ironically, the well-known music critic Nikonov. His first attack came at the Imperial Opera House while watching a performance of Meyerbeer's *The Prophet*. During the third act he became tremulous and sweaty, and his left eye began to twitch uncontrollably. He developed a severe headache and lost consciousness. Nikonov thereafter became a prey to these attacks, each brought on by music and nothing else. Even at a distance, music would trigger epilepsy. As a result, he was tormented by a veritable phobia of hearing music. "If out of doors the sound of an approaching military band reached him, he would stop his ears, and seek refuge in a back street or any handy doorway or shop." Eventually the attacks became more or less controlled with medication. [13]

In contrast, could certain tissues become healthier if "their music" were played? Perhaps. Many healers throughout history have realized the body's capacity to respond to certain music. In 1529, Caelius Aurelianus wrote of a musician who could literally make specific parts of the body dance:

A certain piper would play his instrument over the affected parts and these would begin to throb and palpitate, banishing the pain and bringing relief. [14]

And Aulus Gellius, writing circa 160 A.D., said,

I ran across the statement very recently in the book of Theophrastus *On Inspiration* that many men have believed and put their belief on record, that when gouty pains in the hips are most severe they are relieved if a fluteplayer plays soothing measures. That snake-bites are cured by the music of the flute, when played skillfully and melodiously, is also stated in a book of Democritus, entitled *On Deadly Infections,* in which he shows that the music of the flute is medicine for many ills that flesh is heir to. So very close is the connection between the bodies and the minds of men, and therefore, between physical and mental ailments and their remedies.

It is not just in the charming stories of antiquity that we see the healing power of music. A child psychologist recently reported his experience with an eleven-year-old boy who was diagnosed as a catatonic schizophrenic. The child had not uttered a word in seven years. In one session with him, the therapist played Bach's *Jesu, Joy of Man's Desiring*. The boy began to weep. When the music ended he announced through his tears, "That is the most powerful music I have ever heard; now I can speak!"[15]

If the body can respond so decisively to music, it must in some sense *be* music. As Goethe put it, if the eye were not in some measure the sun, it could not know the sun.

In addition to the physical body, other manifestations of the physical world are being transcribed into music. Scientist Robert C. Morrison of East Carolina University in North Carolina has developed computer programs that will translate patterns of numerical data into musical tones. He points out that the ear is a much more sensitive instrument than the eye for recognizing patterns. Thus through the medium of music a person could distinguish recurrent themes in chemical analyses, economic indicators, and other patterns of data too complex to allow ready analysis either mathematically or visually. In quality control systems, an investigator could listen for disharmonies in the music instead of looking for mathematical irregularities.[16]

The physical world also can be experienced by bringing the sense of touch into play. Scientists Cavid W. Abraham, Ralph L. Hollis and Septimiu E. Salcudean at the IBM Thomas J. Watson Research Center in Yorktown Heights, New York, have developed a "magic wrist" that converts complex images from a scanning electron microscope, an instrument that can display the surface atoms of a material, into three-dimensional movements. This permits the person wearing the wrist device actually to feel the atomic surface structures of metals and alloys. The IBM group plans also to attach their magic wrist to an atomic-force microscope, which measures the attractive forces binding metals together, which would allow a person to experience firsthand the affinities between the constituent chemicals.[17] This will allow the investigator to feel what is going on at the atomic level—literally to "have a feeling" for the substance with which he or she is working.

Similar attempts have been made in medicine and surgery. One eye surgeon is seeking to apply the magic wrist in doing retinal surgery. Presumably anything that would magnify one's sense of touch would create an advantage in performing delicate surgical procedures, which now are done by relying primarily on vision. This would be like having one's fingertips in the cutting edge of the scalpel.[18]

One can imagine a multi-sensory device that not only would transcribe the body's DNA into music as Ohno has done, but translate it into kinesthetic stimuli as well—a kind of "magic ear" and "magic wrist" combined. This would allow us to hear *and* feel what is going on inside our DNA and other body parts, allowing grander visions of the body than anything contained in the machine view.

One can also imagine diagnostic devices that make use of these capabilities. Today the various X-ray and scanning devices give the physician primarily visual images of the function of certain organs—thyroid, lung, liver, kidney, and others. Based on the appearance of these images, the physician judges whether or not the organ "looks" normal. But rather than saying only that there appears to be a "spot" on the lung or a mass in the liver, the new devices might allow the diagnostician to detect bodily disharmonies using nonvisual senses—to say, e.g., that the lung tissue sounds out of key, that there are sour notes coming from the thyroid, or that the kidney is off beat—or, while wearing his magic wrist, that these organs literally do not feel right.

Today the practice of medicine is regarded largely as an intellectual affair. These diagnostic methods would go far beyond the intellect, however, and engage the senses and sensitivities of the physician in a much broader way. Although they would make the practice of medicine more demanding, they almost certainly would bring new meaning and greater fulfillment to being a doctor because they would call forth more of his or her innate human potential. And these breakthroughs just might make the practice of medicine easier. Just as the introduction of the stethoscope expanded what physicians could hear, these new tools similarly would expand the reach of the senses and thus provide the physician with more information on which to base his or her judgments.

The body as music makes possible a different view of medical practitioners. Rather than referring to a cold and indifferent physician as having a poor bedside manner or few communication skills, he or she might be described as being "tone deaf" or having a "tin ear"—a music illiterate, unable to sense or evoke the intrinsic musicality of the body. On the other hand the gifted healer might be regarded as having "perfect pitch," an extensive repertoire, or as *maestro*.

Larry Dossey, M.D.

Physiologist Robert S. Root-Bernstein, of Michigan State University in East Lansing, has written of the need for a *sensual science*. Tools such as those above could revolutionize the way physicians and young scientists in general perceive the physical world. They would speed discovery, he suggests, by enhancing the creative process by allowing a first-hand, immediate knowledge of the natural world. Root-Bernstein points out that many of the greatest scientists had the ability to relate sensually to their object of investigation. A typical recent example is Nobel prize-winning geneticist Barbara McClintock, who attributed her astonishing insights to a highly developed "feeling for the organism." The great neuroanatomist, histologist, and Nobelist Santiago Ramón y Cajal also possessed this ability. Sir Charles Sherrington, the legendary English neurologist who studied with him, reported:

He treated the microscopic scene as thought it were alive and were inhabited by beings which felt and did and hoped and tried even as we do. . . . He would envisage the sperm cells as activated by a sort of passionate urge in their rivalry for penetration into the ovum cell.[19]

Sherrington, one of the greatest neurologists in the history of medicine, was also able to see the body in highly novel ways. He coined one of the most endearing terms to describe the human brain—the "enchanted loom"—which, in the context of the body as music, translates easily into a musical instrument: a magic harp, lyre, piano.

In his admirable book *Nada Brahma: The World Is Sound*, musicologist and writer Joachim-Ernst Berendt observes that in Latin the term meaning "to sound through something" is *personare*. "Thus," he states,

. . . at the basis of the concept of the *person* . . . stands a concept of sound: "through the tone." If nothing sounds through from the bottom of the being, a human being is human biologically, at best, but is not a *per-son*, because he does not live through the *son* (the tone, the sound). He does not live the sound which is the world.[20]

The trick is to hear the music that is the body. If we can do so, the meaning of the body can be transformed. It becomes not a blind, silent, doomed machine but a glorious composition, a part of God's oeuvre: the Great Tone.

Endnotes

1. Lynn Keegan, Environment: Protecting our personal and planetary home, in B. M. Dossey, L. Keegan, C. E. Guzzetta, and L. G. Kolkmeier, *Holistic Nursing: A Handbook for Practice* (Rockville, Maryland: Aspen Publishers, Inc., 1988), pp. 183–185.
2. Mary Smith, Human-environment process: a test of Rogers' principle of integrality, *Advances in Nursing Science*, vol. 9, no. 1 (October 1986), pp. 21–28.
3. Larry Ephron's comment provided by Brad Lemley of Bath, Maine; personal communication, September 1987.
4. B. Lown, et al., Basis for recurring ventricular fibrillation in the absence of coronary artery disease and its management, *New England Journal of Medicine* vol. 294, no. 12, March 18, 1976, pp. 623–629.
5. The research documenting the healthful benefits of Transcendental Meditation is extensive and impressive. Further information can be obtained by writing the Department of Physiology, Maharishi International University, Fairfield, Iowa.
6. M. Cooper and M. Aygen, Effect of meditation on blood cholesterol and blood pressure, *Journal of the Israel Medical Association* vol. 95, no. 1, July 2, 1978.
7. Heinrich Heine quoted in Macdonald Critchley, Ecstatic and synaesthetic experiences during musical perception, *Music and the Brain: Studies in the Neurology of Music*, Macdonald Critchley and R. A. Henson, eds. (London: William Heinemann Medical Books Limited, 1977), p. 217.
8. Susumu Ohno and Midori Ohno, The all pervasive principle of repetitious recurrence governs not only coding sequence construction but also human endeavor in musical composition, *Immunogenetics* 24:71–78, 1986. See also Susumu Ohno and Marty Jabara, Repeats of base oligomers ($N = 3n \pm 1$ or 2) as immortal coding sequences of the primeval world: Construction of coding sequences is based upon the principle of musical composition, *Chemica Scripta* 1986, 26B, 43–49. Grateful thanks to Charles Eagle, Ph.D., Chairman of the Department of Music Therapy, Southern Methodist University, for introducing me to the work of Dr. Susumu Ohno.
9. Professor Ohno's process is, of course, an arbitrary one. There are many musical systems world-wide, each of which would yield different results if its tones were transposed onto the genetic code, and if the resulting tones were harmonized and divided into the discrete notations and beats

characteristic of that particular form of music. The point is that DNA and music can be related to each other, not that the music that results from this process conforms invariably to that of a particular cultural tradition.

10. Lawrence LeShan, *The Dilemma of Psychology* (New York: Dutton, 1990), p. 19.
11. Frank Wilczek and Betsy Devine, *Longing for the Harmonies* (W. W. Norton, 1989).
12. Joachim-Ernst Berendt, *Nada Brahma: The World Is Sound* (Rochester, Vermont: Destiny Books, 1987), p. 171.
13. Macdonald Critchley, "Musicogenic Epilepsy," in Critchley and Henson, eds., *Music and the Brain*, op. cit., pp. 346–7.
14. Quoted in R. A. Henson, "Neurological Aspects of Musical Experience," in M. Critchley and R. A. Henson, eds., *Music and the Brain*, op. cit., p. 6.
15. Personal communication, source anonymous, September 1990.
16. Robert S. Root-Bernstein, "Sensual Education," *The Sciences*, vol. 30, no. 5, September/October 1990, pp. 12–14.
17. Ibid., p. 14.
18. Ibid., p. 14.
19. Ibid., p. 13.
20. Joachim-Ernst Berendt, op. cit., p. 171.

6

Healing the Tone of the Body
Through Network Chiropractic
DONALD M. EPSTEIN, D.C.

To see the forms that sound produces is a miracle. Hans Jenny's cymatic forms remind us that every tone, frequency and instrument creates a wide variety of patterns. As every shape and substance has a unique sound correlation, so every resonant chamber has a corresponding tone.

Dr. Donald Epstein reminds us that the origins of Chiropractic are tone and vibratory waves in the body. Listening to the breath and voice as spinal adjustments are made give us insight into the emerging awareness that the body itself is tone.

Roger's friend called me the morning after Roger had three chiropractic spinal adjustments asking if I could see him right away, as he was "going through some real tough stuff." A few minutes later I walked into Roger's room to see his body shaking and covered in a cold sweat and his hands trembling. He was crying, which he never did. This was not just any cry, it was a deep soul cry. He was on all fours, a waste basket in front of him, retching violently with a deep grunt from his core. This wailing grunt was the type of sound that comes from a punched lower gut. He was rocking back and forth on both knees and sobbing between dry heaves.

At first observation you would say that Roger was ill and needed attention. But Roger was in an accelerated state of release and healing. His spinal system (the conduit of consciousness and tone expressed through the body) was free of interference. I knew this seeming illness was an expression of his resident intelligence, setting him free from undigested life events which were lodged in his nervous system and his being.

Roger had repressed his emotions most of his life. He had eventually sought relief from the emotion stored in his being through drug use. About a dozen years ago he had gone through heroin addiction withdrawal. Now he was reexperiencing the withdrawal experience he thought was complete twelve years ago.

Later that day Roger said that when he released the deep low tones alternated with sobbing, an underlying tension that had always been present disappeared. The world was different.

Roger may not have needed to empty his stomach contents through vomiting. He did need to "throw up" that which no longer served his evolving sense of self. The process occurred without his trying, autonomically, as Roger surrendered to a process which appeared to have a rhythm of its own. The contracture of the retching created audible tones. Roger resonated with and released through sound the tensions that were trapped within his nervous system.

When that lower tone was completely released, Roger regained his calm. A few minutes later as he arched his back, a higher tone was released, demonstrating the relationship between another spinal region and a different sound. This continued until several tones and several spinal regions were freed. Finally he clenched his fists and punched the bed, letting out a roar resonating with rage. He collapsed on the bed, arms outstretched, neck in extension, arms open wide like a bird in flight. He reached a place of peace that he had never before experienced.

Helen had been trying to balance her life. Her perpetual motion and involvement in life left little or no room for her to feel her emotions or listen to her inner voice. Her neck was "such an annoyance." Within a few moments after a specific spinal chiropractic adjustment Helen started humming, and giggling. She hummed, giggled, and laughed most of the day for the next four days. "I just couldn't stop humming and laughing. Everything seems so silly. Oh God, I feel like such a child," she said.

Helen was able to listen to her inner voice once again, without even trying. She could no longer avoid the reality that she was now someone very different from the Helen she thought she had been.

At six days old, Joshua was brought to me by his mother. He had not nursed since birth and was now jaundiced. His breath was rapid and shallow, and he did not respond to outside noises. He did not even cry. His eyes were closed, and he would not open them even to look at his mother. With fists clenched, he opened his mouth and twisted his neck as if trying to cry, but no sound at all came out.

I applied gentle touch to various spinal segments in an attempt to adjust his spine. Joshua coughed a little, and a faint whine was heard. This cry got a little louder. He breathed slower and deeper as his arms opened and his hands relaxed. Later that day his father noticed that Joshua was looking at him and making various sounds, some of them gentle cooing tones. That night Joshua nursed. Within two days he was fully responding to the environment and no longer had a yellow tint to his skin.

Joshua had Down's syndrome. His facial features were profoundly mongoloid. Over the next year his parents were told by capable physicians that his potential was very low, his mental skills would be seriously impaired, and it was improbable that his motor skills would develop enough for him to run or ambulate well. His parents were advised that he would always be profoundly retarded, that he would need heart surgery and most likely eye muscle surgery as well.

Joshua's spine was adjusted at least once weekly for the first couple of years of his life. I have not seen or heard from the family for nearly three years, but I recently received the following letter:

"Dear Donny,

"We've been thinking a lot about you this month. Joshua will be five years old. We wanted to let you know how much he has accomplished.

"Without you, we don't think he would have lived. And even if he did, we know you are a major reason he has accomplished so much.

"Joshua is a very happy and lovable little boy. He can run, jump, and ride his trike. He talks quite a bit and he loves music. The thing we are most proud of is Joshua can read! He is reading from a first grade book and has a sight vocabulary of over 70 words. The professionals do not understand how we got a four-year-old with Down's syndrome to read at a first grade level. They say it is pretty amazing.

"He is still the most healthy child in his preschool. He has only been on antibiotics once, when he had scarletina two months ago and could not go back to school without antibiotics.

"This is one case, Donny, that you not only affected someone's life with Chiropractic, but you changed it. We thank you again!"

What was done to these individuals as a chiropractor was no miracle. I worked according to the concepts of Network Chiropractic, which, like traditional chiropractic, holds that the shape, position, and tension of the spinal system determine the nature of consciousness expressed by the individual. When you are angry your neck comes forward, your spinal cord elongates, and a particular tone is established in the brain, spinal cord, and nerves. When you feel "fluish," or toxic, your shoulders move forward at the same time that your spine elongates, and you slump forward. The tone you resonate with is similar to the feeling of "I can't" or "Why me?" In military posture the spine is straight, without the usual contours or curves. This lengthens the spinal cord also, but the tension set up is one which allows an individual to follow orders without heartfelt conscience.

Daniel David Palmer, the originator of Chiropractic, stated that his discoveries on health, the spine, and the nervous system were founded upon tone. He was reluctant to teach this new practice because he was not able to define the meaning of tone. The first book on Chiropractic, *The Chiropractor's Advisor,* was published in 1910. He explained, as did his son, B. J. Palmer, the developer of Chiropractic, that the nervous system is especially suited as the vehicle for expression of the infinite or universal intelligence in the body. He called the portion of universal intelligence within each individual "innate intelligence": "Intelligence is expressed through the nervous system, which is the means of communication to and from individualized spirit; the condition known as TONE is the tension and the firmness, the resiliency and elasticity of tissue in a state of health, normal existence," explained Palmer. He continued: "The mental and physical condition known as dis-ease is a disordered state because of an unusual amount of tension above or below that of tone." He said further that "normal and abnormal amounts of strain or laxity are due to the position of the osseous (bone) framework, the neuroskeleton, which not only serves as a protector to the nervous system, but also, as a regulator of tension."

Palmer explained the method used in Chiropractic: "Instead of using the knife and drugs, chiropractors substitute hand adjustments of the displaced portion of the neuroskeleton which presses upon or against some portion of the nervous system, which injures (instead of protecting) the filamentous bands of nervous tissue that connect the parts of the nervous system with each other and transmit impulses to the various organs of the body" (D. P. Palmer, *The Chiropractor*, 1914; p. 8; republished 1970 by Health Research, Inc.).

"Philosophy, special or general, is not the foundation upon which I built the science of Chiropractic. Its science is based upon TONE. Tone is the basic principle, the one from which all other principles, which compose the science have sprung," wrote Palmer in 1914 in his book *The Chiropractor* (p. 8).

When B. J. Palmer further developed his father's discovery, the concept of tone was eliminated from the new philosophy, science, and art. B. J. still considered and taught that the purpose of the chiropractic adjustment was to unite the physical with the spiritual. The chiropractic adjustment was to be given with the sole intent of better enabling the resident intelligence to freely express and personify itself. The natural expression of this intelligence or unbound consciousness through our nervous system is our natural state. The spinal distortion which interferes with the flow of this universal consciousness or intelligence (which extends beyond time and space) is called a spinal (vertebral) subluxation.

It was the vision of the Palmers that as innate intelligence flowed in an uninterfered fashion, the prisons, mental institutions, and hospitals would be emptied. The genius allowing inspiration or enlightenment to flow through us would be attainable for each person. As this innate intelligence expressed itself more fully, the educated mind would have free access to its storehouse of wisdom.

The Palmers referred to a second form of consciousness or intelligence, which they called "educated intelligence." This is the sum total of what we have learned during our lifetime. According to Network Chiropractic and holographic models of consciousness, information and experience are expressed and stored throughout the body. Each cell has a perfect all-knowing consciousness (innate tone, innate mind) and a consciousness which has been educated during its lifetime (educated mind, or self). The cell's sense of identity is a combination of the innate intelligence (unlimited) and educated intelligence (limited).

Network Chiropractic was established to extend the traditional chiropractic practices into the reverence of the spiritual health of every individual. It serves to release the innate intelligence within the body and allows clarity that harmonizes mind, body and spirit. The practice called *networking* is an adjustment, not only of bones and nervous system, but of the eternal and temporal systems of health and life.

In my experience the shape, position, tension, and *tone* of the spinal system appear to be mediators of the states of consciousness in every cell of the body. Experience has shown that each type of traumatic event carries a resonant tone which is in phase with the experience. The "non-ascended," "immature," or unresolved consciousness which is expressed in the body-mind, cells, and tissues of the body has characteristic vibration or tone. It is associated repeatedly with characteristic spinal subluxation patterns. These patterns seek to draw consciousness from other regions in order to perpetuate themselves.

Terms like "upright," "hanging loose," "high-strung" are used to relate the observed alteration of tension or tone in the spinal system to attitudes or behavior. Undigested emotional, chemical, psychic, or physical events perpetuate their own consciousness in the body-mind. These blockages to the flow of life energy remain as long as the spinal system resonates with the consciousness or tone of the event. A spinal system with single or multiple vertebral subluxations is less flexible and has a reduced ability to recover from events which have passed or are feared in the future. This compromised spinal system may have difficulty in recovering from the effects of judgment, autosuggestion, and socialized limitations.

In this model all disease or "illness" is an expression of the innate intelligence attempting to reveal itself within the limits of the tones available, but it is limited by the range of spinal tones which the human instrument can sound.

As the spinal subluxation is adjusted in the appropriate phase with which it resonates, cohesive waves of life pass through the individual. These waves propagate more of the same. In the process, the dissonant tones are expressed through the body and the voice.

New perspective and new awareness are part of healing. It is associated with moving beyond the established sense of self. Rather than viewing the movement beyond self as pathology, we view this as necessary for healing to occur. As the innate consciousness contacts the educated consciousness, the self is transformed.

Two conflicting models of transcendence and healing may be considered.

One model states that through releasing aspects of one's self that no longer are relevant, one's sense of self becomes so large that it is without boundaries. In this model self-realization leads to the utmost realization, or as some would say, God.

This model is not fully consistent with the clinical experience of Network Chiropractic, which holds that it is only through an ultimate realization that one can realize the true self. The instant the innate body intelligence contacts the educated mind, self is transformed. Consciousness is changed, matter is altered. Healing occurs. Since the innate intelligence is the creative intelligence which animates, motivates, heals, coordinates, and inspires us, a great personification of this intelligence instantly alters our reality. Thus diagnosis or prognosis of the condition is not as relevant.

Physical, emotional, mental, or social disturbances known as illness are a consequence of vital force (assembled by an all-knowing innate intelligence) which has been redirected, blocked, inhibited. As soon as the infinite consciousness is expressed through the body, that part receiving the consciousness is reborn.

With the awareness of a self greater than what was formerly expressed, there is a discharge. The stomach or intestines may eliminate that which did not honor the digestive system. This may be through vomiting or diarrhea. The lungs and bronchi may expand beyond their sense of self, and mucus or coughing may be produced. Fever, sweating, pain, cramping, inflammation, and altered urination are other means by which the innate mind creates a discharge of the trapped tones produced by a subluxated spinal system.

The adjustment of the spinal subluxation, applied in a particular sequence or phasing system, appears rather consistently to promote reorchestration of the symphony of educated and innate mind. It does this without suggestion, without advice, without the individual trying to do anything. When innate body intelligence resonates in the educated mind, there is a miracle of integrated healing.

I have seen cases of paralysis healed and the effects of altered or blocked life expression, labeled as almost any disease, resolved during or subsequent to chiropractic adjustments. But these are not miracles. When there is an appropriate change in tone in the spinal system, the music played by each cell of the body changes. Healing and balance occur.

A recipient of Network Chiropractic described his recent journey on the path of healing. He reported that a small pea-size lump appeared under the skin on the inside of his right arm near the elbow joint. Immediately he became fearful and remembered his cousin's fatal ordeal with cancer which began with a lump in his arm.

After the initial reaction of alarm, he meditated. He felt a reassurance from a deep part of himself that a detoxification was beginning and knew that it would be in his best interest to get cleared out as much as possible. He listened to this voice within telling him to trust the process and did not go to a doctor, to the dismay of his family.

The lump increased in size and tenderness and became the size of a marble. It was accompanied by a series of clear outs; a term unique to Network Chiropractic, meaning "integrated healing adjustments." Small infected sores broke out on most of his fingers and the lump grew in size and soreness until it was the size of a walnut and protruded considerably. His lymph glands became enlarged and he ran a low-grade fever. The lump started to burn and throb with considerable intensity.

He increased adjustments to one or two a day. After each clearing adjustment, the burning and throbbing sensations would ease. He had no doubt that his body was going through a major release or discharge. After two months a scab formed. The lump decreased in size and there was seepage. During this period he lost ten pounds and had little appetite. A week later the scab broke off revealing fresh tissue developing. New tissue filled in the minor remnant of cavity behind the swelling, which continued to drain.

Throughout this process he did not interfere but simply allowed his innate intelligence to release this foreign matter. He wrote, "I do not know the source or the reason about this detoxification. However I recognize that my body is finally releasing something filled with anger that never belonged to me. My frequent adjustments helped me to be present with the process in complete trust. This process has deepened my appreciation and respect for the Network Chiropractic Model, and has been a vivid demonstration of its innate power."

The miracle is not in the condition that healed but in this man's greater contact between his innate intelligence and his educated mind. The magic is in the natural awareness, trust, and respect for life that develops in an individual as a consequence of this form of healing. The change in a person's attitudes about self, about life, and his or her awe of life are the true miracles.

This new trust and awareness results naturally from a spinal system cleared of interference—a system that exceeds the most glorious instrument ever made by human hand—that is properly tuned to serve the Composer of all creation. It is available to all. To quote Don Campbell in *The Roar of Silence,* "Exploring the inner world . . . does not require study, travel, or devotion to a guru . . . it is simple. We need only to have the courage to see God within ourselves as a unique reflection of all time, knowledge, and ever abundant love."

7

Theme and Variations:
Testimonies Old and New
LANCE W. BRUNNER

I was not prepared for the miracle that was about to happen.
Norman Cousins[1]

Each illness has a musical solution. The shorter and more complete the solution—the greater the musical talent of the physician. Sickness demands manifold solutions. The selection of the most appropriate solution determines the talent of the physician.

Novalis

"Snakebites are cured by music of the flute when played skillfully and melodiously," says a medical text called *On Deadly Infections,* attributed to Democritus, a Greek born in the mid-fifth century B.C.[2] Theophrastus, a student of both Plato and Aristotle, noted in his work *On Inspiration* that "sufferers from sciatica were permanently freed from it if someone played the *aulos* over the place in the Phrygian *harmonia.*"[3]

Homer and other bards sang of even more miraculous claims of music's power in its ability to fend off plague. One account tells us of Terpander, who "went to Sparta . . . and cured the people there by means of music, releasing Sparta . . . from the grip of the plague."[4]

Ancient writings are filled with testimonies to music's power to perform miracles of healing or transformation, whether in ancient Greece or Rome, in the Bible, or other ancient texts.[5]

Modern readers tend to dismiss these claims as fanciful myths: touching and quaint, at best, or silly and absurd, at worst. Our more rational worldview does not accept the lofty assertions of such testimony without some scientifically validated proof. None of the ancient writers could offer explanations of the healing process that would satisfy us, given the technical state of science and medicine at the time. That music did, in fact, have a major role in such realms as moral and psychological development, the transformation of minds and the healing of bodies is not in question for these ancient witnesses. But words, by their very nature, could not "prove" what happened so long ago, nor capture the vividness of the music now so remote.

As a musicologist specializing in the music of the Middle Ages, such references in the ancient texts have always held a special fascination for me, especially in their symbolic or metaphorical meanings. However, it was not until I had some of my own extraordinary experiences with music's healing powers that I began to look at the ancient testimonies in a different light, to take an interest in the possibilities of literal meanings, as well. At the same time, I began to discover a number of what I consider to be modern counterparts to the ancient texts suggesting to me that, far from isolated voices from a "primitive" and naive past, these early references to music's miraculous powers, particularly in healing, form the part of an ongoing theme throughout human history that is still very much alive in our own time. Indeed, people like Norman Cousins or Alfred Tomatis[6] today are telling of their own experiences of musical miracles, reminding us that there may very well be something to be rediscovered and explored in the long chain of testimonies. Scholars like Joscelyn Godwin have systematically explored what Godwin called "the musical branch of the Perennial Tradition," in making available translations of, as well as offering interpretive essays on, contributions to the subject from ancient Greece to the twentieth century.[7] We might look at this tradition as a type of "theme and variations," of which we can continue to be a part as we explore the way music can transform our own lives.

The miraculous powers of music are, of course, by no means restricted to Western civilization. Non-Western cultures have their own rich legacies of musical miracles, as anthropologists and ethnomusicologists have long been discovering.[8] In passing over this vast and fascinating field of material in which music is often attributed magical power, I cite only a single passage by an Indian writer testifying of the powers of *ragas* (an important genre of the music of India based on continuous elaboration of specific scale patterns): patterns):

> When the Rag[a]s are sung in the proper season and time and with perfect knowledge of the science, an absolute sense of calm and inner satisfaction is derived, hardly to be expressed. In such a state of perfection the Rag[a]s are supposed to be possessed of supernatural powers. . . . They are benefactors of humanity by curing various bodily ailments. They charm the element of nature, and invoke fire and water, in short, *perform miracles.*[9] [My italics.]

In the present essay I would simply like to add my voice to the others in this volume by pointing to some of the recent testimonies that have helped bring me back to both the historical and non-Western references to musical miracles and to the present moment, as it were, and a new relationship to the world of music. That "new" relationship is actually a very old one, perhaps even primeval, that can allow us to become a part of this tradition, not as passive observers, but as creatively engaged participants. I intend these remarks to be no more than an invitation for readers to "listen for themselves" and discover what truths they can experience in these variations on the theme of music and miracles. The more this happens—the more we can move these phenomena from the periphery of curiosity and fascinating concepts and testimonies of others to the center of our lived experience—the more music will be able to exert its power, not only in individual miracles, but in transforming the way we view such fundamental issues as health and healing.

Norman Cousins

Let me begin by summarizing Norman Cousins's testimony alluded to in the epigraph. In *Anatomy of an Illness,* Cousins told his remarkable story of recovery from a crippling illness. Through laughter and will power and his partnership with a physician, he was able to mobilize his body's own healing mechanisms to overcome a seemingly hopeless situation. This healing experience was so powerful that Cousins spent a good part of the rest of his life, some twenty-five years, trying to better understand and write about those powers inherent in each of us that can be mobilized for our own healing. A writer and editor by profession, he was asked in 1978, at the age of sixty-three, to join the faculty of the UCLA School of Medicine to teach literature to medical students. All the while he was keenly observing in both literary references and lived experience how the mind and the emotions play a role in the healing process.

In a chapter from *Anatomy of an Illness* called "Creativity and Longevity," Cousins recounted his meetings with Pablo Casals and Albert Schweitzer, both of whom were renowned musicians. It was just a few weeks before Casal's ninetieth birthday when Cousins visited him in his home in Puerto Rico. When he arose in the morning, Casals could barely drag himself around. As Cousins describes the *maestro:*

His various infirmities made it difficult for him to dress himself. Judging from his difficulty in walking and from the way he held his arms, I guessed he was suffering from rheumatoid arthritis. His emphysema was evident in his labored breathing. He came into the living room on Marta's [his young wife's] arm. He was badly stooped. His head was pitched forward and he walked with a shuffle. His hands were swollen and his fingers were clenched.[10]

Casals headed for the piano, and Cousins bore witness to a remarkable transformation:

I was not prepared for the miracle that was about to happen. The fingers slowly unlocked and reached toward the keys like the buds of a plant toward the sunlight. His back straightened. He seemed to breathe more freely. Now his fingers settled on the keys. Then came the opening bars of Bach's *Wohltemperierte Klavier,* played with great sensitivity and control. . . . He hummed as he played, then said that Bach spoke to him here—and he placed his hand over his heart.

Then he plunged into a Brahms concerto and his fingers, now agile and powerful, raced across the keyboard with dazzling speed. His entire body seemed fused with the music; it was no longer stiff and shrunken but supple and graceful and completely freed of its arthritic coils.

Having finished the piece, he stood up by himself, far straighter and taller than when he had come into the room. He walked to the breakfast table with no trace of shuffle, ate heartily, talked animatedly, finished the meal, then went for a walk on the beach.[11]

Cousins witnessed the same process later in the day ("Twice in one day I had seen the miracle"). He attributed the miracle not directly to the music itself, but to the more general realms of creativity and purpose, which clearly triggered biochemical reactions: "Creativity for Pablo Casals was the source of his own cortisone. It is doubtful whether any anti-inflammatory medication he would have taken would have been as powerful or as safe as the substances produced by the interaction of his mind and body."[12]

Writing in the 1970s with access to research findings in the field that has become known as psychoneuroimmunology, Cousins was able to describe some of the apparent biochemical reactions Casals went through in his musical transformations to a degree that would have been unthinkable in the ancient world. Yet, as to just how music served as agent in this process, we are left in as much mystery as with our Homeric witnesses. It is also clear from the word "longevity" in the chapter title of Cousins' work that Cousins was also testifying to a succession of miracles that, for people like Casals and Schweitzer, results in long and productive lives, in which one of the central creative forces is music. Cousins, in any case, was not a musical researcher, but a keen observer and witness to the miracles of healing occurring in his own and others' lives. It is comforting to know that after his death in November, 1990, his quest to understand those processes and invite others to explore and celebrate in them goes on on many fronts.

"Music and Health" Conferences

Over the past few years, I have had the privilege of hearing the testimonies of dozens of individuals on the quest to understand the ways in which music can function in human health. I am referring, in particular, to three remarkable two-day conferences on "Music and Health" held at Eastern Kentucky University in 1986, 1988, and 1990. The conferences were created and organized primarily by Professor Arthur Harvey.[13] They were co-sponsored by Eastern Kentucky University's College of Allied Health and by Music and Health Services Foundation, which Arthur Harvey and I founded in 1986 to help disseminate information about research and opportunities associated with the therapeutic and health promoting uses of music. One of the roles I played at each conference was to summarize the presentations and draw conclusions from each day's program.

In summarizing each of the three conferences, one is struck with the enormous range and diversity of the programs and with the number of people who are drawn to work with music in endless varieties of therapeutic applications. We had presenters from various musical fields, including music therapy and music education, performance and composition, musicology, and even the recording industry. Medical personnel were also on hand, including physicians and researchers, nurses, physical therapists, psychiatrists, and psychologists. Social workers who use music in their work as well as entrepreneurs and inventors were represented. There were those folks who had become musicians, in a sense, by learning to listen in profound new ways that helped transform their lives and health, and they simply wanted to share their experience. Although it is impossible in a limited space to do justice to the richness of these presentations, to the uniqueness and the details of each, I can attest that these voices, taken as a group, provide a powerful testimony to the power of music to perform miracles, big and little, in the quest for leading healthy, sane lives. I share here only a few examples, some solo voices, taken from a much larger chorus.

Healing Harps

When I listen to Professor Ronald Price of Northern Illinois University tell about his life and music's role in it, I am drawn back to the type of Greek testimonies cited at the beginning of this essay. The miracles he describes seem just as fanciful and beyond rational comprehension—certainly beyond what medical science can neatly explain. Yet there he stands: radiant proof for the claims that music can produce miracles of healing, even if, as in the ancient accounts, such claims still defy explanation.

Price was embarking on what seemed to be a long and distinguished career as a French horn player and teacher when he was struck, in his mid-twenties, with the onset of a degenerative Parkinsonian condition. He began to lose control of his motor functions as his nervous system deteriorated, and he had to give up his instrument. His prognosis was grim, with little hope of recovering his health and a normal life. Doctors confirmed at this time the presence of cerebral palsy.

Somehow Price was drawn to the harp and quickly experienced a miracle. He found that after pulling on the strings of a harp for several hours, his symptoms began to disappear! He decided to take up his new "medicine" in a serious way and eventually became a professional harpist, playing three or four hours a day. Such performance activity has kept him relatively symptom-free—and free to lead a full and exciting life. The harp's miracle with Price was not a complete healing, however, anymore than Casals's piano performances permanently cured his arthritis. Price concedes that when he does not play the harp for three or more days, back come the symptoms. One side of his face begins to slacken, his speech becomes garbled and he begins to drool, he loses control of his left arm and leg, and he has severe perceptual problems. Still, the nontoxic "medication" of performing on the harp has allowed him the freedom of otherwise good health. Although there is no satisfactory scientific explanation of how playing the harp specifically palliated Price's symptoms, the results were so dramatic he naturally wanted to see if they could be replicated with other sufferers of neurological disorders.

At the 1988 Music and Health Conference his ensemble, Healing Harps, gave a performance and discussed their work as performing musicians and the "side effects" in the realm of health.[14] The ensemble grew out of a research project in music therapy conducted at Northern Illinois University, a project that had its roots in work begun by Dr. Price nearly twenty years earlier.[15] At the time of the conference three of the six members of the ensemble had disabilities. The objective for the Healing Harps, however, is to focus exclusively on musicianship and humaneness; the term therapy is not used. Nevertheless, some of the therapeutic results of the engagement in music-making, as with Ronald Price, are miraculous.

Angie M. was a twenty-three-year-old member of the ensemble in 1988. She had severe disabilities when she joined the group nine months before the conference. Born three months prematurely, her left arm and leg were notably affected by cerebral palsy. Surgical procedures and physical therapy administered when she was a child helped increase the function of her left leg, but she was never able to extend her left arm away from her side, to turn her hand over, or to use the fingers of her left hand. After nine months with the group, Angie had developed good mobility of her left arm and independent dexterity of her fingers that produced a strong, well-centered sound from the harp. Her miraculous improvement through making music with the harp lay well beyond what the best surgeon or other medical practitioners could have hoped to achieve.

One of the goals of the group is to work with medical clinicians to help explain and understand the mechanisms of such remarkable results. At this point, however, the primary goal of the ensemble is still celebrating by making music, and if that produces a miracle or two along the way, that, too, is worth celebrating. Oliver Sacks shares some similar stories of musical miracles in *Awakenings* (New York: Harper, 1983); for example: "This power of music to integrate and cure, to liberate the Parkinsonian and give him freedom while it lasts ('You are the music/while the music lasts,' T. S. Eliot), is quite fundamental, and seen in every patient" (p. 60, n. 45); "There are still a few things which bring her together, or which recall her former unbroken self. Music calms her, relieves her distraction, and gives her—if briefly—its coherence and concord" (p. 160); "Mercifully, what medication cannot achieve, music, action, or art can do—at least for the time that it lasts" (p. 330); or, citing E. M. Forester, "The Arts are not drugs. They are not guaranteed to act when taken. Something as mysterious and capricious as the creative impulse has to be released before they can act" (p. 283). I am grateful to Todd Garland for pointing these references out to me.

Medical Music

Kay Gardner is an accomplished performer and composer who has had a long-standing interest in the healing dimensions of music. She made presentations at all three "Music and Healing" conferences. In 1988 Gardner told of an experience she had while her father, who had Alzheimer's disease, was dying:

I found . . . that Don Campbell's *Crystal Meditations*, music which pulses between the brain's alpha and theta rhythms, enabled us to verbally communicate for twenty minutes, where attempting communication without this music was impossible for more than twenty seconds at a time. Dad's brain was able to entrain with the music at a deeper level than where the dis-ease was.[16]

Gardner had recently been invited to Yale University to meet with anesthesiologists to discuss the uses of music before and after operations. She observed that in a number of countries, including Italy, France, Germany, and Poland, music was already a part of surgical procedures.[17] Her presentation at the 1988 Music and Health Conference outlined the nine components of composing specifically medical music. She explored the various parameters and how each might function in given medical situations. As systematic and rigorous as her approaches are, she acknowledges a great deal that cannot be quantified. She mentioned, for example, her contact with a woman from Maine who had a painful shoulder dislocation. Gardner discovered that playing her recording of the Chopin Second Piano Concerto freed the woman from pain. What it was about this piece— or this *performance* of the piece—that relieved her pain cannot be measured or easily understood. Until such things are better understood, we can safely classify such phenomena as "miracles."

Life-Saving Lullabies

At the 1990 Music and Health Conference, Terry Woodford related that a miracle he had inadvertently brought about through music profoundly transformed his own life. A successful music producer for such groups as the Temptations and the Supremes and stars like Roy Orbison, Woodford decided to make a recording of ten lullabies with a special beat that could be used for day-care centers. He wanted to use the sound of the human heart as heard where a baby lays its head on an adult's chest to highlight the metrical basis of the lullabies, assuming that it might calm infants and small children and help them sleep better. He did not expect to run into the kind of technical problems he encountered with the sound of the heart, which is rhythmical, of course, but irregular. He spent at least a thousand hours, stretching his considerable skills as a sound technician, to get the recorded heart to beat as regularly as a metronome, so that it could be placed into the fabric of the songs. Woodford was gratified with the enthusiastic reception the tapes had at the one hundred and fifty day-care centers to which he had sent complimentary copies, but he could not have imagined at the time another reception and use the tape would find.

An experiment carried out on fifty-nine newborn babies at Helen Keller Hospital, near his Alabama home, revealed that 94 percent of crying babies fell asleep right away without a bottle or pacifier. Somehow a copy of his *Baby-Go-to-Sleep* tape found its way into the hospital of the University of Alabama at Birmingham, where nurses were using it in the cardiac recovery unit for infants recovering from open heart surgery. A baby there, struggling against the respirator, was about to die when the nurses tried the lullabies. To everyone's amazement, the baby calmed down, went to sleep, and lived! Woodford described his response:

I could hardly breathe. Babies were recovering from open heart surgery, and to see their immediate response to a lullaby tape, instead of having to be injected with sedatives, changed my whole value system. In the music business, you measure success by your last record, how high it went on the charts. But the minute you see that music can calm a baby, give it the rest it needs to survive and live . . . well, that's real success.

Woodford sold his million-dollar-a-year recording business to start, with his wife Lola Scobey (who shared the presentation with Woodford at the 1990 conference), what is now Audio-Therapy Innovations. The initial tape was sold in department and infant specialty stores, but all profits were used to make more tapes, which are still supplied free to pediatricians, hospitals, and institutions that serve children.[18]

The success of the tape is a kind of miracle in itself. By early 1992 some 20,000 tapes have been given away to individuals or institutions that serve children, and the tape is now being used in at least 4,000 hospitals and health care facilities. The tapes and audio-mattress systems are now being used in 400 of the 460 neonatal intensive care units in the United States. The mattresses allow the tape to be used for premature babies in their isolettes. Lying in a fetal position with their ears to the mattresses, only the babies can hear the tapes. The testimonies of individual miracles the original and new tapes have facilitated are staggering in their number and range. There are testimonies about otherwise healthy babies (and their parents) who were unable to sleep until they used the tape and numerous accounts of infants in severe pain and crisis, such as those in neonatal intensive care units, burn victims, babies born addicted to crack cocaine, or infants and children who are undergoing chemotherapy. Furthermore, new tapes are being used with adults and geriatric patients with remarkable success.

Woodford referred to his new path engendered by the simple lullabies as "a journey into my own ignorance," discovering the emptiness of focusing on using the power of music to make money, when that power can be used to heal. He and his wife have done all in their power to give this simple gift away as an act of loving-kindness and compassion. When they talk about its effectiveness, they do not focus on technical explanations, which in any case are elusive at this point. "The mind," Woodford explains, "has the ability to censor out offensive sounds and focus on what is pleasing." It is thus possible for an infant to hear the soft strains of the lullabies and exclude the range of noises and other intrusive stimulants that one finds, say, in an intensive care unit.

When Woodford and Scobey speak, they focus on the simple miracle that the music really *does* work again and again, and they trust that its widespread effectiveness will lead to successful research, which in turn will lead to greater acceptance of others who work with the power of music in the healing process. It is remarkable to see the way a few simple songs coming from the heart (literally and figuratively) are transforming not only individual lives, like Woodford and Scobey's, and the tens of thousands the music has helped, but the attitudes and practices of institutions as well.

A Caveat

There are many other witnesses to music's power that I could invoke here, but I trust that those I have mentioned will attest to the continuity of the tradition that stretches from the ancient world to the present. Before closing, however, I would like to mention a discussion that took place during the 1988 conference, in response to an incident that occurred there. A young woman received a demonstration treatment on the *B.E.T.A.R.*, an apparatus designed by Peter Kelly in which a person lying on a platform is bathed and totally engulfed in music, pulsed with music and vibration. After the treatment the woman had such a barrage of thoughts and images running uncontrollably through her mind that she feared she was having an attack of psychosis and began to panic. There were skilled practitioners on hand who dealt with the crisis, which was resolved without serious consequences. The experience was, in fact, one of catharsis. But her initial crisis and distress raised important ethical issues related to working with music in certain therapeutic situations. As we continue to expand our use of music for healing and transformation, the group agreed, we need to proceed responsibly, fully aware that what we do may have powerful and unexpected effects on individuals. Musicians will need to work along with trained psychologists or other professionals to address situations that may arise as a result of a patient's interactions with music.

The Vast Darkness

In closing I would like to retell a story that cultural anthropologist Gregory Bateson was fond of telling about the philosopher Alfred

North Whitehead and his famous student Bertrand Russell. Whitehead had invited Russell to Harvard to give a lecture to a general audience on Einstein's theory of relativity, which was rather new at the time. After Russell spoke, Whitehead publicly thanked him for making a clear and brilliant exposition of a very complex subject, but he also thanked him especially "for leaving unobscured the vast darkness of the subject." If Whitehead was poking fun at his former student, putting him in his place, he was also paying him a compliment for not focusing just on the tiny corner of the field that we can understand and explain. Bateson, always open to discovering "the patterns which connect," pointed out that "every textbook is devoted to the project of obscuring the vast darkness of the subject."[19] Of course, it is important to learn what is known and available, he argues, but we need to be aware, and be willing to explore, what we do not know, which is, in Bateson's words, "how the world fits together."

I think Bateson's little story and reminder are instructive for those working with music and health, where so much remains beyond what can easily be quantified and measured, where the most spectacular results seem still to be miracles, rather than predictable outcomes of a prescribed technique or approach. But the miracles that can ensue from music's interacting with body and mind seem quite commonplace if we look at the full sweep of the testimonies, the many variations on the theme. With this growing weight of evidence, it seems absurd to be trapped in the tiny corner of our knowledge that can be reliably proven in a laboratory by reducing a complex whole to one or two variables. Our miracles are a way of waking us up to new possibilities—or ancient ones—which someday may yield to clearer explanations of the ways music can operate in human health. These miracles can help transform the very ways we experience and understand the world.

There are ways of listening, it would seem, that allow us to embrace "the vast darkness" of our body/mind that can lead to miracles of healing. Going beyond the confines of our rational, discursive minds and experiencing other modes of consciousness, we can participate more fully in the process of our lives. For our counterparts in the ancient world or from other cultures, this participatory consciousness was apparently part of their way of experiencing the world. For us, however, steeped in a mechanistic world view, there is need to reconnect with the wisdom of this mode of knowing.[20] Music is a means for reestablishing such connectedness, making us more whole. But that is the topic of another article. Here, I simply wanted to call attention to the tradition of music and miracles by pointing to some of the witnesses along the way.

"I think we've only scratched the surface on using the power of music as a healing tool," noted Terry Woodford.[21] It seems clear from historical testimony that this process may be one of *re*-discovering some perennial truths, but incorporating such techniques into modern medicine will certainly be a new variation on the theme. Expanding the range of therapeutic modalities to include music will make medicine more humane and personal, while allowing the patient to take a more active role in the healing process. There are enormous possibilities for the ways in which music can be incorporated into healing. The Music and Health conferences highlighted a number of possibilities, encouraging further research and applications. I fully anticipate increased, albeit gradual, acceptance of these approaches in medical practice. However, there is no need to wait passively for this transformation. We already have enough models and examples to incorporate musical medicine actively into our lives. As more variations on the theme are developed, others are bound to listen—and that is what it takes.

Endnotes

1. *Anatomy of an Illness as Perceived by the Patient* (New York: W. W. Norton, 1979), p. 72.
2. Bruno Meinicke, "Music and Medicine in Classical Antiquity," in *Music and Medicine,* Dorothy M. Schullian and Max Schoen, eds. (New York: Schuman, 1948), p. 81.
3. Andrew Barker, *Greek Musical Writings Volume I: The Musician and his Art* (Cambridge: Cambridge University Press, 1984), p. 281.
4. Ibid., p. 247.
5. See, for example, the still useful collection of essays in Schullian and Schoen's *Music and Medicine.* For a cursory survey, see Rosalie R. Pratt, "The Historical Relationship between Music and Medicine," in *The Third International Symposium on Music in Medicine, Education, and Therapy for the Handicapped,* Rosalie R. Pratt, ed. (Lanham, MD: University Press of America, 1985), pp. 237–269. For a more detailed study, see Werner F. Kuemmel, *Musik und Medizin. Ihre Wechselbeziehungen in Theorie und Praxis von 800 bis 1800* (Freiburg: Karl Alber, 1977).
6. Dr. Alfred Tomatis's work is becoming more widely known outside his

native France. For the remarkable account of how he rediscovered the healing power of Gregorian Chant, see Don Campbell's *Music: Physician for Times to Come* (Wheaton, IL: Theosophical Publishing House, 1991).

7. See especially Joscelyn Godwin, *Harmonies of Heaven and Earth* (Rochester, VT: Inner Traditions International, 1987), which contains an extensive bibliography on the subject. For editions of the texts in translation, see his *Music, Mysticism, and Magic. A Sourcebook* (London: Routledge and Kegan Paul, 1986).

8. Music plays an important part in shamanic traditions. See, for example, Gilbert Rouget, *Music and Trance* (Chicago: University of Chicago Press, 1985), or essays in *Shamanism: An Expanded View of Reality,* compiled by Shirley Nicholson (Wheaton, IL: Theosophical Publishing House, 1987), pp. 13, 90–93, 240–241, et passim. The work of Ruth-Inge Heinze, a contributor to the present collection, in the area of shamanism has also been very important.

9. As cited in Dane Rudhyar, *The Magic of Tone and the Art of Music* (Boulder: Shambhala, 1982), p. 175.

10. Norman Cousins, *Anatomy of an Illness as Perceived by the Patient* (New York: Norton, 1979), p. 72.

11. Ibid., pp. 72–73.

12. Ibid., page 74.

13. Professor Harvey recently left the faculty of Eastern Kentucky University to be Director of Music Ministries at Waialae Baptist Church in Honolulu. His work on attitudinal music is described in chapter 11 of Don G. Campbell, *Music: Physician for Times to Come*, Quest Books, 1991.

14. Professor Price and Elizabeth Cifani, who is head of harp studies at Northern Illinois University, made a presentation that discussed background, philosophy, and goals of the ensemble. A copy of their remarks is contained in the "Conference Proceedings" for the Music and Health Second National Conference, April 7–8, 1988, compiled by Dr. Arthur W. Harvey, pp. 86–89.

15. See Ronald D. Price, "Hope for the Troubled," *American Harpists Journal* (Spring, 1973).

16. Kay Gardner, "On Composing Medical Music," 1988 "Conference Proceedings," p. 15. See Therese Schroeder-Sheker's essay in this volume for other music in working with the dying. Don Campbell was also a presenter at the Music and Health Conferences in 1986 and 1988. Since he is a contributor to this volume, I let him testify himself to the numerous musical miracles he has witnessed and experienced. His *Crystal Meditations* is on Spirit Records and is available through IMHE, Box 1244, Boulder, CO. 80306, phone 303-443-8484.

17. For more information on music and anesthesiology, see the proceedings of the First International Symposium on Music and Medicine, December 1982: *Anxiety, Pain and Music in Anesthesia,* R. Droh and R. Spintge, eds. (Basel: Roche Editions, 1983).

Lance W. Brunner

18. To obtain copies of the tapes or more information, contact Audio Therapy Innovations; P.O. Box 550, Colorado Springs, CO 80901; or call 1-800-537-7748.
19. Gregory Bateson, "The Pattern Which Connects," lecture at Esalen Institute (December 1978). Cassette available on Dolphin Tapes through Esalen, Big Sur, CA.
20. For two excellent studies that deal with incorporating aspects of ancient wisdom into the modern world, see Morris Berman, *The Reenchantment of the World* (Ithaca: Cornell University Press, 1981) and Stanislav Grof, ed., *Ancient Wisdom and Modern Science* (Albany: State University of New York Press, 1984).
21. "The Tape that Puts Crying Babies to Sleep," *Western New York Family Magazine* (March, 1992).

8

A Sonic Birth

RON MINSON, M.D.

We were ushered into a cold, white, visually sterile room with a single medical examining table. On that table was a tiny baby with vibrant red hair. She drew me across the room like a powerful magnet. Almost exactly one year after the death of our baby Melissa, we took our new daughter home to meet her brother and sister. We named her Erica. There were problems with Erica from our very first day together. She cried and screamed inconsolably. Nothing we did seemed to calm her. To make matters worse she was plagued by recurring ear infections that kept her ill and in pain through much of her early childhood. Erica was being forced to pay a high price for her very existence, and the price was going to keep going up.

Erica entered the toddler stage as a delightful, if developmentally delayed child. She learned to speak later than usual and had difficulty expressing herself. She was painfully accident prone.

Her alert first grade teacher brought to our attention Erica's poor grasp of reading, spelling and mathematics. Coupled with Erica's inability to express herself well and her occasionally disruptive behavior, these problems suggested that Erica might have a learning disability. Our fears were confirmed. For Erica this particular learning problem manifested itself in an inability to sound out letters. She couldn't reproduce the sounds because she was unable to hear them correctly. This situation was complicated by a phenomenon unique to dyslexia: Erica's brain reversed printed letters. This meant that what she learned with her ears and what she perceived with her eyes had little or nothing in common. (A rapidly increasing body of clinical evidence relates learning disabilities to problems of the ear and auditory processing.)

The consensus of the experts was that Erica was not ready to move on to the second grade. We reluctantly agreed to hold her back, but placed her in another school in a futile attempt to avoid stigmatizing her. As with most families who have a member with a disability, more and more parental attention was being focused on Erica. She was also enrolled in private special education classes for language and speech. Unfortunately, our efforts had the opposite of the desired effect; she viewed herself as a failure.

We contributed to the problem because we didn't understand it. Simplistically, we just thought that the solution was for Erica to work harder in order to overcome her handicap. We failed in our efforts because we failed to see that she was trying as hard as she could.

This constant pressure to succeed, combined with a steady diet of failure, began to have a seriously negative effect on Erica's behavior. She had difficulty accepting reality and became withdrawn.

Fourth grade marked the beginning of a dramatic change in Erica's view of herself and the world in which she was living. She saw the disintegration of my marriage, which moved through separation to divorce, as further evidence that nothing could be counted on, no one was going to give her the stability and unconditional acceptance she so desperately needed.

Though we were now living apart, the bond between Erica and me was not severed. In fact, taking on the mantle of matchmaker, she engineered a meeting between me and Kate O'Brien. When Kate and I decided to be married, we were delighted to discover that Erica wanted to live with us. However, what we hadn't counted on was sabotage. She (unconsciously) transformed herself into an implacable adolescent warrior. Instead of peace, love and understanding, we found ourselves in an emotionally ruthless struggle.

As Erica's focus in the family became more and more destructive, her academic efforts suffered greatly. Our concern for her increasingly hostile behavior grew, as did my concern for her ability to succeed in school. Her will to learn was evaporating. She became sullen and withdrawn and started experiencing significant bouts of depression.

By the end of junior high two unpleasant facts were clear to us. The first was that the school system had washed its hands of Erica. Our second realization was that Erica had truly given up on herself.

During her eleventh grade year things came to a head. On a personal level she now refused to accept any responsibility for her own actions. Her motivation and self-esteem slipped even farther down, and she sank into a deeper state of depression. Psychotherapy seemed to have little effect on her. Finally, half way through the year she hit some invisible wall. Her tolerance for school disintegrated completely, and she dropped out.

She cycled through a series of low skill, low paying jobs from which she was invariably fired. She found herself eighteen years old, living at home, out of school, fighting with her mother, alienated from the rest of her family and deeply depressed. Helpless and hopeless, her thoughts turned to death.

We found ourselves in a state of agonizing helplessness. Nothing we did seemed to make any difference. We were all truly desperate.

Unexpectedly, we got a small ray of hope. A friend brought me an article entitled "A Dyslexified World," by Paul Madaule, and insisted that I read it. Madaule wrote as one who suffered from dyslexia himself. His description of the alienation caused by dyslexia was so cogent and powerful that I realized that none of us in Erica's world had even begun to comprehend the horrifying grasp that her learning disability had on her. Madaule also wrote about a therapeutic program that had helped him overcome his dyslexia.

The program was called the Tomatis Method. Although relatively new in North America, the Tomatis Method was reported to have been used with excellent results in Europe for more than twenty years. The program was developed by a French ear, nose and throat physician, psychologist and internationally recognized expert on auditory problems, Dr. Alfred A. Tomatis.

I had never heard of Dr. Tomatis or his method. But some hope, no matter how slim, seemed much better than no hope at all. I asked Erica if she would be willing to visit the Tomatis Center in Phoenix, and she agreed. That decision had a profound effect on both our lives.

Within a few days we visited the center. I was unclear about how and why the program worked. But, I took the leap of faith and signed Erica up. I also signed up for the program. On some deep intuitive level I saw that it could also enhance my well-being.

As unlikely as it sounded to me, the program used listening to effect change in both the body and the mind, and used music to effect that change. By presenting music in a unique way, our ability to truly listen is awakened and our desire to express ourselves is stimulated.

In humans the ear is the first sensory organ to develop. It is fully functional four-and-a-half months before we are born. In the womb the sounds we hear—our mother's breathing, her heartbeat and especially her voice—stimulate our brain and fire electrical charges into our cortex. It is the nourishment provided by these electrical charges that enhances our mental function and spurs the proper development of the brain and the central nervous system. Because the ear is an active channel to the brain and nervous system, it acts as a battery, constantly charging and stimulating them both. This stimulus is critical not only to our body's ability to grow properly and develop muscle tone and coordination, but to our ability to both hear and listen—and ultimately learn and understand.

Erica's biological mother unintentionally denied her the continuity of her voice—the thread that provides the positive intrauterine and post-birth experience so critical in fostering the ability to bond with others. Without that experience we may lack the capacity to bond. Without that capacity we can never be fully human. But Erica was also robbed of the desire to listen and to communicate effectively. Her repeated physiological problems, like her ear infections, further diminished both her desire and her actual physical capacity to master communication in all its forms.

An important underlying idea in the Tomatis Method is that listening is learned and must be accompanied by the desire to communicate. If listening is learned incorrectly—so that information is distorted and cannot be understood—it must be relearned. If desire is lacking, it must be rekindled. This relearning or retraining process is at the heart of the Tomatis Method. As Dr. Tomatis said, "When hearing gives way to listening, one's awareness increases, the will is aroused and all aspects of our being are involved at the same time. Listening is intimately tied up with the ability to actively attune the ear to a particular sound signal, with both intention and desire to communicate."

The program involves a course of audio stimulation generated by using the music of Mozart. But why use music to create this change? And why specifically Mozart's? For centuries the healing professions have known of the profound emotional, psychological and physical effects of music. But it was Dr. Tomatis who discovered the particular efficacy of Mozart's music.

For two hundred years musicians, composers, conductors, critics and historians have described Mozart's music as transcendent and divine. These same experts often talk about something ineffable in his music that defies description or analysis. During the course of the development of the Tomatis Method, the music of Mozart proved to be universally accepted and effective in evoking the full listening function. After listening to Mozart's music, people from virtually every culture on the planet feel more creative, intelligent, empowered and motivated. Dr. Tomatis believes that this is because Mozart's intellectual and spiritual genius, not his personality, entered into the music. Because of this, when we listen to his music we are free to be in touch with the light within ourselves, rather than in touch with the creator of the music.

But the day Erica and I started the Tomatis Program, I didn't have an understanding of the theory and the science of the program. All I knew was that finally someone held out some hope for Erica.

And so it began, two hours a day, both of us listening to Mozart and Gregorian chants. The music soon began to sound scratchy as the low frequencies were filtered out. It was strange but not unpleasant. We listened to the music by both air conduction and conduction through the bones of the head. As the sound switched back and forth between the two formats, a grating effect was created that produced intermittent changes in the music.

As we filled our days with routine activities after our sessions, I felt that Erica was starting to communicate and share with me on some level we had never reached before. I sensed that the time was ripe for a real discussion. Perhaps now I could understand her suicidal urges and why she didn't seem to feel my love for her. I needed to know why she pushed away our past offers of help. And for the first time, I wanted to know these things about her, not to change her or fix her, but simply to understand. In some subtle yet profound way, my listening had been changed.

The time was right. That night in our hotel room we had a deep and transforming talk. She reacted as if some massive emotional dam had burst. She described how she had never felt wanted, beginning with her adoption, plaintively detailing the pain of not knowing her birth mother and describing the crushing rejection that came from the knowledge that her mother did not want her. She told me how she had come to feel incompetent, stupid, even ugly. She confessed that her life was a prison sentence and that she was just "doing time" until her sentence was up. To Erica, love, joy, life and the future were meaningless terms.

I was amazed at how articulate and clear she was. For the first time she was using language as an effective tool for communicating her deepest feelings. She painted a picture of a life so filled with emotional rejection that I understood how death could seem a welcome solution. I marveled at the courage it took for her to keep on living.

As I listened to a litany of pain about her disability, her adoption, her school and her anger at my former wife Nancy, Kate and me, I was acutely distressed. I wanted to interrupt her, as I had done so often in the past, with assurances of our love for her. But this time I listened silently, finally willing to allow her to be completely and totally heard. It was an incredible emotional catharsis for us both. Understandably we were both in tears as together we experienced the pain of her life, step by traumatic step. We cried and laughed and felt connected in a special new way. I apologized to her for never understanding before, and she absolved me, saying, "That's o.k., Pop, you didn't know." She was right. I hadn't known. And she hadn't been able to express it before either. That night she told me that she felt truly listened to and heard for the first time. Never before in her life had she felt so connected to another human being. As we continued to talk there was something in her voice I had never heard before. It was the sound of hope. We were not out of the woods yet. But with Erica finally ventilating years of anger and hurt in a healthy manner, the path to healing was at last opening.

By the fifth day of the program Erica began to manifest other changes in her behavior. Her sleep pattern changed. She started waking up feeling pleasant instead of hostile. Literally overnight, the severe depression that was inexorably pushing her toward suicide vanished. I was astounded, delighted and perplexed. What I was witnessing flew in the face of all my clinical experience as a psychiatrist. What's more, it was happening without medications, without the usual analysis, catharsis and abreactions I had been taught were necessary for the resolution of conflict.

With her depression lifted, Erica's thoughts of death and suicide dissipated quickly. She claimed that things were clearer and that she was able to remember better. Even her spelling showed a dramatic improvement. As I watched these changes take place I realized that Erica was awakening to the possibilities of her own life. She recognized these changes herself by telling me repeatedly, "My mind just works better."

As the days progressed her mood, overall energy, body posture and mental attitude all improved. Oddly enough, at the same time the clumsiness she had experienced as a small child returned. It was as if her body was saying to her, "You will have to reintegrate your physical coordination because you didn't get it done right the first time." She made giant emotional strides, becoming much more willing to speak out for herself and about herself. She was able to articulate how she felt. She started taking emotional risks and became more open and honest. Most important, she made major progress in overcoming her fear of rejection. By the time the program was completed she had stopped overreacting emotionally, and her behavior had become appropriate in virtually every area.

In the two months after completing the program, Erica made a giant leap in maturity. She was now able to process the math we take for granted. In one instance, while dining out, she added an upside-down dinner check. This simple triumph, which would have been impossible just two scant months before, exhilarated her and thrilled us.

Now the changes were coming dizzyingly fast. She began to have dreams and plans for her future. She rapidly matured in her ability to develop and maintain personal relationships. This included the ability to set and hold realistic limits and to expect a level of respect from her relationship partners. She began to acknowledge her own intelligence. As she joyously told me one day, "I always thought I was smart, Pop, but I couldn't prove it before." Even her voice became animated and expressive, no longer flat and atonal. As I watched this happen, my belief in her ability to survive and even succeed in life grew.

I am convinced that the mechanism that triggered these changes was the filtered music of Mozart. The Tomatis Method had transformed the music to recreate the sonic environment of the prebirth intrauterine state of listening. In effect, Erica was sent back to a time when her desire to listen was still intact, a time before she lost the sustaining and nourishing thread of her mother's voice. For, as Dr. Tomatis later told me, "Mozart is a very good mother."

That final week, Erica wasn't the only one experiencing changes. I too was being taught to be what I call a "true listener." This ability helped me endure the flood of emotion that spilled from Erica that night in the hotel room. But an improved ability to listen was just the beginning. By my fourth day, significant changes began to manifest themselves. Suddenly I was wide awake after only four or five hours of sleep. Yet I awoke refreshed and rested. I felt more relaxed, too.

During the next four or five days I often found myself tearful. It seemed to me that the tears were a mixture of grief for old pains and tears of joy for new self-discovery. I could feel those tears washing out old sadnesses. The process was inspiring, as if something was touching my core and releasing emotional experiences that had been weighing down my soul. With my inner self freer and lighter, something vital and new was brought to the surface—a sense of joy and hope, not just for Erica, but for myself as well.

Even my voice was affected. By practicing techniques taught in the program, I achieved a fuller, more resonant voice. This in turn helped me feel more self-confident and fully present in the world. In a very real sense I discovered my own voice, the one that is unique to me, rather than the conditioned voice that was a product of my parents and early emotional traumas.

I was also taught a vocalization technique called toning, a type of nonverbal vocal expression. By practicing toning I was able to release emotional and physical constrictions created by my subconscious mind. In effect, my body remembered emotional pain I had experienced long before my ability to verbalize was developed. This preverbal emotional pain had lain trapped inside my body, totally unnoticed by my conscious mind. Through toning I was able to release these old hurts without analyzing or dissecting them. I did not have to understand them. I did not have to relive them. I simply had to let them go and they were gone. Each time this occurred it triggered a wave of tears and a feeling of being cleansed. For me the process was like dropping emotional ballast, old unneeded baggage that impaired my ability to get on with my new life. Looking back on that period I can see that by letting go of those old pains I became more willing to commit to all types of relationships. Because I was able to reduce my fears of rejection, a problem which had plagued me from my childhood, I also became less threatened by criticism.

I learned many things undergoing the Tomatis Method. But as a psychiatrist, the most surprising was a new-found ability to articulate what had been an unconscious dissatisfaction with the limitations of conventional psychotherapy. I had spent years in psychotherapy in order to understand myself and my craft. I had mastered the techniques of my discipline and spent even more years applying them as a psychotherapist to help others. Yet psychiatry had utterly failed to reach my preverbal problems and experiences, and I was sure that it was not reaching similar problems in my patients. When these problems are not released, the ability consistently to feel good about ourselves is blocked.

The Tomatis Method is an incredibly dynamic channel for personal change. It is a simple and effective way of speeding the process of personal growth and development, either by itself or as an adjunct to psychotherapy.

Over the next three months, I gradually perceived a series of deeper changes. A physical knot that had lived in my stomach for more than thirty years had vanished. I was clearly happier with myself and consequently much happier with and tolerant of others. As a trained psychotherapist, I found the most significant thing was that all these changes were generated internally, not from any interpretation by others.

The physical and emotional changes I witnessed taking place with Erica electrified me. I felt compelled to track down how and why the program worked. During the next two years I made repeated trips to Europe to investigate the Tomatis Method in greater detail. I visited centers in Spain, Belgium and Greece. Ultimately, I was fortunate enough to study directly with Dr. Tomatis in his Paris facility. In 1990 I returned to the United States and, along with Kate, established a pilot Tomatis program in Prescott, Arizona. In January of 1991 a fully accredited Tomatis Center opened in Denver, Colorado.

After completing the Tomatis program, Erica finished high school. Today she is enrolled in college in a vocational/technical program studying graphic design. For her life has changed from something to be endured to something to be enjoyed—a process of a constant unfolding of new choices and opportunities. Her depression is gone. She continues to develop the emotional and psychological tools she needs to successfully shape a positive life for herself. She can articulate how she feels and describe what she wants out of that life. She is operating in a realistic way. She is happier. She has hope. And all of us in the Minson family share that hope.

9
Composing Self-Health

PAT MOFFITT COOK

Each musical environment that I have placed myself in, as composer, performer, teacher, listener, and student, has worked its miracles on me. In June, 1990, I was required to shift my equilibrium and seek health and wholeness due to physical dissonance. Music and sound became my therapists and dear friends. I have learned throughout my process that hearing God's rhythm in the soul is truly the magic of life. The pulse unfolds as you learn to listen, and sets up a sympathetic vibration among the body, mind and spirit. For those who are able to hear, this unity becomes a living truth. Within this union and understanding, there is love, acceptance of life's challenges, hope, and uncovering of unknown depths.

Emotional crisis, physical affliction, and spiritual deprivation break our wholeness. When we are not in sync with our natural rhythms, these dissonant realities are sounded. Evidence of this is found in the daily news: the growing health crisis worldwide, and the atrocity of world abuse and irresponsibility toward children. In general, our society is not able to listen. We do not resonate with the natural vibratory laws of creation. Individual and community vibrations are grinding against one another, engulfing existence in a growing dissonance. If we do not seek, first as individuals and then in community, harmonious resolutions to this living vibratory dissonance, then our world will vibrate uncontrollably and, like a glass, break and shatter. This call to listen is seldom heard unless we are threatened in some very personal way. Only then do we hurry to discover where the harmony lives in us and in the world.

The Search for Healing

I had been experiencing discomfort in my left side and lower back for some time. Finally in June, 1990, while still living in Dallas, my doctor discovered a pelvic mass. The next day was spent in the hospital for more tests and discussions of treatment. Without surgery, it would be difficult to know the nature of the mass. At first we agreed upon a conservative approach. When this failed my doctor recommended surgery. Instantly my wholeness was threatened.

In such instances, whether from emotional or physical affliction, an opening is forced in the self. A tear in the psyche invites fear and dissonance to quickly adhere to our thoughts, emotions, and energy. The fear sets up a vibratory pattern with its own life force, foreign to our mind and body but invading them swiftly, stealing positive energy. At this point the quest for health is not limited to the body. It engages the psyche, which then calls upon the spirit. They must all work together in order to restore wholeness. Many dimensions of change become activated demanding that healing occur on all operative levels.

My doctor wanted to schedule immediate surgery. I shared my knowledge about natural healing and diet, but my questions were met with impatience. He assured me there were no alternatives and time was important. "You cannot heal yourself," he said. "This is pathological and surgery is the only way."

Perhaps he was right, but I was unable to make a decision. My experience and background in alternative healing was deeply ingrained. I asked him if he would monitor my condition while I pursued a course of natural healing. His answer came by letter. He politely fired me as a patient because of our philosophical differences. My philosophical view to seek health and wholeness on the many operative levels on which we live was not met with understanding and support. This was true with both traditional and several nontraditional therapists I consulted after being diagnosed. From the beginning I had to find my own way. Music became the crucial healing element in my journey.

I knew, from many years of travel in third world countries and participation in ritual music and prayer, that words and song have subtle powers to penetrate our porous being. They remind our spirits and bodies to stir. While living in Asia I attended numerous forms of healings. Whether physical, spiritual, or psychological, all were based on vibratory prescriptions. Specific dances, chants, or prayers were often the primary care given to many. I remember my Chinese/Indonesian teacher of martial and healing arts telling me that *Gerakan Ular* (the snake movements) aids persons with liver ailments and blood disease. The vibration created by the body, moving like the snake, stimulates the liver and results in detoxification. The immune system is also boosted. Asthma and poor eyesight could be healed by exercises and short movements from Pekoe Kun (in Indonesian, *Gerakan Bangau Puti,* white crane movements). A child or adult imitating the spreading of the crane's wings from various positions stimulates the lungs and brings energy and blood flow to the eyes. In fact my new eyeglass prescription showed improved vision when I returned to the States. At the Chinese and Balinese funerals I attended, the family and guests spoke and chanted prayers during the cremation to help the soul continue on its journey and to avoid disorientation during the transition from body death to spirit life. Worldwide, grieving, prayers and songs accompany this transformation.

The practice of supporting transition and healing with vibration has always interested me. I began to apply and train in music-centered therapies and graduate academic studies that most attracted me for my personal process. These included toning, Guided Imagery and Music (GIM), the Tomatis Method, and doctoral work in music with applied psychology and eventually medical courses. In addition, new approaches kept evolving with my own compositions, prayers, songs, and selective music listening. My compositional background was crucial in composing health.

A musical composition is a perfect model for understanding wholeness. Melodic themes, rhythms, harmony, instrumentation and the voice weave together and produce, through time, a picture, mood, or statement. Transitions within a musical composition happen as the composer develops the themes in the work. New directions exit artfully and with understanding from the original theme. Transitions serve and enhance the integrity of the whole composition. This may require a key or tempo change, with new tone colors emerging and supporting an accelerando and crescendo. The development may push and build tension, awaiting breakthroughs, release, and completion.

I view the healing process this way. To change our present state we must make a vibratory transition. To make the transition we must access greater understanding and inner knowing. Music helps us to find access. We are healing different aspects of ourselves. Suddenly and miraculously, we break through limiting, self-imposed filters and experience a higher life harmonic. These breakthroughs and transitions, both subtle and sudden, have been numerous for me over the last two years, facilitated by the music-centered methods mentioned earlier. Their effect on me has ranged from pain reduction and chemical and physiological changes to psychological healing and the amplification of spirit. I would like to share two of these experiences with you.

Spreading My Wings

At 5:00 A.M. I went to the beach for my morning meditation. I had scheduled a Guided Imagery and Music session for later in the day. I knew I had to open myself as much as possible for a healing process to take place. In the back of my mind were the latest negative sonogram report, thoughts about surgery, and self-doubt. The sound and motion of ocean waves entrained my breathing and began to wash away my fears and expectations. The self became emptied. My will had to be removed and replaced with total acceptance of God's will. It took almost three hours before this attunement became real. Then it was time to go back for the imagery session and allow the GIM process to work on me.

After a spoken introduction, Brahms' *Piano Concerto No. 2, allegro non troppo,* began. The music seemed harsh, and I could not fall into a deeper state of consciousness. The striking piano keys imposed themselves on my relaxed body. I knew I had to make room for deepening, so I let go and remained open. When the Brahms was over I relaxed, and the second piece began. At a certain point tremendous pressure pushed down through my chest and solar plexus. I remember having difficulty speaking. I recognized the name of this pressure and named it. "It's Will," I exclaimed, "It's Will." I was actually experiencing a physical, energetic sensation, "Will." After this turning point many sacred symbols literally rose up out of my body. One was a huge book from which images, time periods, and more symbology emerged. Each image and sensation had remarkable presence. They lived in me. A sense of belonging to the past, present, and future all at once came over me.

The music shifted, and the pressure subsided. I imagined an Egyptian sarcophagus lying beside me. The sculpted face and painted body of a king dressed the surface. The moment I acknowledged its presence, things began to happen beyond my understanding. A small black bird entered my pelvic area. My body felt on fire. Heat radiated from the spine, chest, pelvic area, and face. A new kind of pressure came. I was experiencing pain in my solar plexus. One of the facilitators placed her hand there. There was so much light inside my body and under my eyeshades that I kept checking to see if my eyes were really closed. I began to feel strange. A merging of consciousness was taking place.

The back of my head hurt. My energy and awareness began to spin to the right, then to the left, in slow motion. The black bird began to grow, increasing in strength and force. For a moment I was not sure that my physical body could contain this enormous energy. I reported this to my facilitator, but as soon as the words left my mouth, I knew that I was strong enough. The bird was unfolding inside my body. "It's unfolding," I exclaimed. Over my shoulder I heard someone say, "I'm unfolding, say it, Pat." I repeated her words several times. I was unfolding. I had become this magnificent, now glorious white bird. My heart was set free.

While unfoldment took place, my physical body assumed appropriate positions necessary to accommodate this overpowering energy. I held a yoga posture for quite some time, I was told. It was as if my psyche and spirit were spreading their wings while the physical body went through a chiropractic adjustment simultaneously as a result. My pelvic area and lower back were in pain. One of the three women facilitating my session was trained in Reiki. She applied her skills to my areas of discomfort. The three facilitators circled me with arms stretched out. They were holding and protecting the space. This allowed me to experience fully what was happening without being afraid. No one else could come close. I was also aware of the facilitators' energy and intention. There was alchemy in our union.

After quite some time I felt the bird leaving. My heart was wide open and my senses were incredibly heightened. As her presence slipped away, slowly I came back to consciousness. I could feel the imprint of the bird in my body. I learned later that Horus was the Egyptian bird god associated with healing. A small sculpted Horus was used in Egyptian healing rituals. I had no way of knowing this prior to my session that day.

The session left me open and in physical discomfort. My trainer suggested that I swim in the ocean and let the salt water soothe the aches. I felt wonderful and free inside. A new level of healing the spirit, mind, and body had taken place. The music had altered my consciousness while facilitating a birth necessary for new transitions. It awakened my wisdom and inner healer.

I knew when I returned home I would again seek new themes in composing health. Prior to this experience I had become discouraged and felt trapped by my treatment choices. I immediately sought medical monitoring and support with renewed confidence and an open mind. I found very supportive doctors and medical technicians in Seattle and a doctor of Chinese Medicine in Sante Fe, New Mexico.

Tomatis and Toning

Another opportunity to remove self-limiting filters presented itself in March, 1991. Following our move to Bainbridge Island in Washington, I flew to Phoenix to study with Dr. Alfred Tomatis, the renowned ear, nose and throat specialist. I had a private conference with him about my audiogram (a listening test charting both air and bone conduction) taken at the onset of the two-week workshop. He pointed out that I was having difficulty in the intestinal and pelvic area. He felt that through sound stimulation my problem would disappear. I was amazed and intrigued as a patient and researcher.

I asked if the Tomatis Method could cure or help fight a disease such as cancer. He replied that all illness can be healed with sound. A prescribed program on the Electronic Ear (a listening device) could revitalize the cells and help boost the immune system. I asked about surgery. Dr. Tomatis said charging the brain and cells with high frequency sound will give a person energy. Energy is necessary for healing. Under anesthesia the body is shut down; the cells do not work at their optimum. The listening program revitalizes the cells and aids recovery. It was unclear what my condition was. There was enough information to make it frightening, but not conclusive enough to name it.

I was able to do another two-week Tomatis listening program at the Dallas Listening Centre in the summer of 1991 while teaching a program for the talented and gifted at Southern Methodist University. A new listening test was taken and a prescription for listening and active audio-vocal work was given. During the first three days of the program I experienced discomfort in the pelvic area and left leg. These areas seemed to be more aggravated with the active audio vocal work rather than with the passive listening. The discomfort passed and gave way to a noticeable improvement in vitality. My appetite increased, and I began to feel new inner strength. I was being tuned up and recharged with the filtered music of Mozart and Gregorian chant. My cells were given new energy to help me balance and progress toward body-mind integration.

The Tomatis sound therapy further sensitized my inner listening skills. My awareness of inner-body sounds became acute. A highly skilled body worker gave me a session during my stay in Dallas. As he manipulated different areas, I could hear independent pulses, and at times single tones sounded clearly. I imitated aloud what I heard. It felt like discharges of crystalized energy, or the awareness of vibratory patterns and intensity, in different energy and body locations. I was listening to blood flow, to the nervous system, to tensions and inner energy themes. Once again sound and music opened new doors of self-discovery and healing.

Together with the Tomatis Method and GIM, I maintained a discipline of toning. Vocal toning was the first music-centered therapy in my healing process. The daily discipline gave me insights into emotions and tensions that had crystallized. Directing sound, through the voice and imagination, to various parts of the body resonated and dissolved these crystallized areas. Openings began to occur. I became energized and felt a sense of well-being. This kept me in touch with my body. I started paying attention to the specific pitches I was most attracted to. I resonated with these pitches first, and then vibrated my pelvic area with my deepest vocal tones.

Each night after toning I would pray through original song. The intervals chosen to compose my prayer melody depended on mood, need, or inspiration. The starting pitch of E-flat or middle C often began each half-hour session. I found the intervals of a perfect fourth, minor second, and perfect fifth most attractive. They were often separated by melismatic embellishments. The tempo was always slow and attuned to the breath and heartbeat. I began to notice pain reduction, less anxiety, and greater joy.

The Effect of Great Music

To get in touch with music that allows access to the unconscious and inner depths, one must listen to the masterpieces of baroque, classical, romantic and impressionist composers who have encoded many of their works with messages of divine inspiration and unity. When we experience this unity, while in altered states of consciousness, we align ourselves to the vibratory laws of creation, its harmony and rhythm, thereby reminding our body, mind, and spirit how to function properly again. Great compositions offer those who listen passkeys to personal transformation and the understanding of wholeness.

I have had remarkable experiences with "Paradisium" from Fauré's *Requiem*, Vaughan Williams' *Symphony No. 5*, *Romanza* and *The Lark Ascending*. My continued quest for health and wholeness has led me to rediscover the music dramas of Wagner, including *Tannhauser*, *Lohengrin*, *Parsifal*, and *der Ring des Nibelungen*. Whether composers use dissonant harmonies suspended endlessly, waiting for resolution, or glorious augmented and major chords marching stoically, the heart and mind are challenged to open to new inner spaces and territories of awareness.

For this reason, because of my direct experience, it saddens me to see the growing lack of interest in teaching of and exposure to great music. Perhaps if music schools could offer courses in uncovering the soul of great music, discussing its power and purpose as well as its historical and theoretical background, they would overcome this lack of enthusiasm. We live in an age of spiritual emergency. More than ever we seek purpose, reason for being, and connection with self and God. Music invites us to attune ourselves with inner motion. It gives wings to emotions, dreams, and prayers.

Music is a powerful surgical tool. It can open blocked passageways of the mind and emotions, much as a koan given by a Zen Master that changes students' entire view of life in an instant. The Tibetan deity Manjusri, remover of obstacles, holding the sword in his many hands, cuts the illusion out of our lives so that realization and enlightment can enter. Music becomes the scalpel or Manjusri's sword, penetrating our minds and bodies. What is left in the newly created space is a higher vibration of physical, mental, and spiritual well-being.

The Journey Continues

I decided to have surgery in January of 1992. By that time I had investigated several doctors and surgeons. I found one that I trusted who would perform surgery according to my wishes. I used Helen

Bonny's "Operating and Recovery Room" classical music tapes, one of the *Music RX* tapes that have been reviewed and tested for these specific procedures. I had my tape recorder strapped to the gurney as they rolled me to the operating room waiting area. It was unclear who would take charge and make sure the music was played during surgery. I was told to ask the anesthesiologist. Before anyone came to prepare me for surgery, I scanned the holding area and felt calm and ready. A peaceful and wonderful presence came over me before any drugs were administered. Somehow my cup was filled, and I was able to surrender completely. This profound moment has stayed with me.

Soon the anesthesiologist arrived and not only agreed to play music but brought his own tape recorder. He became my friend, making sure my wishes were fulfilled. He put the music on as they rolled me into the O.R. and later asked the nurse to put my earphones on me in the recovery room. My psyche had a place to rest during surgery. The operation went very well, and I was out of recovery quickly. Homeopathic remedies to combat anesthesia and bruising were air-expressed directly to me at the hospital. There was no guarantee the hospital would allow me to take these remedies, so between nurse checks my husband gave me the prescribed dosage for anesthesia. There was an immediate sobering effect. My doctor was surprised at how alert I was when he checked on me several hours later. He had planned to come back, thinking I would not be alert enough, but agreed to stay and discuss what had happened. That night I took the remedy for bruising. Because the surgery was a video laparoscopy, with three small incisions, instead of one where they open the belly, I took only two doses, not expecting much bruising. I took very little pain medication while in the hospital. I didn't need it. I just needed rest and time to let a two-year journey have a resting point. Interestingly enough, I stayed awake most of that first night due to nurses monitoring and asking questions about music and healing.

The mass they found on my left ovary was not cancer. They were able to remove the mass and other scar tissue they found in the pelvic area, created by a disease called *Endometriosis*. Surgery, as I suspected from the beginning, was not necessarily a cure. The treatment for this disease is often subsequent surgeries and drugs. I refused both.

Now I knew what I was dealing with and could proceed, once

again, on a natural path to prevent recurrence. From surgical intervention I gained what I needed, a definite diagnosis. Together with the music-centered therapies, I had explored homeopathy, acupuncture and Chinese medicine. They were all beneficial in giving energy, relieving symptoms, eliminating accompanying problems, and supporting the further development of body and energy awareness. Needless to say, my journey became a firsthand experiment with a touch of adventure. It was a marriage of medical and alternative healing traditions. The person going through the process becomes an integral part of each step. My body, mind, and spirit were attended to.

Recovery time imposed many new rhythms. It forced me to listen and open more deeply. I let go of old ideas and patterns. At times I experienced just being. I saw many aspects of my old self lining up and begging for attention before I said good-bye to them. The openings in my body were symbolic. I now needed time to grow. This sensitive period created new pathways for me.

Recovery was a transition in my composition of health. Prior to this period I had numerous themes and rhythms congested in me. Like any good composer, it was time to weed out the lesser themes. I listened for returning themes that fit my composition of wholeness and included them in the future development of my work. Composing self-health is a fascinating responsibility and journey. I am now aware of an emerging melody and vibration that is truly mine and of the spirit.

These trainings, realizations, and therapies were, and still are, themes in composing health. I had woven in as major themes what would help me recognize and achieve a sense of wholeness. The mass on my left side has been a gift that I have unwrapped over and over. With this deep-seated understanding, I continue in my process, feeling the tension, release, and crescendo toward health and wholeness. I am grateful that the miracles of music and sound were ever available and loyal to my healing journey.

III

Instruments and Healing

Some people may ask, Why are the monks performing publicly what should be private rites? Perhaps these people feel that secret teachings should not be turned into a theatrical spectacle. But they needn't be concerned. The secret interior path and its processes are things which the ordinary eye and ear cannot perceive. What is seen outside is totally different. Based on their inner achievement, the Yogis can unfold energies which can serve the benefit of the entire country, such as in ceremonies which consecrate images and icons, exorcise negative forces, prevent natural disasters and epidemics, and uplift the spirit of the times. Thus, from a certain point of view, these ceremonies have a great benefit for the whole society.

His Holiness the Dalai Lama
Commentary on the popular chanting performances
of the Gyuto and Gyume monks in the West

Chanted prayer and invocation, private and collective, have always taken a place of power in religious practice. In his book Rediscovering the Soul, *Larry Dossey openly discusses the actual and vital influence of prayer on hospital patients. Learning how to pray effectively may very well depend on the quality of the inner sound, the inner voice and the tone of emotion in the devotee.*

In this section the panoramic powers of ear and voice are explored. Here audible and inaudible tones and the powers of sound made inside the body and on instruments begin to take on form and defined method. These serve as important new modes of physical and emotional treatment, as well as inspiration for spiritual practice. Then Jeanne Achterberg joins me for an informal interview on imagery, music and treatments.

Four remarkable musician-researchers share interesting aspects of sound. Anthropologist Ruth-Inge Heinze introduces us to a simple and profound technique of tapping into the inner worlds through drumming. Melinda Maxfield writes of her innovative doctoral research on drumming patterns and the ancient Chinese oracle, I Ching. *Don Wright tells of the ancient Andean water jars known as Peruvian whistling vessels. Their modern reemergence brings mystical experiences, visions and healing to many who have experienced them. David Darling and Bonnie Insull invite us to experience the transformational powers of improvised music, no matter what our background. These troubadors of the future give hope to all the wounded musicians who were not allowed in the choir or band . . . . and reassure musicians that there is little reason to worry about performance quality in the intuitive recreational process. The Force is always with us when music and sound are allowed to manifest!*

Last in this section is an interview with the chantmaster and abbot of the Gyuto Monastery of Tibetan Buddhism conducted during a visit of the Gyuto Tantric Choir to Houston, Texas. Their evocative overtone singing style, introduced to the West by Huston Smith in his documentary Requiem for a Faith, *has now opened many ears to the power of spiritual prayer produced by the voice singing many notes of a chord simultaneously.*

10

Miracles of Voice and Ear:
A Bulletin Board
DON G. CAMPBELL

Miracles are connected with stories. The contrast between the rhythms of normal perception and those of an unexpected or exceptional event creates episodes that draw attention to a miracle. Jean Houston says that a miracle is "a sensorial cooperation with an awareness of an eternal incident."

This article is a collage of stories, news clips, research materials and ideas. Reading the pieces presented here is like changing channels on television to sample news, weather, sports and stories that are broadcast simultaneously. The pieces are intended to spark an attentiveness to contrasting incidences that, woven together, suggest a fresh way of perceiving the voice and ear. They show the connection between vocal patterns, personality and health, and they reveal the power of sound, music and tone to affect body, mind and spirit in both healthful and harmful ways.

Music—Let's Split (Newsweek, July 12, 1990)

Music can do magical things, especially in Canada. First there was the 7-Eleven Store in British Columbia that piped Muzak into the parking lot to keep teenagers from loitering. Out blasted the Mantovani and the kids scattered, leaving only a wake of Slurpee cups. Now downtown businesses in Edmonton, Alberta, are playing Bach and Mozart in a city park to drive away drug dealers and their clients. Police say drug activity in the park has dropped dramatically since Johann and Wolfgang arrived.

"The secret is in your voice. The secret is in your bones. The secret is in your voice. Listen. You must learn to listen." She said this over and over to me. I visited this eccentric old Russian lady monthly for nearly six years. "The secret is in your voice, in your bones, in your voice." I agreed casually. What I really wanted to learn from this wise woman was her association with the mystical world. She had been a Theosophist most of her life, practiced *Mazdasden*, a Swiss system of exercise and tone, met Nicholas Roerich, led an Agni Yoga group, privately practiced ancient Orthodox Christian rituals, taught music in a Catholic girls' school for fifty years, and kept secrets.

> God guard me from those thoughts
> Men think in the mind alone
> He that sings a lasting song
> Thinks in the marrow-bone
> William Butler Yeats

In 1970, when I met Maria Pavlovna Marsoff, she was eighty-four. I was just over one quarter of her age. Her family was killed in Russia and Poland. She fled to Japan to endure two major earthquakes, a horrific war and the American occupation. She made her living by teaching piano and spent every day rigorously studying *The Secret Doctrine,* H. P. Blavatsky's source book of esoteric wisdom, singing magical spiritual songs from a descendant of Saint Germain, and practicing forms of curative eurhythmy developed by Rudolph Steiner.

In all the years I knew this remarkable lady, she always seemed tied to an obligation of secrecy to an inner world, an inner teacher, an inner way of knowing. She would attend Russian Orthodox liturgies at the holy seasons, Catholic mass at school, and use the Japanese religious holidays to honor the Eastern traditions. Since I was already a trained musician and had studied voice and conducting, her comments about the secrets in the voice and bones almost went unnoticed until a decade later when I heard about the astonishing effects of chanting, emphasizing the vibration in the bones, being used in France to charge and alter the body and brain. Alfred Tomatis, a Parisian physician, had developed decades of research that began to open the secrets of the ears and the bones.

Don G. Campbell

TV Host's voice triggers epileptic seizure
(Associated Press Release, July 11, 1991)

New York. A neurologist reports in a prestigious medical journal that a woman got epileptic seizures by hearing the voice of "Entertainment Tonight" co-host Mary Hart. Symptoms included an upset feeling in the pit of her stomach, a sense of pressure in her head and mental confusion, said Dr. Vekat Ramani, who reported the case in today's issue of the *New England Journal of Medicine.*

The religious use of repeated phrases for prayers and invocations depends on the rhythm of the sounded tones as much as on the meaning of the words. Quintilian, a first-century philosopher, was one of the first to express interest in the connection between the voice, the body and the spirit. By the year 1600, Giovanbattista della Porta, a physician in Naples, Italy, had attempted to systematize and analyze the many factors that the voice reveals about the body. Eastern and Western philosophers have long recognized the significance of the voice, the word, the vocalization, but with little concrete understanding until the middle of this century.

Now Hear This—If You Can (*Time,* August 5, 1991, paraphrased)

About 28 million Americans suffer severe hearing loss. The most hazardous pastimes by far are hunting and target shooting, but "car booms," cassette players with earphones and rock concerts are serious detriments. When you lose your hearing you lose, to some degree, one of our most vital attributes, the ability to interact with your environment.

Good News About Noise
(*U.S. News and World Report,* September 9, 1991)

After years of making the world an increasingly noisy place, engineers finally are helping create a little peace and quiet—by raising even more of a racket. The weapon they are using is called anti-noise: an acoustic mirror image of a bothersome noise that, when mixed with the original noisy sound, creates the sound of silence. Conceived in the 1930s, the idea of using one sound to quiet another only recently became technologically feasible.

Chants, mantras, litanies, zikirs and choruses all impel the voice to repeat sound patterns. The stabilization of the breath's rhythm, the subtle movements of the tongue and larynx, and the volume of sound all create subtle modifications in the brain, eyes, and muscles. Long periods (over three minutes) of self-produced repetitive sounds bring about relaxation, lower brain waves, increase warmth in the hands and create a feeling of being centered. When the sounds are long and vowel-centered, the effect is greater.

Journal of the American Medical Association, September 11, 1991

Imagine a form of Therapy which benefits nearly every user in terms of increased vitality, renewed motor skills, increased mobility, and easing of pain. Imagine, too, that it is able to reach some patients whose physical condition isolates and immobilizes them. It can sometimes create a setting in which they are able to tap into remembered reserves of memory and ability, however transiently. Then imagine that it costs almost nothing. Such a therapy would be worth investigating, and that is just what music therapists have requested in their first discussion of this subject with the Senate Special Committee on Aging [in 1991].

The electronic ear, a device developed by Dr. Alfred Tomatis in Paris, transmits sound frequencies to a listener by air and bone conduction. Highly filtered tapes of Mozart's music and Gregorian chants powerfully affect people with speech and attention disorders. For many people, physical and emotional changes take place over a period of a few months. This electronic device alters the voice in its richness, expression and continuity. It repatterns the hearing range, the focus of listening and the attention span. After fifty to a hundred hours of listening to filtered music of Mozart and Gregorian chant through the skull bones and ear, concentration, thought and communication skills begin to be retrained.

Headphones and Exercise: A Bad Connection
(*Woman's Day*, August 13, 1991)

Wearing stereo headphones while you jog, bike or do any aerobic exercise can lead to deafness, according to a study at the University of Louisville School of Medicine. During aerobic exercises, your body pumps blood and oxygen into your arms and legs, leaving the delicate linings of your inner ears dangerously unprotected. Dullness and ringing in your ears are warning signs of a hearing loss.

Three New Theories to Consider about the Voice and Ear

The First Law of Tomatis: "The voice contains only what the ear hears," or in more scientific language, "The larynx emits only the harmonics that the ear can hear." If a subject emits a vowel sound into a microphone that filters out a band of frequencies and returns the sound to headphones on the subject's ears, the subject no longer emits the band that was cut out.

The Second Law of Tomatis: "If a defective ear is given the capability of hearing the lost or impaired frequencies correctly, these are instantly and unconsciously restored to the vocal emission." The comparison of auditory curves before and after using the electronic ear of Dr. Tomatis (having restored hearing in the impaired frequency bands) easily demonstrates the resulting recuperation of the vocal pattern.

The Third Law of Tomatis: "Auditory stimulation maintained for a determined period modifies, by retention, the self-listening faculty of the subject and consequently his phonation." The function of the ear brings into play the modifying muscles of the bone and muscle system of the middle ear. The system that produces speech, on the other hand, works under the action of a series of muscles which operate the larynx, the cheeks and mouth cavity, the tongue and the lips. Both hearing and phonation muscles are controlled by nerves that are under the same neuronal command. In adults, this system is perfectly adjusted to the ethnic auditory pattern corresponding to the mother tongue. However, if the hearing is modified by introducing into the self-checking circuit an electronic ear tuned to a different way of speaking—to a foreign language for example—the whole neuromuscular circuit of the subject starts to work at the foreign rhythm. Thus, a memory of the new mode is gradually built up by cerebral memorizing of this new activity and by muscular action.

Dr. Billie Thompson calls them "mEARacles,"—these dramatic personal changes that occur when the ear is reeducated through the Tomatis Method of listening training. The program is powerful because it comprehensively integrates the neurological listening-learning-language connection. People of all ages have broken out of self-limiting behaviors at the Sound Listening and Learning Center in Phoenix.

Elaine came to the Phoenix Center to receive help for her nonreading nine-year-old son Chris. He had a long history of failure, lack of motivation, depression and withdrawal. He had worked with a tutor for years and also been in therapy. His mother said, "We knew we were losing Chris more and more each day. Continual therapy, medication and no amount of love seemed to help." Like many other parents, Christopher's parents knew he was bright, but learning and life were overwhelmingly difficult for him.

After a few months of "listening treatments" on the electronic ear using specifically filtered recordings of his mother's voice, Gregorian chant and Mozart's music, Chris began to do his homework without prompting. His grade point average rose from .8 to 3.5, and he began to read books for pleasure.

Tune Therapy (*USA Today*, May 30, 1991)

Schizophrenics are less likely to hear imaginary voices if they hum softly, says a study in the newsletter of the U.S. Alcohol, Drug Abuse and Mental Health Administration. Evidence indicates patients who hear voices are using speech muscles without producing sounds, and somehow that triggers hallucinations. Doctors at the UCLA Research Center at Camarillo State Hospital theorized humming would interfere with inaudible muscle activity. They asked 20 schizophrenics to hum: 59% had fewer hallucinations.

The most important history of the connection of voice and ear with physical well-being began its mature, modern research stage through Gregory Bateson, cultural anthropologist, in a project conducted at the Stanford University School of Medicine in San Francisco. This project, funded by the Rockefeller Foundation in the late 1940s and early 1950s, revealed that the voice is a precise and very important instrument for diagnosing neurotic disturbances as well as treating physical and neurotic conditions. One of the many conclusions of this vital study is that vocal analysis is an essential key in the interpretation of neurotic and psychotic behavior.

Paul Moses, M.D., found a recurring pattern in the vocal analysis of his schizophrenic patients. The characteristics of these vocal symptoms are obvious to the discriminating ear:

1. The voices were more rhythmic than melodious.
2. Voice registers were separated, with a dominance in the high head tone voice.
3. There was little nasal resonance.
4. The voice could not glide; it always moved scale-wise or jumped.
5. Inappropriate accents were evident in the speaking voice.

As new vocal techniques were introduced into the speaking voice and into the humming voice, some of the neurotic and psychotic patterns disappeared. Singing was of little help, but the humming, speaking and creative vocal dialogue with the patients modified their behavior.

At the Institute for Music, Health and Education in Boulder, Colorado, extensive research has been done with the audiological listening assessment (Tomatis Method), blended with the Bateson-Moses project. As a result, the creative use of toning, humming in different registers of the voice for extended amounts of time, and daily repetition of long vowel sounds holds out great hope for the application of sound for self-healing.

> Likewise the Spirit helps us in our weakness; for we do not know how to pray as we ought, but the Spirit intercedes for us with sighs and groans [tones] too deep for words.
>
> Romans 8:26

Since the early 1970s Sandra Seagal, Ph.D., a Jungian analyst, has been researching the character of the voice through voice spectographs, body movements and manners of thinking. She is able to detect the lifelong learning styles and the manners of expression, learning and communication. Schools are being developed in Israel, Sweden, Canada and the United States based on what is called "human personality dynamics" (physical, emotional and mental traits) that are observable in all people. The Human Personality Training program gives specific tools for teachers and business people to observe the conceptual, structural, relational, organizational, tactical and operational patterns from the voice and body. This process pinpoints the differences and unique qualities of the voices of mentally centered, emotionally centered and physically centered people.

Mother Tongue May Influence Musical Ear
(*Science News*, December 1, 1990)

When a Briton and a Californian listen to Beethoven's *Fifth Symphony*, they may not hear the same things. New research indicates that people who speak different dialects of a language perceive tonal patterns in strikingly different ways, supporting long standing speculations that speech characteristics influence the way people hear music. Diana Deutsch of the University of California, San Diego, set out to investigate a musical paradox she had discovered four years ago. This phenomenon, called the tritone paradox, occurred when she electronically removed specific "overtones" from a series of two computer generated pitches separated by a half octave, an interval called a tritone. Overtones normally help listeners identify the octave of a note. Without them, the octave becomes ambiguous.

The awareness that each voice has a unique print, insignia or signature is interwoven through the preceding pages. It is just now being realized how specific frequencies and patterns received through the skin, bones and air can alter attention, emotions and physical conditions.

Long sessions of using the relaxed vowel sounds of the voice can efficiently promote physical well-being. In *The Roar of Silence*, I wrote about the healing effects I personally experienced from toning. Others have reported regained use of limbs, improved motor skills, realignment of dislocated bones and elimination of pain. For years I have observed notable responses to toning among people altering their addictions to drugs, and have seen stroke patients' improved facility for language and motor function. I know of people with arthritis and severe back pain being eased as their symptoms diminish with drumming and the use of a sonic table. I have seen remarkable results from psychotherapy used with music and imagery in the GIM system. I have observed Alzheimer patients radically come to memory and attention with the help of music. I am aware of the remarkable progress of autistic and dyslexic children through the air and bone conduction stimulation by the electronic ear. I have seen a nearly paralyzed arm move on command through the power of tone in the voice. I know of teenagers with severe burns who are soothed by Michael Jackson's music. I have sung "Amazing Grace" in overtones to a comatose loved one and received a response. I have sat with critically ill, poor people in Haiti who died with a glowing presence while singing gospel hymns. I have seen the crippled walk at evangelistic services that used prayer and song. I have read of levitation, spiritual transformations and even resurrections through repeated chants, mantras and litanies. Music and miracles? Yes!

> . . . seek out a man who is skillful in playing the harp; and when the evil spirit from God is upon you, he will play it and you will be well.
> Samuel 16:14–16

The interweaving of the patterns of this patchwork in sound, healing, and transformation are revealed in miracles: spontaneous remission through sound, the secrets of the voice, brain and bones, and the glory of great music. Yet the ultimate healing lies in the power to listen, attune and harmonize with the consistent energy of life, the music of the spheres, the great Tone.

References

Ackerman, Diane. *A Natural History of the Senses*. Random House, New York, 1990.

Baken, R. J. *Clinical Measurement of Speech and Voice*. College Hill Press, Boston, 1972.

Berendt, Joachim-Ernst. *The Third Ear: On Listening to the World*. Element Books, London, 1988.

Bruscia, Kenneth E., ed. *Case Studies in Music Therapy.* Barcelona Publishers, Phoenixville, PA., 1991.

Campbell, Don G. *A Hundred Ways to Improve Teaching with YOUR Voice and Music.* Zephyr Press, Tucson, AZ, 1992.

—————. *Heal Yourself With Your Own Voice.* Sounds True, Boulder, CO, 1990.

—————. *Introduction to the Musical Brain.* MMB Music, St. Louis, 1983.

—————. *Music: Physician for Times to Come.* Quest Books, Wheaton, Ill., 1991.

—————. *Rhythms of Learning, Creative Tools for Academic Development.* Zephyr Press, Tucson, AZ, 1991.

—————. *The Roar of Silence.* Quest Books, Wheaton, Ill., 1989.

Deutsch, Diana, ed. *The Psychology of Music.* Academic Press, New York, 1982.

Dossey, Larry. *Meaning and Medicine.* Bantam, New York, 1992.

Gardner, Kay. *Sounding the Inner Landscape: Music as Medicine.* Caduceus Publications, Stonington, ME, 1990.

Heenan, Edward F., ed. *Mystery, Magic & Miracle: Religion in a Post-Aquarian Age.* Prentice-Hall, Englewood Cliffs, NJ, 1973.

Helle, Jean. *Miracles.* David McKay Company, New York, 1952.

Lee, Mathew H. M. *Rehabilitation, Music and Human Well-Being.* MMB Music, St. Louis, 1989.

Lewis, C. S. *Miracles, A Preliminary Study.* MacMillan, New York, 1947.

McClellan, Randall. *The Healing Forces of Music.* Element Books, London, 1988.

Monden, Louis. *Signs and Wonders.* Desclee Company, New York, 1966.

Moule, C. D. F., ed. *Miracles: Cambridge Studies in their Philosophy and History.* A. R. Mowbray & Co., London, 1965.

Murphet, Howard. *Sai Baba: Man of Miracles.* Frederick Muller, London, 1971.

Stehli, Annabel. *The Sound of a Miracle: A Child's Triumph over Autism.* Doubleday, New York, 1991.

Tomatis, Alfred A. *The Conscious Ear.* Station Hill Press, Barrytown, New York, 1991.

Werbeck-Svardstrom, Valborg. *Uncovering the Voice.* Steiner Press, London, 1980.

For an updated biography of over 1200 titles on music and its relationship to health and education, please contact IMHE, P.O. Box 1244, Boulder, CO 80306.

For further information on music, healing, and music and sound therapy contact:

The Institute for Music, Health and Education
Don G. Campbell, Director
  P.O. Box 1244
  Boulder, CO 80306
  303-443-8484
The National Association of Music Therapy
  8455 Colesville Road, Suite 930
  Silver Spring, MD 20910
  301-589-3300
The American Association of Music Therapy
  P.O. Box 80012
  Valley Forge, PA 19484
  215-265-4006
International Society for Music in Medicine
  Dr. Ralph Springe, Executive Director
  Sportkrankenhaus Hellersen
  Paulmannshoher Strasse 17
  D-5880 Ludenscheid, Germany
Sound Listening, Tomatis North America
  Billie Thompson, Director
  2701 E. Camelback, Suite 205
  Phoenix, AZ 85016
  602-381-0086
International Arts-Medicine Association
  3600 Market Street
  Philadelphia, PA 19104
Mid-Atlantic Institute for Guided Imagery and Music
  Sara Jane Stokes, Director
  Box 4655
  Virginia Beach, VA 23454

For Books, Materials and Recordings on Music and Healing contact:
  Institute for Music, Health and Education, Catalogue Services, P.O. Box
  1244, Boulder, CO 80306, tel. 303-443-8484
  Magna Music, 10370 Page Industrial Blvd., St. Louis, MO 63132, tel.
  1-800-543-3771
Music Therapists
  Kenneth Bruscia, Ph.D., RMT, DC, Temple University, Department of
  Music Education and Therapy, 1938 Park Mall, TU 298-00, Phila-
  delphia, PA 19122
  Virginia Clarkson, MMT, CMT, RMT-BC, 112 Livingston St., #C1,
  New Haven, CT 06511
  Barbara Crowe, MMT, RMT-BC, Department of Music Therapy, Arizona
  State University, Tempe, AZ 85287
  Laurie Rugenstein, MMT, RMT-BC, Naropa Institute, P.O. Box 1435,
  Boulder, CO 80306

11

Drumming, Shamanic Work and Healing:
An Interview by Don G. Campbell

JEANNE ACHTERBERG

Jeanne Achterberg and I had a discussion about music, miracles, healing and transformative energies. We explored how creative arts, especially sound, assist in moving energy in the healing process. Her research with imagery, suggestion and health has often been accompanied with music, drumming and sound.

Don Campbell: Jeanne, what do you believe entering into shamanic states does healthwise to the body?

Jeanne Achterberg: For one thing, it seems to coordinate brain function. That is also associated with the imagery of well-being, so well-being can become the goal to achieve. The shamanistic trance state is one that is historically associated with healing.

Don: What do you think healing meant historically?

Jeanne: It probably meant the same thing to people as it does now. People would go in sick and suffering and expect to be fixed. In some cultures people would enter the healing with family disruptions or individual depressions or various types of symptoms and hope to have those resolved or reversed.

Don: I'm curious, in your and your husband's work in hospitals, what have you noticed using drumming in the pain clinic?

Jeanne: Drumming does some interesting things. It seems to have anesthetic results. Looking back historically and traditionally one could say that is what they were probably doing with drums, music and sound. With the onset of trance relief would occur. Drumming has been used with insomniacs and sleep disorders with success.

Don: Have you noticed if pain reduction occurs with recordings and headphones as it does with full room speaker?

Jeanne: It does work, but I'm sure that there is also something wonderful about live drumming that would be more effective. Still we have gotten remarkable results from tapes.

Don: Are other people studying the effects of drumming?

Jeanne: Let me tell you about a recent dissertation. This important work on sound was developed by my student Mo Maxfield at the Institute of Transpersonal Psychology. She has been a longtime practitioner of shamanistic disciplines. She observed wave patterns and images in naive subjects in a controlled study with three groups. One group had traditional shamanic drumming in which she used a very fine recording. The other group had something very interesting which she developed called the *I Ching* drumming. She has taken the patterns of the *I Ching* and drummed them. It is phenomenal. In the hexagrams when there is a solid line you get one drum beat (♩) and when there is a broken line you get two (♩♩). (See the chapter in this book by Melinda Maxfield.)

She uses five drummers, so sometimes three will be playing one series and two will be playing the other. It is very interesting drumming.

These subjects had never participated in any ceremonial drumming, so that was not an element, since they had no expectations as she measured their images and their comments. She gathered a lot of findings. The most noteworthy was that within ten to twelve minutes into the session the people hearing the shamanic drumming had a dramatic, significant increase in theta waves. All of us that do shamanic work know that if you go on a journey, the brain waves alter after ten minutes or so. If it doesn't happen then, it doesn't happen at all. It rarely happens before then.

Dr. Maxfield measured theta, alpha and beta waves. In the free improvisational drumming there was no change throughout the session. In the *I Ching* drumming, there was some increase in *theta*, but nothing like with the shamanic drumming. In the shamanic group they had full-blown shamanic experiences, with visions and dream-like experiences. This is the first controlled study looking into this thousands-of-years-old practice.

Don: I understand you also use heartbeat recordings that work like a sedative. Do you know my album on that?

Jeanne: No, because we did that work a long, long time ago.

Don: I would be curious to see if it works effectively. One side of the record is just heartbeats and the second has simple melodies with the heartbeats.

Besides drumming, I am interested in your intuitive sense of the use of sound in the healing process—like Medieval music in the church context or like the tarantella spider bite healing dance of southern Italy. Do you have any speculations about how music facilitates the process of physical change?

Jeanne: I can only relate it back to research, where repetitive sound with ritual techniques, plus expectation of the intervention of God or the supernatural, allows other psychological phenomena to unfold. Physically, any kind of sound that is repetitive, such as a metronome or other tones, has a regulating effect upon the biological functioning.

Don: What do you sense in this emerging field of New Age music? How do albums like my *Crystal Meditations,* which has repetitive patterns, compare with other kinds of very ambient music with no rhythmic pattern, but that is very popular and seems to have results. I mean music such as Steve Halpern's *Spectrum Suite* work or Brian Eno's *Thursday Afternoon.*

Jeanne: I think that the availability of these albums has enhanced awareness of the effects of music. Brugh Joy is using high frequency sound almost exclusively in his workshops and healing sessions, very complex with mood changes throughout, like the sound track of *The Mission.* People report incredible experiences with it.

I remember one study on pediatric oncology where subjects picked their music. They had good results as long as they were allowed to choose. But nothing we gave them made any difference if they did not like it.

Don: That's important.

Jeanne: If given the chance to select what they wanted and do with it what they wanted, it could work for them. Some of them hated all of it, some of them tolerated it and some loved it. They all loved things like *Deep Breakfast* by Ray Lynch. I think people don't have associations with those kinds of sounds, unless they are professional classical musicians.

Don: Do you find that the use of music with your imagery processes is more effective or less?

Jeanne: For a long time we tried to put music behind the imaging, but it was problematic to find the correct pieces. What I suggest now is that the person imaging put on background music that they think will assist the process. They pick different things.

Don: Are these patients in hospitals?

Jeanne: No, mostly people I see individually.

Don: Do you think music in general, if it is the right music, really facilitates the speed of healing?

Jeanne: For some people this works and other people find it distracting. Since the latter are less auditory, we try something different for them. I think 60 to 70 percent can find music they like that works for them.

Don: Speak of your own story about your jaw operation and the use of music, and how you experimented on yourself.

Jeanne: The musical pieces that I asked for were grounding, to carry me through the surgical process. You and I had a talk, and I used your selections "Memories of the Alhambra" and the Mozart piece from *Cosmic Classics*. I didn't want any aery-fairy music. I wanted to feel alive and not come out of surgery thinking I was dead. I used pieces before surgery and in the recovery room to remind me that I was okay and coming back. These pieces were very helpful for that kind of grounding.

Don: What do you see emerging for the next century for creative arts therapies?

Jeanne: I think there will be more health professionals and musicians functioning at the bedside with good-looking, colorful outfits. Everything is going to free up. We have gone on too long with those drab lab coats and hospital garb. With creativity, things are going to continue to get better.

We have a library of relaxation and music tapes for pediatric oncology, and we are trying to encourage their use. Since they are doing more bone marrow transplants, which requires a lot of morphine, I feel that using sound and music certainly helps here with pain control. The future of music in physical therapy is very promising.

12

Inner Listening

RUTH-INGE HEINZE

Just as dreams reveal the innermost experiences of our lives, the process of listening to music allows the profound language of the unconscious to emerge into conscious awareness.

During my workshops on "The Use of Sound in Healing," participants experience the balancing of mind, emotions, and psyche. Their creativity is stimulated and, most of all, they are offered a safe structure for the arising of messages which, though received, have been retained on less accessible levels of the mind.

We are constantly receiving messages, but most of the incoming information remains unprocessed. Our autonomic nervous system, for example, tries to prevent systems-overload and screens out information which does not seem to be important for our survival. "Education" at home, at school, and during our professional training and the opinions of our peer groups establish even tighter grids to filter out "irrelevant" information. This repressed information seems to rise to consciousness only under stress and during traumatic events, at times when we are ill prepared for such messages. Thus, only a small amount of incoming information gets a chance to rise to a level where it can be consciously received.

How can we counteract this rather dangerous "censorship"? Research like that at Maimonides Dream Laboratory has shown how unprocessed information can be brought to consciousness. Research on sonic driving—that is, using sound to access different states of consciousness—has added another technique to our tool chest for information retrieval. Archaeological evidence indicates that the effects of drumming and rattling on the central nervous system must have been known in prehistoric time. Also chanting, whether in a religious or nonreligious context, produces shifts in consciousness (see Tomatis quoted in Wilson, 1991:13–16).

Neurophysiological changes produced by drumming were investigated early in this century, by Dr. Adolf Meyer (Torrey, 1972:94). The research on rhythmic sensory stimulation continued in the 1930s. V. Y. and W. G. Walters then found in the 1940s that "when a very large group of sensory units can be excited simultaneously and rhythmically, . . . the central electrical response is correspondingly larger" (quoted in Heinze, 1988:85). Rhythmic stimulation can have a profound effect on one's body and mind.

Jilek (quoted in Heinze, 1988:85) elicited responses to auditory driving at the fundamental of each stimulus frequency (3, 4, 6, and 8 beats per second). Neher (1961, 1962, also quoted in Heinze, 1988:86) exposed clinically and electroencephalographically normal individuals to low-frequency high-amplitude acoustic stimulations produced by instruments similar to the deerskin drums used by North American Indians and observed that different sound frequencies were transmitted along different nerve pathways in the brain. (He had, however, reinforced the acoustic effect by flashing lights and did not control for all variables.)

The research continues. Melinda Maxfield, for example, wrote her dissertation on the neurophysiological effects of drumming. She recorded the temporary changes in brain wave activity as well as the imagery induced under specific circumstances and has laid the groundwork for more substantive research. (See chapter by Melinda Maxfield in this volume.) Also noteworthy is Felicitas Goodman's book (1990) in which she discussed her extensive research on the effect of rattling, combined with certain body postures, on her workshop participants.

Check Your Mailbox

Turning to my own research in the field of information retrieval, I want to give an example from a drumming session I conducted in Salt Lake City in August, 1991. During my inductions, I explain an exercise called "checking your mailbox," designed to access information which has not risen to consciousness because so-called "undesirable" information has been filtered out. In the exercise the facilitator drums while participants empty their minds and observe the contents that arise.[1] On this occasion after a brief induction explaining how to ride on the sound of the drum, I beat the drum (one from the Taos Reservation, New Mexico) for ten minutes, using 3 beats per second. The following is an excerpt from a report tape-recorded immediately after the session:

"Everything happened with a great deal of urgency. I was just caught up by the drum. I started down by the edge of the water and ran up to where I could see the opening of the cave. . . .

"I became a green and gold snake that began to spiral around and around. I spiraled down into the earth. I was very long with no arms but filled with enormous energy—spiraling, spiraling, spiraling down.

"When I got down, I started doubling back and curled up, almost like a gorgon's knot. Then I backed out, through myself, like shedding my skin, and was myself again.

"I was on a beach and saw this small vortex. I was swirling, thinking that the hole might go away before I got to it. So I jumped in.

"I came out in water. I was under water. I was a fish for a time and then I became myself again, swimming along with the fish. I was perfectly comfortable in the water. Then I came shooting out like I was a tidal wave—just enormous energy!

"After I had shot out, I found that I was turning into a large cat, like a leopard. I was racing across this big plain, racing and racing.

"Then I came to this huge tree where the branches seemed to have been knocked off. I ran straight up the tree—higher and higher and higher—until I was so high it was unbelievable. I looked down and it was far too high to come back down again. So, I thought that what I had better do is snap this tree off at the base. I started to sway back and forth, again and again, to snap the tree but it was far too resilient. Then I just pulled back and flipped myself off.

"I turned into a bird! I was a seagull and I could fly."

This woman commented on her report: "So this is the message: I thought that I was aiming too high, that I was trying to get too high, that my aspirations were too great. I thought I was going to have to snap off and go back to the base, but once I got to the top of the tree I knew I could fly. I can fly!"

Earlier in the workshop, she had confirmed my observations of some physical problems which seemed to restrict her activities. She also had severe doubts about her energy level. Her liberating report speaks for itself. It was the strongest reaction I have witnessed so far in my years of facilitating drum journeys. The experience surprised this woman as well as everybody else present. Her exuberance was physically visible and shifted her into a new mode of action, so that in the following days she embarked on a series of new activities. Her energy had, indeed, "unexpectedly" risen from the depth!

A Precognitive Vision

Before I began my research into information retrieval forty-two years ago, I myself had received a message after listening to Bruch's violin concerto in a relaxed mood. In 1949, I worked as an actress at a theater near the German-Polish border. Performances had been scheduled during the Christmas holidays, so I could not visit my family in Berlin. I decided to use free hours to relax and meditate. I wanted to experience again the peace of mind which is so necessary for being productive. I wanted to "take inventory" of where I was at the moment.

Though I was raised Lutheran, my faith is not based on any dogma. I was not avoiding the religious issue at Christmas, though, and looked for a candle to perform a small ritual of my own. During the winter solstice, many people celebrate the birth of a child in whom they set their hopes, or they participate in a festival of light to overcome anxiety and darkness.

After I lit the candle, I turned on the radio. One station was broadcasting Bruch's violin concerto, which seemed to fit the occasion. I do not remember all the stages of transformation I went through, but I do remember that the music became the vehicle which carried me to a different level of consciousness.

The next morning, I awoke at dawn, still feeling weightless, peaceful, and in harmony with the world around me. I realized that something unusual had happened and that I had to write it down immediately, so as not to lose the experience.

During the dream or vision, I felt that I was in a large house with many rooms. To test whether I was dreaming or awake, I pinched myself and felt the pain. I was in a house where people can stay overnight—a caravansary or a large shelter for pilgrims.

I was wandering along endless floors with many rooms, right and left, but all the doors were closed. Somebody approached me, and I cannot remember whether I actually saw a human shape or just heard

131

a human voice that told me that I could not stay, there was no room for me. "Not yet," said the voice. Why did an unknown caller forbid me to be in this house to which I felt myself drawn? I asked. Somebody responded by giving me a basket that could be used for collecting fruit. Something was moving inside the basket—a red cat, purring and wanting to be caressed. Was she to be my guide?

As soon as I touched the red cat, the house, the basket, and the cat disappeared. I was walking in a large garden, though I cannot remember leaving the house.

The garden was on a slope, bordering a lake. People were walking up and down, talking to each other softly. It sounded like the murmuring of a spring—or the purring of a cat. The men, women, and children did not wear ordinary clothes but simple gowns of a gray-bluish color. Under the blinding sun, all colors in the garden faded away.

Through the bright haze, a man left the crowd and came toward me. He was my uncle, the brother of my mother. I had always been attracted to his cheerful and generous personality. While he was talking to me, I suddenly realized that all the other people in the garden had already died. I recognized dead friends, relatives, and neighbors. At the same moment, I also realized that my uncle and I were the only living beings in the garden. It seemed strange, but there was nothing unnatural about it. I again pressed my thumb nail against my palm to test whether I was dreaming or awake, and again I felt the pain.

When I asked my uncle why we were in this garden, he led me to a building on the left that looked like a mausoleum. We entered and saw two sarcophagi. A neighbor who had been close to me when I was a child was resting in one, and my uncle lay down in the other. I asked him why. He had talked to me freely before, and he continued to move his lips, but I could not hear a sound. It was like being under water where you can see, but all the sounds are blunted. Trying to understand him and wanting to make myself understood, I woke up.

After I notated what I remembered, I put the report in an envelope, sealed it, and gave it to a fellow actor, telling him to open it only when I asked him to do so.

After that, my work, performances and rehearsals, required my full attention. Six weeks later, during lunch at the theater's cafeteria, the mail was distributed, and there was a letter from my parents. My colleague asked me why I was so quiet. I gave him my parents' letter and told him to open the sealed envelope. My parents wrote that the neighbor who had been lying in a sarcophagus had died at the time I had seen him in my dream/vision, and that my uncle, at the same time, had been rushed to a hospital and had died there three weeks later.

It seems that the music had increased my sensitivity to respond to thoughts of people who had not been consciously "on my mind" but who had wanted to communicate with me before they transcended.

A Message from Beyond the Grave

To illustrate further that unprocessed information needs to arise to conscious levels, I want to relate another experience I monitored at a philosophers' retreat in the hills near Pescadero, California, in early 1990. Somebody had heard about my method of "checking your mailbox" and invited me to drum. After a brief induction period during which I explained that participants should relax, clear their minds, and use the drum beat as a vehicle to explore unknown areas in their minds, I drummed (3–4 beats per second) for ten minutes.

Immediately, after the drum stopped, a physicist from Stanford reported:

"Ruth's drumming was soft and lulling and rhythmic. I believe she gave the suggestion that we go down to a beach and enter a cave we found there, but I was already off on other paths. . . . I suddenly received the image of a white bird. . . . I got on the bird and was taken high in the sky over the vast distance—to my father's grave site on Cape Cod. I saw the grey granite plaque with a Star of David made out of twigs.[2]

"I then saw my father rise up from the grave, ghostlike, and the message conveyed was: he had accepted his death and my mother has freed him,[3] allowing him to rise. He, too, has freed himself from his ties to her, which had been keeping him from claiming his spirithood.[4] I felt too, that, in learning that he wasn't physical any more, he would be freed from the illness and suffering that had overtaken him in his later years. I hoped that my dreams of him would now change to ones where he was healthy again.[5]

"This was a tearful experience for me, and I could not keep from crying as I shared my journey with the group.

"The next day, I found six twigs on the path, exactly like the ones in my vision. I have put them in my father's goblet and will eventually arrange them in the form of a Star of David."

This information retrieval speaks for itself. Neither this woman nor the people around her had thought of her father during our day together before the drumming. It seems the message from beyond the grave could arise because the right circumstances were provided.

Information Retrieval

I want to close with reminding us to "check our mailboxes" regularly. There may be messages that tell us about sources of energy we have not known before or messages that speak of the innermost needs of our body, emotions, mind, and soul. There may be messages that point to "unfinished business" and messages that convey the thoughts of people who have no other way of communicating with us. The reasons for information retrieval are almost infinite.

"Checking your mailbox" is a simple tool that is most effective when we can clear our minds from superimposed grids of understanding. Most of all, we have to find the right environment (sacred space) where we can trust the facilitator, so that we can allow ourselves to become open and receptive, without interference from the outside and without interfering in the process ourselves. Sound then will open the doors of our perception so that we can receive and understand those "hidden" messages consciously.

Endnotes

1. Important considerations for a successful information retrieval:
   (a) to purify body, feelings and mind by breathing (sigh of relief—sweeping with increased intensity); shake your body free of tension (Qi Gong exercise); smudge (with sage or incense); possibly wash hands and face, and drink some water;
   (b) to empty your mind (no active imagination), suspend judgment;
   (c) to find an entrance into the earth (go down stairs and keep going or enter a cave on the beach or go down the root of a tree, etc.). Remember how you got in and try to return the same way, thus paving a highway into the less conscious regions of your mind, so that you can access the different levels and states of consciousness more easily next time;
   (d) to use the drum as a vehicle (return to the drum beat when you are "stuck"); the drum can also serve as a weapon (with which you can overcome obstacles or ward off negativity);
   (e) not to change anything! If something frightens you, go toward it (it may change by itself) or go past it (no need to play the hero), the drum will help you to continue;

(f) to be in the moment, just observe (like sitting in a movie theater looking at a blank screen, not knowing which movie will be played);

(g) when something is unclear, to ask questions. Sometimes the answers will be very clear, sometimes they will emerge in symbolic forms; sometimes you will have to say "come again!";

(h) to enter such journey only under the guidance of a trained practitioner who is monitoring not only the drumming but is watching the faces of all present. Latent traumata are bound to come up and have to be talked through immediately. Never touch a latent psychosis!!!

(i) to write down the experience immediately after the drumming and a brief period of return because our mind tends to change the content over time. Looking at the written record later, we can then continue to process the journey.

2. The description of the plaque is accurate and there is a Star of David carved in it, but there is nothing brown and no twigs.

3. My parents were extremely close and always very much in love.

4. According to Seth, the dead very often find themselves in an out-of-body stage, not knowing and/or not accepting the fact that they have died. People have very different intensities of connection to physical reality. For some, years of our time may pass before they accept their deaths. Some choose to reincarnate right away; some may take a century; some may choose not to return to physical reality at all. According to Seth, all of this must be understood in the context of simultaneous time: Time *is* simultaneous, he says. All of our reincarnational existences occur "at once." "Re"-incarnation is a psychological construct of our linear time sense, which is itself an artifact of our physical reality.

5. My father who suffered from asthma and emphysema had difficulty breathing most of the time. In virtually all of my dreams about him at that time, he had been sick and/or weak. . . . I rarely dream of him now, but think about him every day.

References

Campbell, Don. (1991) *Music: Physician for Times to Come.* Wheaton, IL: Quest Books.

————. (1989) *Healing Power of Tone and Chant.* Wheaton, IL: Quest Books.

Gardner, Kay. (1990) *Sounding the Inner Landscape: Music the Inner Medicine.* Stonington, ME: Caduceus Publications.

Goodman, Felicitas D. (1990) *Where the Spirits Ride the Wind, Trance Journeys and Other Ecstatic Experiences.* Bloomington, IN: Indiana University Press.

Hamel, Peter Michael. (1978) *Through Music to the Self*, transl. from German by Peter Lemesurier. Boulder, CO: Shambhala/Random House.

Heinze, Ruth-Inge. (1988) *Trance and Healing in Southeast Asia Today.* Berkeley/Bangkok: Independent Scholars of Asia, Inc./White Lotus, Ltd.

Hodges, Donald A., ed. (1985) *Handbook of Music Psychology.* Kendall/Hunt Publishing Co.

Meyer, Leonard B. (1961) *Emotion and Meaning in Music.* Chicago, IL: University of Chicago Press.

Neher, Andrew A. (1962) "A Physiological Explanation of Unusual Behavior in Ceremonies Involving Drums," *Human Biology,* 34, pp. 152–160.

————. (1961) "Auditory Driving Observed with Scalp Electrodes in Normal Subjects," *EEG and Clinical Neurophysiology,* 13, pp. 449–451.

Prophet, Elizabeth Clare. (Spring 1981) "Sound, Life's Integrating Phenomenon," *The Cosmic Revolution, A Magazine for Higher Consciousness,* 2:1, pp. 24–33.

Quincy, Cheri and Joel Alter. (1987) "Sonic Resonance and Its Interactions with the Dynamic of Cerebral Spinal Fluid in Relation to Focus of Attention," *Proceedings of the Third International Conference on the Study of Shamanism and Alternate Modes of Healing, 1986,* ed. Ruth-Inge Heinze. Berkeley, CA: Independent Scholars of Asia, Inc., pp. 164–168.

Rouget, Gilbert. (1985) *Music and Trance.* Chicago/London: University of Chicago Press.

Rubik, Beverly. (1990). "Music at the Heart of Life: Toward a Resonant Model of Health and Healing," *Proceedings of the Sixth International Conference on the Study of Shamanism and Alternate Modes of Healing, 1989,* ed. Ruth-Inge Heinze. Berkeley, CA: Independent Scholars of Asia, Inc., pp. 16–20.

Tomatis, Alfred. (1963) *L'Oreille et le Langage.* Bourges, France: Imprimerie Tardy.

Torrey, E. Fuller. (1972) *Witchdoctors and Psychiatrists, The Common Roots of Psychotherapy and Its Future.* New York: Harper and Row, Publishers.

Wilson, Tim. (1991) "Chant: The Healing Powers of Voice and Ear," *Music, Physician for Times to Come.* Wheaton, IL: Quest Books, pp. 11–28.

13

The Journey of the Drum

MELINDA C. MAXFIELD

> Where I come from we say that rhythm is the soul of life, because the whole universe revolves around rhythm, and when we get out of rhythm, that's when we get into trouble. For this reason the drum, next to the human voice, is our most important instrument. It is special.
>
> Babatunde Olatunji, Nigerian drummer

Why is it that the oral traditions of many indigenous cultures say that percussion in general and rhythmic drumming in particular facilitate communication with the spiritual world? Why does Nevill Drury, author of *The Elements of Shamanism*, write, "One thing never ceases to amaze me—that within an hour or so of drumming, ordinary city folk are able to tap extraordinary mythic realities that they have never dreamed of."

I was a graduate student at the Institute of Transpersonal Psychology in the fall of 1986 when I experienced my first "drum journey." The course was "Shamanism," a synthesis of universal principles of the wisdom of native cultures, taught by Angeles Arrien, a cross-cultural anthropologist and Basque folklore specialist. I was told to decide which world, upper or lower, I wished to visit. I decided to journey to the lower world in search of my power animal. I was to image an appropriate entry to the lower world. I was to ask any

This article also appears in Angeles Arrien, *The Four Fold Way; Indigenous Wisdoms Applied in Contemporary Times*. (Harper and Row), 1992.

animal that appeared if it was my power animal. The power animal would reappear three or four times or sustain connection.

The journey for me was profound. I experienced vivid visual and somatic imagery, incorporating classic shamanic and archetypal themes. I was intrigued. There was nothing in my paradigm about "the way the world worked" that could account for my powerful images and emotional reactions. I mean, after all, I was in the middle of the suburb of Menlo Park, California, in a classroom with many other students, at three o'clock in the afternoon. How could this be? And what exactly is "shamanism," anyway?

Shamanism and the Shamanic Journey

Roger Walsh, in *The Spirit of Shamanism,* defines *shamanism* as "a family of traditions whose practitioners focus on voluntarily entering altered states of consciousness in which they experience themselves or their spirits traveling to other realms at will and interacting with other entities to serve their community."

Shamans are often referred to as "technicians of the sacred" and "masters of ecstasy." The shaman may journey to the upper world or the lower world. Images that are traditionally associated with an upper world journey include: climbing a mountain, tree, cliff, rainbow, ladder, etc.; ascending into the sky; flying and meeting a teacher or guide. The upper world journey may be particularly ecstatic. In the lower world journey, the shaman may experience images of entering into the earth through a cave, a hollow tree stump, a water hole, a tunnel, or a tube and finding his or her power animal and animal allies. The lower world is traditionally a place of tests and challenges.

To accomplish the shamanic journey, the shaman enters into a specific type of altered state of consciousness which requires that he or she remain alert and aware. In this state, the shaman is able to move at will between ordinary and nonordinary reality. Michael Harner designates this proactive state as a Shamanic State of Consciousness (SSC). There are various techniques for entering into the SSC, including sensory deprivation, fasting, fatigue, hyperventilation, dancing, singing or chanting, drumming, exposure to extremes of temperature, using hallucinogenic substances, and the set and setting dictated by the beliefs and ritualized ceremonies of the culture.

Journey Drumming

It was three years and many drum journeys later when I decided to train as a drummer. Several friends joined me, and we drummed on a regular basis. I had a wondering: Would it be possible to drum the *I Ching?* Yes, it was. The *I Ching*, or *Book of Changes*, is an ancient book of Chinese wisdom consisting of sixty-four hexagrams, each dealing with aspects and issues surrounding archetypal or universal energies. Each hexagram consists of six lines; these lines are either solid — or broken — — . Drumming patterns were derived from the hexagrams, the solid line representing one full beat and the broken line a half-beat. We drummed the *I Ching*, writing music and taking people on journeys. The question persisted: Why is it that beating the drum in this way can facilitate such powerful experiences? How could this tool be used in psychotherapy? Dream work? Healing?

From my own subjective experiences, I hypothesized that I was entering into an altered state of consciousness of some kind, related to, but not the same as, a meditative state. If this were so, then possibly it could be tested by measuring the electrical activity of the brain with an electroencephalogram machine (EEG). (Charles Tart defines an altered state of consciousness [ASC] as one in which a given individual "clearly feels a *qualitative* shift in his pattern of mental functioning, that is he feels not just a quantitative shift [more or less alert, more or less visual imagery, sharper or duller, etc.], but also that some quality or qualities of his mental processes are *different*.")

What would happen, I wondered, if I were to take some naive subjects, people who knew nothing about shamanism or drum journeys, into a biofeedback laboratory and have them experience the drumming? Could various drumming patterns be associated with specific brain wave activity? Would the subjective experience of percussion in general and rhythmic drumming in particular elicit images or sensations with a common theme? As I wrote my dissertation proposal, I decided that if it were not accepted, I would do the research anyway. My dissertation topic had "found me."

Brain Wave Frequency and EEG

To understand the results of this research, it is necessary to know some basic facts about EEG and brain wave frequencies. EEG is an instrument that produces a drawing of the various brain wave patterns. EEG waves are classified according to how many times a single wave occurs over a period of one second; this is known as wave frequency. Wave frequency is measured in terms of cycles per second, or Hertz (Hz), and by wavelength. For example, a wave completing three cycles in one second is called 3 Hertz (Hz) or three per second.

There are four major types of brain wave patterns, or *frequency bands:* delta, theta, alpha, and beta.

delta	theta	alpha	beta
. . . .	. . .	. . . .	. . . . . .
1	4	8	13HZ (Frequency)
1000	250	125	77ms (Wave Length)

Delta (under 4 Hz) is the longest and slowest wave, i.e., this wave will repeat itself less than four times in one second. This wave is associated with sleep or unconsciousness.

Theta waves (4 Hz to 8 Hz) are usually associated with drowsy, near-unconscious states, such as the threshold period just before waking or sleeping. This rhythm has also been connected to states of reverie and hypnogogic or dreamlike imagery. Often these images are startling or surprising. For many people, it is difficult to maintain consciousness during theta without some sort of training, such as meditation.

Alpha (8 Hz to 13 Hz) is associated with states of relaxation and general well-being. Alpha generally appears in the occipital region of the brain (the visual cortex) when the eyes are closed. Consciousness is alert but unfocused, or focused on the interior world.

Beta (over 13 Hz) is associated with active attention and focus on the exterior world, such as normal, everyday activities. Beta is also present during states of tension, anxiety, fear, and alarm.

Research has confirmed that such spiritual practices as yoga and meditation produce changes in the electrical activity of the brain, leading to an increase in alpha and/or theta rhythms, and theta is found to be a characteristic brain wave pattern of long-term meditators. These meditators are able to keep their self-awareness intact, remaining alert in this "twilight state of consciousness."

Theory and Speculation

I was not the only one who had wondered about the connection between the drum and the spiritual realm. Other investigators, such as anthropologist R. Needham, had similar queries. He states that he finds "the common report, encountered again and again in ethnographical literature that a shaman beats a drum in order to establish contact with the spirits," and "All over the world it is found that percussion by any means whatever that will produce it, permits or accompanies communication with the other world." He asks, "How is one to make sense of the association between percussion and the spiritual world?" and states, "The question seems not to have been asked . . . just why he beats a drum, and why this banging noise is essential if he is to communicate with spiritual powers."

This universally observed phenomenon has been well documented but remains unexplained. There are, however, many theories and much speculation: Are these effects caused by the elements of cultural conditioning, imagination, superstition? Is it the rhythm? Is it the monotony? Is there a physiological process involved? To date, there has been only a limited amount of scientific research on the physiological and neurophysiological effects of drumming. It was not until the pioneering work of Andrew Neher that acoustic stimulation in connection with the drum was tested. He supposedly confirmed the theory that rhythmic drumming can act as an auditory driving mechanism, bringing the brain into resonant frequency with an external auditory stimulus; however, his findings are thought by some to be critically flawed because he did not control for movement artifact.

Wolfgang Jilek, researching the drum beat frequencies contained in the ritual dances of the Salish Indians, found that the predominant frequency of the rhythmic drumming was four to seven cycles per second, the theta wave EEG frequency of the human brain. He hypothesized, as did Neher, that this frequency would be the most effective aid to entering an altered state of consciousness.

An immense body of ethnographic literature cites the many and varied uses of the drum within the secular and religious activities of cultures. The specific uses of this instrument are as diverse as the cultures which employ them. These uses include: ritual and ceremony involving calendrical feasts; harvest and sowing; healing and sacrifice; celestial observations such as solstice or equinox; rites of passage such as birth, death, initiation, or marriage; processions; lunar rites; hunting; warfare; etc. Each culture has its own pattern of rhythms that are incorporated into ritual and ceremony.

The use of the drum in shamanic journeying is somewhat different from other uses, and practitioners claim that the drum is indispensable to their shamanic work. They say that they use it to enter into an altered state of consciousness and to travel to other realms and realities, interacting with the spirit world for the benefit of their community. They say they ride their drum through the air; it is their "horse," their "rainbow-bridge" between the physical and spiritual worlds. Mircea Eliade, author of *Shamanism: Archaic Techniques of Ecstasy*, emphasizes that "the shamanic drum is distinguished from all other instruments of the 'magic of noise' precisely by the fact that it makes possible an ecstatic experience." Shamanic drumming, in the majority of cases, consists of a steady, monotonous beat of 3 to 4½ beats per second.

Into the Laboratory

My research was conducted with the biofeedback technology of MindCenter Corporation. This multiuser system is composed of four modules, each designed to block external sound and light. The participants were able to lie down, the traditional journey posture. Each module contains a sound system. From these modules, four cortical sites are monitored for theta, alpha, and beta brain wave activity. Bipolar (left and right) channels were recorded from scalp electrodes placed on the four cortical sites: left and right parieto-temporal lobes and left and right parieto-central lobes.

Twelve participants were divided into three groups and monitored for EEG frequency response to three separate drumming tapes, which I and my drummers had recorded in a commercial sound studio. These tapes included: Shamanic Drumming, at approximately 4 to 4½ beats per second; I Ching Drumming, at approximately 3 to 4 beats per second; and Free Drumming, which incorporates no sustained rhythmic pattern. Four cortical sites, bilateral parieto-temporal and parieto-central areas, were monitored for each participant during three sessions. No journey preparations were given; the participants were told to relax, to listen to the drumming tapes, and to try to be still, as any body movement was likely to create artifact.

At the conclusion of the sessions, each participant prepared a brief written account and was given a tape-recorded interview of his or her subjective experience. These subjective experiences were then categorized according to recurring themes and consensual topics.

Results

This research supports the theories that suggest that the use of the drum by indigenous cultures in ritual and ceremony *has specific neurophysiological effects and the ability to elicit temporary changes in brain wave activity,* and thereby facilitates imagery and possible entry into an ASC (altered state of consciousness), especially the SSC (shamanic state of consciousness).

A pattern that incorporates approximately 4 to 4½ beats per second is the most inducting for theta gain. Seven of the twelve participants showed varying degrees of increased theta during Shamanic Drumming.

Drumming in general and rhythmic drumming in particular often *induces imagery that is ceremonial and ritualistic in content and is an effective tool for entering into a nonordinary or altered state of consciousness (ASC) even when it is extracted from cultural ritual, ceremony, and intent.* It is interesting to note that all twelve participants had some imagery, visual and/or somatic. For eight of these twelve, the images were vivid. This fact speaks to the power of the inducting force of the drumbeat in general, and the patterns of the Shamanic and I Ching Drumming in particular, to enhance imaging capabilities. It is hypothesized that the enhanced imagery capability is a direct result of theta frequency gain.

The pattern of the drumbeat as it relates to beats per second can be correlated with resulting temporary changes in brain wave frequency (cycles per second) and/or subjective experience, *provided the drumming pattern is sustained for at least thirteen to fifteen minutes.* In many instances, there is an accelerated shift in frequency increase or diminishment at minute nine, most notably for theta and alpha. According to field observations and subjective reports, the period of time required for most people to be affected/inducted by drumming appears to be thirteen to fifteen minutes. Generally, a rapid increase or diminishment of theta and/or alpha is seen to the fifteen-minute point, with a gradual gain or diminishment on to the twenty-minute point. This corresponds with the findings of meditation research as to the time required for optimum physiological response and, according to Angeles Arrien, to the oral teachings of some indigenous cultures concerning auditory stimulation.

The drumming also elicits subjective experiences and images with common themes. The first twelve categories are the common themes as synthesized from participants' verbal and written reports of their experiences in one or more sessions during the drumming. These include:

- *Loss of Time Continuum (LTC).* Seven of the twelve participants were aware of and stated that they had lost the time continuum, thus having no clear sense of the length of the drumming session.
- *Movement Sensations.* This category includes the experience of feeling: the body or parts of the body pulsating or expanding; pressure on the body or parts of the body, especially the head, throat, and chest; energy moving in waves through the body; sensations of flying, spiraling, dancing, running, etc. Ten of the twelve participants experienced one or more of the movement sensations categories.
- *Energized.* Nine of the twelve participants mentioned specifically that they became energized during and/or immediately after the drumming session.
- *Temperature Fluctuations (Cold/Hot).* Six of the twelve participants experienced sudden changes in temperature (e.g., chills, being flooded with warmth, sweating).
- *Relaxed, Sharp/Clear.* Five of the twelve participants noticed that they felt particularly relaxed, sharp, and clear. This was usually in lieu of emotions.
- *Discomfort.* Five of the twelve participants mentioned specifically that they were in varying states of emotional or physical discomfort.
- *Out-of-Body Experience (OBE)/Visitations.* Three of the twelve participants stated that they had the experience of leaving the module or being visited by a presence or a person during the session. This category is differentiated from Journey (see below) in that no traditional shamanic imagery was present.
- *Images:*
Vivid Imagery: All twelve participants had some imagery. Eight of

the twelve commented on experiencing vivid visual or sensate (somatic) images.

Natives: Nine of the twelve participants saw or sensed African, Tahitian, Eskimo, or Native American peoples. These natives were usually participating in rituals and/or ceremonies involving dancing, singing, or chanting, hunting, or drumming.

Animals/Landscape: Seven of the twelve participants reported a wide range of animal and landscape imagery.

People: Nine of the twelve participants imaged childhood friends or important people from their past, faceless teachers, non-native drummers, unidentified faces, etc.

Journey: Five of the twelve participants' description of their experiences included classic shamanic journey imagery, such as: going into a hole or a cave; being shot through a tube or a tunnel; spiraling up or down; being initiated; climbing an inverted tree; meeting power animals and helping allies.

• *Nonordinary or altered states of consciousness (ASC).* A majority of the participants, in one or more sessions, were conscious of the fact that there had been a qualitative shift in mental functioning, and the twelve themes as synthesized from the participants' oral and written reports may be correlated with Ludwig's delineations of features that tend to be characteristic of most ASCs. Eight of the twelve participants experienced at least one episode that was a journey, OBE, or a visitation; the data suggests that they achieved an altered state of consciousness (ASC). There was a total of thirteen such episodes for the thirty-five individual sessions.

Honoring All The Ways

It seems that there is validity for the ancient oral traditions that link the drumbeat with nonordinary realities. How many other spiritual traditions hold tools for us to use for healing of mind, body, and spirit? We can no longer afford to dismiss them as the product of an overactive imagination, superstition, or outright psychopathology and charlatanism.

Most indigenous cultures do not separate psychological from spiritual processes. Charles Tart emphasizes that "many primitive peoples . . . believe that almost every normal adult has the ability to go into a trance state and be possessed by a god; the adult who cannot do this is a psychological cripple." Michael Harner states, "It is extremely difficult for an unprejudiced judgment to be made about the validity of the experiences in the contrasting state of consciousness. . . . The persons most prejudiced against a concept of nonordinary reality are those who have never experienced it."

It is now time to bridge the separate and often isolated disciplines of medicine, psychology, religion, anthropology, ethnomusicology, science, sociology, etc. If researchers in each of these areas continue to work in the vacuum of his or her own discipline, the exact nature of certain continually reported phenomena may never be found.

References

Arrien, A. (1989). Personal communication.

Achterberg, J. (1985). *Imagery In Healing: Shamanism and Modern Medicine*. Boston: Shambhala.

Drury, N. (1989). *Elements of Shamanism*. Longmead, Shaftesbury, Dorset: Element Books.

Eliade, M. (1964). *Shamanism: Archaic Techniques of Ecstasy*. (W. R. Trask, Trans.). Princeton: Princeton University Press.

Harner, M. J. (1980). *The Way of the Shaman: A Guide to Power and Healing*. San Francisco: Harper and Row.

Hart, M. (1990). *Drumming at the Edge of Magic*. New York: Harper Collins.

I Ching Book of Changes. (3rd ed.) (1950). R. W. Wilhelm, Trans.; rendered into English by C. F. Baynes.) Princeton: Princeton University Press. (Bollingen Series XIX.)

Jilek, W. G. (1982). Altered states of consciousness in North American Indian ceremonials. *Ethos*, 10, 326–343.

Ludwig, A. G. (1968). Altered states of consciousness. In R. Prince (Ed.). *Trance and Possession States* (pp. 69–95). Montreal: R. M. Bucke Memorial Society, McGill University.

Needham, R. (1979). Percussion and transition. In W. A. Lessa & E. Z. Vogt (Eds.). *Reader in Comparative Religion* (pp. 311–317). New York: Harper and Row. (Reprinted from *Man*. 2 [1967], 606–614.)

Neher, A. (1961). Auditory driving observed with scalp electrodes in normal subjects. *EEG and Clinical Neurophysiology*, 13, 449–451.

Neher, A. (1962). A physiological explanation of unusual behavior in ceremonies involving drums. *Human Biology*, 34(2), May 1962, 151–160.

Tart, C. T. (Ed.). (1972). *Altered States of Consciousness* (2nd ed.). Garden City, N.Y.: Anchor Books, Doubleday & Co., Inc.

Walsh, R. (1990). *The Spirit of Shamanism*. Los Angeles: Jeremy P. Tarcher.

These drumming sessions for many of the participants were a profound entry into a nonordinary state of consciousness. In written reports and taped interviews, each person shared his or her experiences. The following is a brief sample:

Gender: Female
Age: 26
Occupation: Computer Software Sales
Years of School: 16 (BA)

SESSION 1

Body: She felt a "massive clearing in the throat area," and became "charged-up or energized." "I was feeling my head change shapes. My head flattened and pulled in a natural way. . . . There was no thinking about the process. It was all about feeling the sensations and feeling myself smile—no thinking. . . . There was much intensity and clarity. . . . I felt clear; the sound felt clear; the air felt clear—sharp and clear. . . . I felt lulled by the voice and the music."
General Comments: "I had a good time. I was very open to it. . . . The drumming was wonderful." She lost the time continuum and had no idea of the length of the session.

SESSION 2

Body: "The room temperature seemed to change throughout the session and became increasingly colder as the session progressed. . . . I felt strongly that I was inside the drum—not trapped or confined, just touching the insides." She was ill when she arrived for the session with abdominal cramping. She had been in pain for 2 hours before the session and on and off all week. (She was later diagnosed as having a bladder infection.) She said that she felt physically better as the drumming went on. "The drumming did sweep away the pain. By the end of the session, I had no more pain."

"I saw myself running—felt myself running. . . . There was no particular sense of urgency to go to anywhere or from anywhere. . . . There was no scenery, just movement. . . . I saw and felt myself running and had the sensation of running all around me, like I was in a herd. . . . I am running, but there is no scenery, very much like a dream. I was having lots of fun."
Emotions: She experienced very little emotion. She had a "nice sense of crispness, clarity and calmness. . . . There was a neutrality of emotions—a clarity, crispness, peace, but no emotions."

Melinda C. Maxfield

General Comments: "The first session has a clear sense of positive emotions; this time there were not many emotions, I just felt clear and sharp." She once again lost the time continuum, having no idea of the length of the session. "It could have been ten minutes or two hours."

SESSION 3
Body: "I got very tired. . . . I felt like I was definitely out of my body. I had little sense of it most of the time." She thought the drumming had ended, and she was outside the module walking around. This phenomenon occurred twice before the session actually ended. She says that she came in and out of awareness of the drums. She did not know where she went, but the drumming was a nice "welcome back."
Emotions: "The drumming seemed to be on a much narrower range than other days—fewer variations. It seemed to make me tired, and I didn't feel 'charged' the same way as other sessions." There was no sense of the "sharpness" she had felt before. "My mind wanted to take off, and I let it. . . . I left my body. . . ."
Images: She received picture images of the movement of sound. Her awareness of the drumming came in and out throughout the session. She has some sense of being in a jungle-like world at times. "Twice, I thought we had actually finished, when we hadn't." The first time, she found herself outside the module standing beside her mother. (Her mother was assisting the research team in the laboratory.) The second time, she heard the voice of this researcher telling her to come out of the module. She did. There were no electrode wires attached to her head. She joined a group of participants and research assistants who were walking around the room, talking. Each time, she "awoke" to find herself back in the module, aware of the drumming.

Gender: Female
Age: 29
Occupation: Massage Therapist
Years of School: 14

SESSION 1
Body: "I felt a slow, turning sensation, like I was spiraling up or down—like when you drink, but it wasn't like that. It was real slow, very slow. It was a nice feeling, like breathing." She experienced sensations and visuals of flying.

Images: She experienced smells and scenery from her trip to India. She saw an eagle very close up. It was flying over a ravine. . . . She went into a spiraling sensation and lost all sense of time. . . . Then she was at her brother's house. . . .

SESSION 2

Body: She had her hands folded over her stomach. He hands and stomach felt "full" or rounded—bigger than they were. Everything felt rounder. She felt rounder. There were no edges. Everything felt soft, clear and rounded. . . . She experienced strong sensations of movement throughout the session.

Emotions: "I had great anticipation at the very beginning, like something was going to happen. . . ."

Images: She had a strong sensation of movement throughout the session. "I saw a river running through a narrow canyon. The water was even with the top of the canyon and then it dropped deep into a lower canyon. I had a feeling of being there. I felt as though I were moving on the water, although I never saw myself. I didn't seem to have a body. I was flowing with the river toward an opening. . . . I did not drop with the water. I popped above it. Then I was traveling very fast through a heavily forested area. It felt like a hunt. Then I was on the river, flowing towards an opening, a large, black, circular hole, with my feet in front of me. I was being sucked horizontally. . . . As I reached the opening, I grabbed the side walls to keep from falling in. I had the sensations of hanging, although my body was horizontal. I felt the movement of the water below me and the air all around me. What was on the other side (it felt like below) was a long drop and lots of darkness. I hung on and the image faded out. . . . Then, I was underground, looking across a room. It was a cave with a dirt roof above me with a round hole in the ceiling with light shining through. I felt very alert, almost high. . . . I saw a symbol etched in the rock. I remembered that I had seen this symbol in other places during this session, the first time when I was flying above the water, and the second time after I stopped myself from going into the hole."

General Comments: She had a good time and is enjoying herself. "It was weird because it was so different; all kind of stuff was happening. It fell into place like a dream. It had a beginning, a middle, and an end, like a story. It was not so disjointed as last time. I felt like I spaced out in the other one. There was more movement and more action, and I was present most of the time. There was lots of water and movement, not just visual pictures of things." She says that she feels a "little spacey," but basically she is feeling *very* good.

SESSION 3
Body: The session was extremely relaxing for her. . . .
Emotions: She felt very relaxed and drifted in and out of awareness of the drums. . . .
Images: "I heard people talking. They were too far away to hear what they were saying. . . . The voices sounded surrealistic. It happened twice, at the beginning and at the end of the drumming. I got the sensation of being in a circle of people, although I didn't see faces, only the feeling. . . . At one point _____ (her brother, who was in the adjoining module) came into my module and lay down on me. It was like a spirit-form. It felt like a big pillow. . . ."
General Comments: ". . . This drumming was very relaxing. I could listen to it every night before I go to sleep. . . .

Gender: Female
Age: 43
Occupation: Graduate Student
Years of School: 18 (BA, MA)

SESSION 1
Body: "I had twitches originating from the shoulders, sharp, fast and involuntary. There was no warning. They just happened. . . ."

SESSION 2
Body: She reported lots of "body twitches," but no voluntary movements. "They are like a spontaneous release," many times in clusters. Sometimes they involve the head as well as the shoulders. "If I relax into it, there are more of them. . . . It is very much a deep body energy. . . ."

"I mentally danced through most of the drumming. I was sensing and seeing myself." She stated that this mental abandonment to dancing is a new visceral experience for her—the feeling that she wants to do it. "I was doing 'authentic' music the whole time, with different dance patterns, waving and stomping." Later, she felt that she had been dancing in a group of women.
Emotions: There was a general lightness of mood, a playfulness that bordered on a "mental abandon" to the mental dance she performed in her mind—a kind of "abandon to passion." At the end of the

drumming, she was inwardly and perhaps outwardly smiling and totally energized.

After the drumming had stopped, she felt as if someone were massaging her neck and shoulders. She continued to feel a "presence" in the module until she sat up.

Images: ". . . I saw myself as part of a line of Indian women walking up a hill, along a cliff, looking at the village below. This village is where I had been dancing, and the dancing was still going on. I had left the dancing to go with these women; I was one of them. . . ."

"Then an old Indian woman, grey hair in braids in Indian garb, beckoned to me and stayed in my 'mental screen' for awhile. The image was of the head and shoulders. It remained after the drumming stopped. I was left with a 'welcome feeling,' as if I were being welcomed into something." She feels that perhaps this old Indian woman was the "presence" that she felt in the module.

General Comments: "Overall, I mentally danced the whole time." She was both experiencing the dancing and doing it simultaneously. In the post session she stated that she was "on some form of a high" all Wednesday night. (This session occurred Wednesday afternoon.) She felt wonderful. She was grinning all night. She feels that it was some form of a "sustained altered state." . . . She stated that she had never before experienced such a strong flow of "psychic energy."

SESSION 3

Body: She had such intense body spasms that much of her EEG records had to be deleted as artifact. At one point, in the middle of the drumming, her whole body shook violently. "After that wave, which felt like fire-crackers exploding, I saw sparks. . . . Towards the end, I went through another intense spasm. My arms wanted to fly. I had to work hard to keep them from cutting loose and pulling out the electrodes in the possible flailing. This is similar to flailing I have experienced in deep hypnotic trance."

"Following this series of spasms, I got very cold and am still cold as I write this. . . . I am still cold and sweating simultaneously and slightly light-headed."

Images: "The stream of images was rapid and hard to catch and recall. There were so many." The images are not being recalled in the order in which they arose. "In the beginning, there was the sense

151

of an Eskimo in a double-headed canoe. . . . Right after the Eskimos, in the beginning, I saw an abstract symbol that became a seal that beckoned me. I joined it and swam through a sea of blue calm. . . . I became a swimming projectile, moving very rapidly . . . propelling myself with wavy motions of my body and tail."

"Following each of the two most intense spasms, I had the image of a streaming Infinity symbol—streaming in that there was a flying going on, very rapidly moving as if a stream of electrodes were moving. . . ."

Gender: Male
Age: 33
Occupation: Design Checker
Years of School: 15

SESSION 3
Body: "My neck seemed to tighten up a little at the start, but then the warmth sensations took over my body, and I was completely relaxed. . . . The warm sensations came in again later. They started at the feet and went right up to my head."
Emotions: "I had warmth in my mind and happiness in my body. . . ."
Images: He wanted to try to go outside to "dream," but he couldn't get there. "I went to the same dream-place as on Wednesday. . . . There was a room like this (the interview room) lighting-wise with two to five people there. When I looked at their faces, they were blank. They had hair and ears, but no nose, mouth or eyes. They were talking to me. I knew who they were, though." He thinks maybe the people were this researcher and two assistants.
General Comments: "The beat was more regular. . . . I didn't seem to go as far as I went on Wednesday. After each session, I feel great—six inches off the ground!" He feels very energized after the sessions. "It's like doing tai chi for a couple of hours. I didn't want it to stop."

Gender: Male
Age: 50
Occupation: Dep. City Manager
Years of School: 17 (BA+)

SESSION 1

Body: "I felt stiff at first, but then I became extremely energized, relaxed and alert. . . . I did not go to sleep. It (the drumming) took me way the other way (energized and alert). I could feel it happening. . . . It gives me extra energy, an extra boost, and now my whole body feels lighter and energized."

Emotions: "In the beginning, I was thinking, 'Why the hell am I here?' Then I began to feel secure and happy. There was no thinking about day to day issues. I was just more or less experiencing the experience."

Images: "I saw Indians around a campfire in some sort of a spiritual ritual. The ceremony involved using the drums. The Indians, their garbs, and the campfire were very vivid. The images just dropped in. . . . I saw bright colors and the ceremony all around me, in the fresh air, out of doors. . . . Being in the hills and mountains invigorated me."

Post-session note: He realized the next day that he was totally energized, all day.

SESSION 2

Body: "During the latter part of the drumming, I felt the energy level in my body increase and move throughout my body. It moved through me continuously. I still feel it now. . . . As the tape started, I was *very, very* warm. I then cooled off a little, and then got warm again toward the end of the tape as I felt the energy shifting in my body. . . . I had sensations of movement and being shot up through a channel."

Emotions: "I felt happy and somewhat stimulated during the latter part of the tape, particularly when I was on the 'journey.' "

Images: "Immediately, I saw a heart pumping to the beat of the drums. There were two drum beats to every heart beat. . . . I saw an African tribal dance, at night, with big drums and dancers in costumes. I viewed this from a distance." He was focused on the beat of the drums; the dancing was foggy and in the background. "The auditory beat was the main thing. . . . I was suddenly shot through a tunnel of darkness. I felt the movement UP, like being in a channel. I had no clue how I got in it. All of a sudden, I was there. I ended up free in the outer universe. It was dark, but I had a real sense of freedom. It was great. I felt free, excited and relaxed—exhilarated, as if I had let go of something. My body felt a sense of uplifted exhilaration and freedom."

General Comments: "It was good tonight. . . . I went out and ran before I came. I didn't want to feel like I did on Monday night, just coming from work. Tonight I was in a much different place coming in. . . . I have more energy since Monday, especially yesterday (Tuesday). Tuesday, I felt the energy. I knew something had happened to me."

Gender: Female
Age: 41
Occupation: MFCC Therapist
Years of School: 18 (BA+)

SESSION 1
Body: "I had a VERY POWERFUL visceral experience." Her ears were "full," and occasionally her head "got big—it expanded." She felt energy waves up and down her body. At one point, she felt a very heavy pressure on her chest. "The music was coming right into my chest . . . actually there was pressure on the whole body. . . . I felt in a circle. I was experiencing no restraint and yet I was really in my body. . . . The music *was* me. There was no separation. . . . The drums changed tempo, from very, very fast to really, really slow." She heard the different drums and tempos "in different parts of her brain," and each time the rhythms and tempo "totally changed."
Images: "I went down through a tunnel. My body moved and bent with the tunnel and popped up in another part of the earth. . . . I had many, many, *very vivid* images. I was *right there* . . . Indians, smoke, firelight, cat faces of all kinds, mountain lions, prairie-kinds of animals, barn owl. . . . All of it was 'night-time stuff.'. . ."
General Comments: She lost the time continuum; "time had no meaning." After the session, she stated that she was a "space-cadet," and her eyes were out of focus.
NOTE: In her next two sessions, she experienced two very powerful and profound archetypal shamanic journeys. She met her power animal, Big Owl, and was taken through several initiations. She was "ecstatic," "reverential," and "filled with joy."

Gender: Female
Age: 44
Occupation: RN; Massage Therapist
Years of School: 14

SESSION 2

Body: She felt like dancing. She felt inspired and motivated. "I went in with a headache, but it disappeared during the drumming. . . . I had a chill throughout my body during the first few minutes. . . . Generally, I felt very relaxed. The sensations were more audio than visual. . . . I seemed to expand and, more or less, just floated pleasantly."

Emotions: "I felt full of joy and very energized."

Images: Most of her images were in black and white, which surprised her. "I had an image of a drummer's hands playing the drums. The drummer had long, sensitive fingers. . . . I saw Indians dancing."

General Comments: "I feel much better physically than before the session. I had a horrible headache when I came here. I feel like I expanded this time. . . . I feel like I went somewhere, but I don't know where. . . . When I went out, I was still aware of the drums. . . . I was surprised that the session was so short."

SESSION 3

Body: "I experienced relaxation and energy in the 3rd eye area. There was pressure there. I began to feel immobilized, but it was not uncomfortable. It was more like I was in a trance or something. . . . I had slight pressure in my chest and a feeling of an opening of my heart. . . . At one point, I had snake energy all through my body. . . . Seems like I was really gone a couple of times."

Images: "This one was really different—more primal stuff, like an initiation. . . . I was initiated in some African tribal ritual. . . . It was at night, in a jungle. An African shaman in a black and white mask is leading the ceremony. He danced toward me and away from me. It felt like he was my guide. All of these images were in grey, black and white, at night. . . . The masks were made out of wood and painted. They were quite big. They came down to the person's chest. . . . I did not feel threatened. The shaman has a rattle or something. . . . I saw a large snake reclining in a tree. The image was in color. It was like a python, in colors of browns. . . . Then the same snake was coiled and lying on my chest. It couldn't hurt me because of the state I was in. Then there were more snakes, and I felt snake energy in my body and jungles and darkness everywhere. . . . Then I rose above it all into the clear blue sky. I could see fluffy white clouds in the distance and a dark bird circling high above. . . ."

General Comments: ". . . The images were much more somatic this time. . . ."

155

14

Peruvian Whistling Vessels:
Pre-Columbian Instruments that Alter Consciousness through Sound

DON WRIGHT

Just as *magic* and *miracles* have been eliminated from the awareness of the Western world by inhibitions or injunctions created by the reality paradigms of church and science, music has similarly been limited and confined. The paradigm constraining music dictates that music must be produced within the confines of scale, rhythm, and controlled changes of amplitude. Music structured through these controls can produce changes, in emotion, mood, energy level, and desire, and can evoke memories or stimulate fantasy. What this music cannot do easily (without dance, ritual, or chemical enhancement) is induce profound altered states of consciousness. I believe all music that could readily induce these states has been repressed successfully because of the ability of altered states of consciousness to produce an awareness that threatens or supersedes the reality paradigms of church, science, and political states. That music such as this does exist is indicated by Professor Joseph K. Long, of New Hampshire's Plymouth State College:

> Those who attended the 1988 *AASC* Annual Meeting found the Tibetan cymbal playing and Peruvian (Chimu and Moche, mainly) water bottle whistling a treat if not an astonishment. When the first seven participants played the bottles, the response was electrifying. As one of those, I took an immediate interest, realizing that the whistles might well be the most powerful psychedelic and brain stimulant yet discovered. I had realized that there was some suggestion that people *believed* in such an effect from music for millennia.[1]

For approximately two thousand years, cultures existed in Peru that produced the instruments mentioned by Professor Long, instruments which create musical experiences not based upon scale, rhythm, or controlled changes of amplitude. They are multi-chambered whistling vessels assumed to be water bottles by many anthropologists. The assumption is erroneous, in my belief, for several reasons, which include the vessel maker's concern for the vessels' tuning (each vessel being tuned closely around a primary frequency unique to the specific culture which produced the vessel),[2] the ineffectiveness of the vessels in pouring water, and, primarily, the surprisingly effective psycho-acoustical ability of the vessels. These findings are reason enough to suggest that the purpose of these objects is not to be amusing drinking vessels!

Interestingly enough, the production and use of these instruments ceased around 1532, the time period when the conquistadors arrived in the vessel maker's land. It is also curious that although the Spanish in their journals produced a comprehensive account of even the most intimate aspects of the cultures that produced the instruments, there is not one mention of the vessels' use or purpose. Not only did the people of the vessels not share their use with the Spanish, but they had not depicted the vessels in their paintings, weavings, or stelas even before the arrival of the foreigners. This fact seems unusual considering that Peruvian peoples often depicted such personal aspects of their lives as sexual acts and other intimate domestic scenes. This indicates that the vessels played a very special, and most probably, spiritual part in their lives, a part they were not inclined to share with the Spanish "visitors." Could the religious attitude of the conquistadors have influenced the decision not to share the experience of the vessels? I suspect that it did. The vessels were so numerous and common that they were clearly not reserved for a select few in the cultures.

I first encountered the vessels as an undergraduate at Boston College. My major was psychology, and my minor was theology. I was especially interested in consciousness manipulation techniques in both psychology and religion. My mentor and personal friend at Boston College, Professor Daniel Baer, was an expert in these areas; he provided me an opportunity to become quite knowledgeable about them. One day he mentioned that he had acquired a set of amazing instruments that had the ability to induce trance states with their sound. They were clay vessels, about the size of two grapefruits connected together; the front globe was in the shape of an effigy, and the back one had a spout about three inches long sticking up that you could blow into. The set consisted of seven vessels, a number of vessels that produced a peak effect when blown together in a group. I had an opportunity to experience this effect a few nights later at a gathering at the house of a mutual friend. I entered a room in which seven people were sitting in a circle, each blowing a vessel. Other people sat inside the circle or around the outside of it. Immediately, I was lost in an ocean of sensation that dominated my awareness completely. When the playing stopped, I was handed a vessel that a friend had been playing, and, when everyone began playing again, I started to blow through the vessel.

I suddenly realized that I was seeing a huge, "invisible" cylinder in the middle of, and yet larger than the room. The intense shifting, pulsating, and chaotic mixture of vibrations were reflected directly in the cylinder by shifts in the cylinder's wall thickness, transparency, and density. The cylinder extended infinitely up through the ceiling and down through the floor. Within the cylinder was absolute voidness, with a wind of "beyond voidness" blowing through it (I can't explain or describe how I could perceive this, but it was clear beyond question). A buzzing energy was present inside my brain. The experience was similar to a soda straw-sized stream of effervescent bubbles of energy shooting upward through the center of my brain, splashing against the roof of my skull, and pouring over my brain and down through my body. This effect, I noticed, was increasing in intensity. I knew that it would shortly reach an intensity that would be beyond my ability to experience and still remain in control of my awareness.

I decided to stop blowing on the vessel. Immediately, the cylinder disappeared from my visual perception. The buzzing energy continued to increase, however, although at a much slower rate. I placed the vessel on a small table near me and left the room. The rate of increase seemed to be directly related to the extent to which I could still hear the sound. I suddenly recalled that a person in one of the rooms had been playing a guitar. I went to that room; he was still there, but he was not playing. I asked him if he would play again, and he picked up the guitar. His first stroke across the strings abruptly stopped the buzzing effect in my head. The unanticipated nature of this experience affected me so profoundly that it led to my becoming the apprentice of Daniel Stat,[3] the person who discovered the psycho-acoustical nature of the Peruvian whistling vessels and who developed a way to reproduce them.[4] Since then I have produced sets of the vessels for persons or groups who are bringing this experience to others.

My first encounter with the vessels seems to have been far more intense than the experience of others, with the exception of my teacher. Although there are often common themes, the experience of each person is unique. Examples of common themes include being out of the body flying over jungle valleys; being on a mountain cliff overlooking a jungle valley; being in a cave or rounded room; seeing puddles and/or columns of white or bluish-white energy; sensing the presence of ancient or native people; hearing voices (usually all male or all female) conversing clearly but in an unknown language; hearing one excited voice trying to communicate something in an unknown language; hearing beautiful humming or singing with undiscernible words by women; hearing the growl or purring of a huge panther (known to be a panther in some unknown manner); or variations of these themes.

Other examples of experiences while hearing the vessels include that of a man who was crying when the vessels stopped. He explained that he had been traveling all over the world in search of pure spiritual experiences, a journey beyond anything he had found or expected. Another example is that of a woman attending a vessel session I was conducting in a bookstore one evening. I noticed her handing her vessel to her neighbor and leaving the room. After the session, I asked her if she had left for any unusual reason. She told me that she had experienced tinitus in her right ear and partial paralysis in the left half of her face since childhood. During the session, she had suddenly realized that the left side of her face was burning. She went to the bathroom to put cold water on her face, and discovered that the paralysis was gone as was the ringing in her ear. Occasionally, people will realize at the end of the session that they are very angry, sad, anxious, etc. When questioned, these people invariably reveal that they have recently experienced a trauma or are facing an impending traumatic event (i.e., surgery, a terminally ill family member, divorce, etc.). I have come to believe that one of the effects of the vessels is to unblock or facilitate the ventilation of underlying emotional energy.

One of the most exciting results of the vessel experience is the shared state of "clarity and realness" among participants. Although short-term in its observable manifestation, this state is apparent in the dropping of the "social persona," resulting in the new manner in which participants relate. As opposed to the attitudes held before the session, participants seem to be less concerned afterward about perceived differences in importance, intelligence, experience, etc. Participants seem to perceive others as equals without the relatively constant self-observation and judgment that existed before the session. There also seems to be a feeling of happiness and ease, participants enjoying the slightest humorous or pleasant event or expression by smiling or laughing. This state does not appear inappropriate, as it might if observed in a group of chemically-altered people. The participants are clearly grounded and in control, without any indication of intoxication or lack of coordination. I tend to attribute this after-session condition to a discharge of stress during the session and a de-hypnotic effect in which perceptual bias is eliminated.

The manner in which a vessel session is conducted has evolved since the first sessions I heard about and led. I was initially trying to develop a set and setting which would maximize the experience of the vessels. In the beginning this resulted in my developing an increasingly structured ritual for the experience. Through time and experience, I arrived slowly at the realization that more structure and control led to less profound experience for participants. Today I still have some suggestions that I share with participants. These, however, are intended to eliminate distractions that would occur if they were not mentioned.

My current sessions with the vessels begin with instructions to participants that they not to try to control the sound intellectually. If they are not warned, people will occasionally alter the sound by tapping their finger over the air vent in the vessel, by playing some rhythm of their own by pulsating their breath, or in some manner introducing an artificial or contrived element into the unified experience which is occurring for the other participants. This behavior is most probably the result of a reluctance to let go of control and simply experience, a condition which occurs naturally unless willfully avoided. Another instruction is for the participants not to blow too lightly, resulting in not "plugging in" to the unified experience created by the group, and not to blow too hard, producing air pressure so great that the vessel makes no sound at all. The most satisfying way to play the vessel is to allow the natural deflation of the lungs to occur, neither pushing nor holding back the breath. Blowing too lightly may indicate an insecurity about what the experience may be and an attempt to enter it only "lightly," while blowing too hard can probably be attributed to eagerness to "go for it" and realize the fullness of the experience. My last suggestion is that when the blowing stops, everyone remain silent and become aware of their own state of being. A subtle joyous internal state exists within almost everyone immediately after blowing that can easily be missed if the person begins to talk immediately. Because almost all participants have just returned from a unique and profound experience that has probably included some unusual and insightful elements, the natural tendency is to share them immediately and excitedly.

I also always explain before the session begins that each person is personally in control of his or her participation. Each person has the right to stop blowing and just listen or to put the vessel down and leave the experience. The reason for this instruction is two-fold. One reason is that the volume of the sound is loud, and someone with very sensitive or blocked hearing may experience physical discomfort. Interestingly enough, the effect after the session is an increase in hearing sensitivity in almost all cases. The second reason is that not everyone is on the same path or in the same place on their path. What one person is prepared to experience may not be what another person needs or is ready to experience.

What are the vessels doing? Why and how did the ancient cultures develop them, and for what reason? Given the present-day taboos against mind-states exploration, it is highly unlikely that empirical research will be conducted (at least openly) in this new form of self-administered mind change. These and other questions concerning the vessels may, however, be answered through research into the vessel cultures by those archaeologists free of limiting professional protocol, and through the experiences of people who are not afraid to step out of the confines of our present "everyday trances" into new and expanding experiences of reality. The current intimation that the vessels may be inducing an awareness or "awakeness" like that described by Gurdjieff, even if only temporary, is truly exciting. As sets of the vessels come into the hands of more and more researchers, the mystery of the vessels will come closer and closer to being revealed. If properly understood, the vessels or their technology may be the gateway to an awakened, "untranced" human race.

Endnotes

1. Joseph K. Long, in a review of "Animated Earth," *AASD Quarterly, Association for the Anthropological Study of Consciousness*, Vol. 5, 2–3 (June–September 1989).

Don Wright

2. Daniel K. Stat, and Steven Garrett, "Peruvian Whistling Bottles," *Journal of the Acoustical Society of America,* Vol. 62, 2, (August 1977): 449–453.
3. Don Wright, "Peruvian Whistling Vessels, Rebirth of Ancient Sounds of Consciousness," *Sacred Earth News* (Winter 1989).
4. Daniel K. Statnekov, *Animated Earth* (Berkeley: North Atlantic Books, 1987).

15

Music and Improvisation for Self-Expression:

The Work of David Darling and "Music for People"

BONNIE INSULL

For more than two decades, David Darling—cellist, composer, teacher, and passionate friend to anyone wanting to connect with their own musical expression—has been passing along a simple message: musical self-expression is a joyful and healthy means of communication available to absolutely everyone. Believing that expressive sound-making is a birthright and a healing practice for all humans, Darling has been generating enthusiasm in everyone from burned-out classical players to "non-musicians" in his workshops and concerts across the United States, Canada, and Europe.

Eight years ago, David's dedication in giving hundreds of improvisational concerts and "Music for Everyone" workshops spawned the grassroots organization *Music for People,* a networking organization that provides services and support for people who wish to continue their own musical explorations.

It was early December, the dark of the year, and I had never before experienced a despair like this. Each waking hour required conscious effort to move through work and family life without being overwhelmed by numbness and hopelessness. Friends were as helpful as they could be, but the way to recovery was clearly something I needed to find on my own.

So each morning I walked to an abandoned railroad tunnel, well out of human hearing range, and sang. I sang passionately, of grief and anger, of love and hate; and gently, of lullabies and farewells. I sang Gregorian chants and Irish ditties, nonsense songs and terrible war cries. And unfailingly, tears would come with the singing. The songs and the tears jumbled out together until enough had flowed to continue on with the day.

One morning in early February, a sudden physical sensation of glowing well-being—a mantle of beatitude and acceptance—enveloped my entire body as the singing finished. Along with it came the realization that I had passed to the other side of the depression and healed myself with my own music.

Tales of profound personal recovery through music-making come to the *Music for People* office quite regularly, as did this one. It seems that many of us have lost some degree of our emotional, mental or physical well-being by ignoring our expressive needs. People who have regained their health simply by making their own music send us letters, books, photos, music they have composed, and other heartfelt gestures of thanks.

Music as a healing art is not the primary impetus behind *Music for People*. Nonetheless, the interdependence of creative self-expression and personal health is obvious to us from the glowing faces that leave our workshops as well as from the many letters we receive from workshop participants.

Some months after attending a weeklong *Music for Everyone* workshop, Joe wrote us.

Each day after class, I was ready to pack up and drive home. Only on the last day, while we were filling out our "Musical Miracles" diploma and contemplating what we really wanted, did I fully realize that I was ready for major life changes. I was choked up to the point of exploding. For years I've been smothering a blissful little boy and a delightful musician inside me—with the help of parents, vice-presidents, coworkers and wounded lovers.

Since class, I've ended an unhealthy five-year relationship, made plans for a change in job (I'm a V.I.P. in a major corporation), kept a vegetarian diet (curing a food allergy and losing 15 pounds), repaired two suffering relationships with very significant and dear friends and given up marijuana. These aren't trivial changes for me—I've been pondering them for years in some cases. Your teaching was the catalyst I was ready for. I cried every day at your workshop. It hurt deeply to be so aware. Now, that awareness makes me smile every day.

What is it that happens in these workshops that permits so much healing and self-growth to occur? It is simply the acknowledgment that we all need to express ourselves creatively in sound. This need seems to be especially strong in Western culture, since we have relegated music-making to the realm of a select group of people who "know how." It's ironic that typically those who "know how" to make music—trained musicians—feel the most alienated from authentically expressing their emotions in their own music. The workshops provide an opportunity for all people, regardless of level of expertise, to create music together. A unique musical democracy evolves during our workshops, with its own "bill of musical rights":

- Human beings need to express themselves daily in a way that invites physical and emotional release.
- We are all unique creators.
- There are as many different ways to make music as there are people.
- The human voice is the most natural and powerful vehicle for musical self-expression. The differences in our voices add richness and depth to an improvisation.
- Sincerely expressed emotion (anger, pity, fear, joy, etc.) is at the root of meaningful musical expression.
- Music is more fully expressed when the body is involved in musical expression.
- People who can't sing on pitch can be more interesting musically than those who can.
- The European tradition of music is only one sound. All other traditions deserve equal attention.
- Any combination of people and instruments can make music together.
- Improvisation is a unique and positive way to build skills for life-expression.
- In improvisation as in life, we are responsible for the vibrations we send one another.

In each workshop, accessible techniques for improvising are given. What follows are some of the ingredients for improvising music that have been as helpful for the beginner as for the professional.

Warmups

Allow yourself a warmup period, and give yourself permission to do anything that gets you physically warmed up and artistically engaged. Observe whether you need to start in a gentle way or a physically active and dynamic way, and fashion your warmup accordingly. While there is no specific order recommended for the warmup exercises below, it is usually more productive to start with body and voice warmups before playing an instrument. If you pay attention to your physical and emotional needs during your warmup, a natural flow will take place.

Body and Voice Warmups

- Dance in slow motion to your favorite music, involving your whole body. Gradually transform your gentle and flowing movements into a vigorous, rhythmic workout.
- Babble like a baby, letting your fingers and hands imitate what your tongue is doing. Permit yourself to look and feel silly. Babbling can help shake off self-conscious feelings and get you ready to risk something new, especially if you allow your sense of humor into this process.
- Lie on the ground and lift your feet up two or three inches, then rest them on the ground. What you experience is tension . . . release. A universally acknowledged cycle of opposites (in Chinese tradition, this is called Chi Kung) is also the heart of music.
- If your mind gets too involved, or you want to change gears, try this releasing gesture from Tai Ji: put your hands on top of your head; lift them up to the sky as they separate; then let them fall to your sides. This movement can be a way of letting go of whatever preceded it.
- Gentle vocal warmups:

    Take a few deep breaths, and sigh on each exhale. Transform the sigh into an extended note that feels natural and good to your body. Release the sounds, and remember that you are just exploring, not performing.

    Discover your natural singing range by saying your first name in slow motion and centering in on the pitch. Repeat this, extending the length of each sound until you are actually singing a note.

    Sing long vowel sounds. Some of the most instinctive sounds are aaahh, Ha!, oooo, oh?, Yay!, mmmm, Aha!, mm h'mm?, Oho!, Ho!, and Hey! Stay with these sounds long enough to get used to them, exploring new aspects as you sing. Allow your natural attitude of wonder into the process. Let silence occur between each sound, and listen through the silence.

- Energetic physical and vocal warmups:

    When you are ready to be energetic, stand in a half-crouch with your feet apart and your weight balanced over both feet. Shake your hands vigorously, and mimic your hand movements with voice and tongue sounds, making distinct and separate sounds as fast as you can. Using syllables that start with hard consonants (*t, k, d, g, b,* or *p*), make rapid and distinct articulation your goal. Don't go any faster than *your* natural speed. You'll know you're there when the sounds are articulate and clear.

    To improve rhythmic articulation, make up accented nonsense phrases like "***duh***-ga, ***duh***-ga, ***duh***-ga, ***doh***," its reverse "guh-***dah***, guh-***dah***, guh-***dah***, goh," or other phrases that start with hard consonants. Be percussive, precise, assured, and expressive.

- When you feel sufficiently warmed up, explore the full volume range of your voice. Most people can be expressive when being soft and gentle, but many have difficulty finding a commanding and powerful expression. If you have a hard time reaching a loud dynamic level in your warmup, follow an energetic physical warmup by hollering "Hey!" or "Yay!" (rhymes with Hey!) at the top of your volume range, as if in a life-threatening situation, or shouting across a mountaintop. Extend the "Hey" for as long as you can. In our loudest and most enthusiastic shout, repeat "Yay!, Yay!, Yay!, Yay!" for as long as possible (thirty seconds or longer). We call this "getting to your 'Yay!' energy." Finding this dynamic is an important part of being a powerful soloist.

- Hear and incorporate silence in your warmup. Silence is the source of all the mysteries of sound. Let your silence be full of appreciation for the last note sung, or full of anticipation for the note about to happen.

Instrumental Warmups

When you feel in touch with expressing yourself vocally, you are ready to transfer this to an instrument. As in your vocal and physical warmups, honor your own sense of what is right to do at the moment you play.

- Energetic instrumental warmups:

    Get physically involved with your instrument before playing it. Dance with it. Or *pretend* to be playing on it while "playing the

167

heck out of it." "Play" your instrument as if you were your favorite rock star, concert artist, composer or conductor.

Make sounds on your instrument while standing in an athletic position, as if your life were at stake, the room was on fire, or you were about to run a race. Put total personal involvement into your breath and the physical posture of your playing.

Create rhythmic drive by imitating a percussion instrument with your voice and then imitating it as closely as possible on your instrument. This can lead to unconventional and imaginative ways of playing your instrument.

Explore as many different sound textures as you can imagine on your instrument (harmonics, overtones, tremolo trilling, percussive fingering, etc.).

● Gentle instrumental warmups:

Play in the most comfortable and favorite place on your instrument.

Take a phrase you know on your instrument and extend it. Play it inside out, move it to a different place on the instrument, play it loud, play it soft, or play it with a different texture.

Connect your singing to your instrument by singing a phrase and then finding exactly those same pitches on your instrument, translating the emotional feeling as well as the pitches to your instrument.

Improvising a Solo

Absolutely everyone has the capacity to be a powerful soloist in music improvisation. Just as a long journey starts with one step, an improvised solo starts with what we call "One Quality Sound." A "Quality Sound" is one note or tone that authentically expresses how you feel at the moment you sing or play it. Try this: breathe in, and on your outbreath, sing one sound that completely expresses what you are feeling right now. It can be a long sound or a short one, a high one, or a low one. Smile, relax and hold your "Quality Sound" for as long as you want, actively loving it as you are singing it. In our experience, willingness to express truer inner feeling in sound is the most potent tool in music improvisation. It provides catharsis for the performer and compels the listener to awareness.

"One Quality Sound" sung or played is actually the beginning of a melody. By connecting one "Quality Sound" with a second "Quality

Sound," you have made an expressive two-note melody. Longer melodies are simply several "Quality Sounds" in a row. Try improvising a melody in this way. Allow your passage from one sound to the next to be full of the great mysteries of life. Be aware of danger and opportunity as you travel from one note to the next. Melody is a moment by moment experience, so make each ensuing musical sound from the feeling and emotion you are experiencing at the moment. Remember to use SILENCE as one of the musical elements of your melody.

Warming up voice and body appropriately will leave you in an alert and imaginative state, and you want to stay that way for your solo improvisation. Be a powerful soloist by staying committed to your physical and vocal involvement during your improvisation.

Experiment going from your loudest volume level (the one you would use when singing the *Hallelujah Chorus*) to your softest, most tender voice. When you can go from a loud, dramatic place to a soft and mysterious place, you are tapping into your ability to be a powerful musician. As you solo, use anything that helps you stay alert: open your eyes; close your eyes; dance; play or sing as fast and as recklessly as possible, or as softly and tenderly as possible. Use any movements or vocalizations—yelling, whispering, cajoling, laughing, playing or singing loud and high, loud and low, soft and high, soft and low, and so forth—to find your own dynamic as a powerful soloist. All of your raw emotional feelings can become a catalyst for what you are playing.

Your solo may be as long or as short as it needs to be.

Like many things, the more you improvise, the easier and better it becomes.

Improvising in Groups

This section contains suggestions for improvising in a group of two to four people. When improvising in a group, it is important for each improvisor to talk about the experience of one improvisation before going on to the next. Each person needs to be honest about what did or did not work.

Whenever possible, tape record and listen to your improvisations. It can be amazing and instructive to hear your improvisations played back.

Duets

The duet is the most accessible ensemble for improvising: it is simplest to find one other person to play with; it is easier to hear what you are creating; and each person has ample opportunity to explore different dimensions of their artistry (percussionist, pianist, vocalist, and so forth) by switching instruments.

● Solo/Drone

In this structure, the first person improvises a simple melody (remember, an improvised solo is just two or more "Quality Sounds" played one after another), holding out the last note, which is called a drone. A *drone* is simply a sustained note that doesn't change pitch. Its volume or intensity may change, but the pitch stays constant. If you need to breathe while singing a drone, just breathe whenever needed and resume droning. As the first singer ends the solo and begins to drone, the singer nods to the duet partner, who then sings or plays his or her own improvised melody, with the first person's drone serving as accompaniment. When the second singer concludes the solo, he or she holds out the last note with the first singer's drone. The improvisation can be ended at this point by getting louder and signalling a stopping point together, or it can continue by repeating the structure.

Important suggestions for first-time duet-ers: keep your melodies short and give a clear visual and physical signal, such as a nod, when you're ready to switch from soloist to accompanist (the one singing the drone).

● Solo/Ostinato

You can vary the solo/drone structure by replacing the drone with a short repeated rhythmic/melodic pattern known as an *ostinato* (or more simply, a *groove*). Many people find this easier than using the solo/drone structure. Keep your ostinato pattern extremely simple at first. Two or three notes repeated over and over in an easy-to-hear rhythmic pattern works well.

● Imitation

Imitation is one good way to make an improvisation satisfying. Rather than trying to play exactly the same thing as your partner, simply imitate the shape or rhythm in the most natural way for you. For instance, if the first melody starts by going up in pitch and then comes down quickly, start your melody by going up in pitch and then doing anything else you want.

Larger Ensembles

We suggest that four musicians be the size limit for this type of improvisation. If you are in a group much larger than four, take turns playing quartets in front of each other, or divide up and go into different rooms for your improvisations.

• Beginning techniques for quartet improvisations:

One Quality Chord

You can begin a larger musical gathering by sitting in a circle and honoring the silence. Be close enough to touch each other, and breathe in together. Try starting with your heads touching, breathing as a group a relaxed inbreath and outbreath. On the outbreath, each person sings a "Quality Sound," all starting at the same time. You're not trying to sing the same pitch as the group; rather, each of you is simply singing one expressive tone that is comfortable. If your group is new to this, starting together can be a challenge. Here's one way to start a group at exactly the same moment: One person, designated the leader, lifts his or her arm up and then brings it down (like an orchestra conductor), ending the gesture in a finger snap. The group is intently watching this gesture, and sings together on the snap. Once you land on your note, don't move it around or put in rhythms. Simply sustain the pitch that comes on your exhale.

Repeat this until your group has come together. Remembering that your sense of humor is an important element, enjoy the drama and the sounding of your voice. Closing the eyes and being in your own space should be balanced with keeping your eyes open and visually communicating with your fellow improvisors. Your ensemble may wish to stay with this simple process for the entire time, as it is a very satisfying way to sing together. Or you may wish to move on to another structure.

Solo/Drone or Solo/Ostinato

If you want to move on to something else, you can adapt the solo/drone duet structure for your trio or quartet. To adapt it, after the first and second persons' solo, both continue to hold their drone while the third person solos. Continue around the circle in this way, each soloist holding their last note with the others who have already soloed. If you follow the structure, at the end of the solos, all four people will be droning. When you come to this point, be alert! The improvisation may be coming to its end, or it may want to continue on in some unstructured way.

Try this four times, with each person taking a turn starting the improvisation. If your ensemble is new to making music, let this be a short, self-contained improvisation, with each solo lasting no longer than 20 seconds.

Remember to allow time for verbal feedback after each improvisation. Each member of the group needs to be encouraged to share how the experience was for them. Be assured that telling the truth opens up the possibility for a deep learning.

Free Improvisation

Improvising freely and inventing your own structures for group improvisation is an excellent way to challenge your musical creativity. In fact, the structures given above should be looked upon simply as starting points for your own creative ideas. But your ensemble's success in free improvisation will depend upon how well you understand the techniques given above, and how well you can listen and communicate with each other.

In a free improvisation, each person is responsible for the following: being a powerful soloist when you find yourself in that role; being ready to provide a rhythmic groove for others to solo on; using solo/drone or solo/ostinato techniques when appropriate; offering your silence when you don't have a musical idea to give; closing your eyes some of the time, but not all the time; making eye contact at key times during the improvisation; giving the soft instruments or voices in your ensemble room to be heard; and remembering that imitation is one of the most powerful tools for a satisfying musical experience.

Since the main focus of music improvisation for self-expression is making the group successful as a whole, encourage everyone in your ensemble to play a powerful solo at some point during the improvisation. It is important that each person honor the totality of what the group is doing at any given moment.

When playing a free improvisation, don't take a vacation. Be there moment by moment, and be responsive to the natural ending point of your improvisation.

• More advanced structures for quartet improvisation:

Imitating Traditional Musical Forms and Styles

Choose a traditional musical form or style that everyone in your ensemble recognizes in sound or "feeling." For instance, if everyone in your group can tap the feeling of a waltz, then an improvisation can be structured around a "waltz feeling." Other examples are march, funk, ragtime, jig, chorale, lullaby, Dixieland, fugue, blues, gospel, and so forth. During this kind of an improvisation, make use of any of the techniques listed above while staying with the "feeling" (beat, mood, or meter) of the style you've chosen.

ABA Form (The Oreo Cookie)

ABA Form has been used in all kinds of musical styles for centuries. It can be of any length. It begins with a musical statement or theme, moves to something different, and concludes with a return to the original musical statement. Most people find starting and ending an improvisation with the same musical material and putting something different in the middle to be very satisfying. Make the opening statement (the *A* in your *ABA*) distinctive so that it will be easy to recall at the end of the piece.

Think of an oreo cookie: chocolate cracker, creme filling, chocolate cracker, and you've got the *ABA* Form.

Improvising on a Familiar Melody in ABA Form

Here's another way to improvise using the *ABA* Form: Find a melody that everyone in your ensemble knows. Childhood songs like "Row, Row, Row Your Boat," "Jingle Bells," or "Three Blind Mice" work well and are readily accessible to most people. The improvisation starts with the ensemble playing the rhythm (general "feel") of the song together, without needing to play the "right" or "wrong" notes of the song. Then move it into a free improvisation by playing imitative fragments of the familiar melody. The improvisation concludes with a simple restatement of the melody. Thus you've created a piece in *ABA* Form, in which *A* is a familiar melody, *B* is a free improvisation based on the melody, and the concluding *A* is a restatement of the familiar melody.

Improvising in Specific Instrumental Combinations

Incorporate as much instrumental diversity as feasible in your ensemble. If possible, try to include a melody, a bass, and a rhythm section. You can also experiment with putting together instruments of the same family (four celli, four kazoos, four harmonicas, four bells, four clarinets, etc.) to explore the beauty of their sound when played together. If you have two or more ensembles of similar instruments—as in a wind quartet and a percussion quartet—try a call and response or question/answer alternation between them.

Games for Continuing your Musical Growth: Practicing Alone or With Others

The Accent Game

This is a good rhythmic technique for violin, viola, cello, and bass players, to be done plucking or bowing the strings. Go back and forth between two neighboring strings, alternating between them as evenly as possible. When this feels successful, try alternating between three strings, and then four strings. Next, accent one particular string in each pattern (for example, 1-*2*-3-4, 1-*2*-3-4, 1-*2*-3-4, or *1*-2-3, *1*-2-3, *1*-2-3). Accenting in this way will give a sense of excitement with rhythmic playing, and puts the player in touch with syncopations that exist in pop and folk music. Particularly well-suited for the novice string player, this game allows you to lay down a rhythmic framework that's easy for others to play with.

Staying With It

Take a short rhythm pattern or melodic fragment and, using variations in tone, timbre, texture, nuance, and accent, repeat it over and over, learning to extend its beauty through continuity. If you are playing by yourself, try tape recording it and improvising on top of the playback.

Sing What You Play, and Play What You Sing

Find on your instrument the exact pitches of a melody that you can sing. Sing a two- or three-note melody several times before trying to find it on your instrument. If you forget what the melody sounds like while trying to find it, go back and sing it several more times. Increase your expertise by lengthening the melody one note at a time. Also try to find with your voice the exact pitches of a piece that you know on your instrument. If possible to do on your particular instrument, sing in unison with your instrument while playing the tune. This will deepen your experience with your instrument, and you'll connect with the piece of music in a new and exciting way.

Jazz Piano (for the novice)

With your left hand, walk a slow and deliberate ascending or descending line on the piano, making each note a *One*. Play notes that are next to one another and use both black and white keys. Then with your right hand, your voice, or with another player, freely explore jagged melodies and riffs against this steady bass.

Jazz Bass (for novice cellists or bass players)

Like the Jazz Piano game above, the cellist or bassist will play a slow *walking* bass line by sliding his left finger slowly up or down one string while plucking each note as a *One* with the right hand. This invites a melodic improvisation on top.

Wrong Notes

This is a good exercise for anyone who wants to improvise within a tonal context. You'll need to find a piece of music to play with. Anything that changes harmonies slowly will do. (The *Music for People* tape, *Improvising with David Darling, Tape II* was made for working on this technique.) Play notes that sound as *wrong* as possible against the tonal center that is being played. Experiment with playing only wrong notes. Try holding onto a wrong note for too long, then hold onto a wrong note until you can hear a *right* note that resolves it. Finally, try moving to the right note that you hear.

Scale Playing (done in pairs, or alone with a tape recorder)

One person repeats a fragment of a slow descending or ascending scale pattern over and over. The second person finds a way to harmonize with this scale pattern. Stay with this long enough for the improviser to feel successful. Then switch parts, giving each person the opportunity to harmonize over a simple repeated scale pattern. The improviser can also play the Wrong Notes game above while their friend continues to play the scale pattern.

We warmly encourage you to try any of these musical concepts with your children, your coworkers, or your next-door neighbor; bring them to nursing homes, prisons, therapy sessions, or embrace them in your personal routine. You'll find this approach to making music can heal the soul, cut through language, age, or cultural barriers, and provide a shortcut to vital communication. But best of all, it is profoundly fun.

We invite you to rediscover the power of your own musical expression.

"Music for People" welcomes your comments or inquiries.
The Improvising with David Darling tutorial series is available on cassette tape through the MfP Office.
Music for People, RD 4 Box 221A, Keene NH, 03431, (603)352-4941

16

Mysteries of the Spiritual Voice:
An Interview by Don G. Campbell with the Abbot of the Gyuto Tantric University
KHEN RINPOCHE

I have just returned from Tibet, the land where Nicholas Roerich painted scenery that reflects the soul's spectrum on the Roof of the World. The land where Padmasambhava brought Buddhism to flourish in the eighth century. The land where the lineage of fourteen Dalai Lamas have ruled the Gelugpa tradition of Buddhism. The land where over 5,000 temples and monasteries were destroyed by the lack of mindfulness of the Chinese Cultural Revolution. The land where a living esoteric system is still the heart and life of a gentle and peaceful people. The land where one prayerful, religious voice may produce the mysterious sound of four or five pitches at once.

From my first exposure to this distant world of Shambhala, it was the sound that called me. Over twenty years ago, through Alan Watts' lectures and Huston Smith's film *Requiem for a Faith*, single-voice chording caught my attention. The experience of first hearing the monks of the Upper Tantric College (Gyuto) led me into a timeless place where both the sense and concept of music were transcended.

In this style of chanting, each of the eight to fourteen singers produces a chord. The lowest note is usually about two octaves below middle B, C, or D flat, plus another note which is the middle B, C, or D flat, plus a third higher. Actually, the second, fifth, sometimes sixth and tenth harmonics are very prominent. Many other overtones can be observed on a voice spectrograph up to the sixteenth partial.

Explanations of the overtone series and how to begin to make harmonic sounds can be found in Chapter 6 of my book *The Roar of Silence* (Quest, 1990).

A couple of hundred monks outside of Tibet are able to make these sounds in either the Gyuto or Gyume traditions. While in Lhasa, I was able to visit each of these original tantric colleges where the singing tradition is thought to have originated over 450 years ago. New recordings of the choirs of their sister colleges outside Tibet were given to the monks during the summer solstice full moon *puja* (offering ceremony) in Lhasa.

While curiosity is a natural reaction to hearing these sounds, it is when intent, practice, and the contemplative listening are integrated that the fullness of the religious and artistic meaning can come into focus for the Western ear.

The great difference between the Tibetan practice of Buddhism and other Buddhist forms in Asia is the concept of *tantra*. Tantra is a devoted study of the continuity and link between phenomena and mind in terms of energy. Through direct practices, observation of the relationships between inner and outer worlds and contemplation of the "true nature" that exists outside of duality (good and bad, life and death, I and the other), energies are understood and utilized for spiritual transformation. Complex tantric traditions have evolved for centuries.

The complexity of disciplines and doctrines in the four schools of Tibetan Buddhism is enough for numerous lives of study. The intricate and fascinating rituals, the hierarchy of manifestations of deities, art, and architecture are awesomely abundant, even as seen in Tibet today.

It was a privilege to meet with the Venerable Lungri Namgyal, referred to as Khen Rinpoche, during the visit of the Gyuto Tantric Choir to the Rothko Chapel in Houston, Texas, and the Museum of Natural History in New York City. Sincere gratitude is extended to the many people who made this interview possible: the staff of the Rothko Chapel, Frances Thargay at Tibet House in New York City, Dr. Robert Thurman, professor of Buddhist Studies at Columbia University and the Tibetan teachers at Naropa Institute in Boulder, Colorado.

Don Campbell: What is the Tibetan word for "overtone"?

Khen Rinpoche: We do not have a name for it. This is something new that Westerners, in listening to and analyzing our sound, have come up with. We do not have a discussion of this ourselves, this sort of synthetic, synergetic resonance within the vocal cords and so

177

forth. This kind of overtone thing occurs in other musical instruments, like drums—if you hit a drum it has a deep resonance, and also there would be a high-pitched resonance. So it is not that amazing. All voices have certain overtones; however, the human voice does not usually have that degree of multiplicity of overtones. It is very rare, and this is one of the reasons why this chanting, when Huston Smith first discovered it from the Western point of view, was so amazing to people. Those deities who revealed this special technique to the ancient lamas must have wanted to amaze Western scientists!

DC: Are all of the young monks who come to study chant in the Gyuto tradition able to learn this overtone style with extended practice?

Khen Rinpoche: Some cannot learn it at all.

DC: Are there any techniques to help enlarge the larynx or any nonmusical techniques?

Khen Rinpoche: There are no particular mechanical things as a kind of test to show how well someone might be able to develop this—we may do something like have someone practice gargling with water to see how resonant the sound can become. Other than a test like that to get a sense of how someone is going to come along after they have practiced, we do not have any special exercises or anything.

DC: In the West we have certain scales and modes that have a tonal center and at times modulate to other tonal centers. In this style I hear different beginning pitches and consistent modulations. Is there a sense of knowing which tone to start with or does it find itself in relationship to each one of the rituals?

Khen Rinpoche: Usually they start on the same note, and they are composed to begin on the same note; the tradition is handed down so that they would be. Sometimes the individual leaders of the chant, depending on the characteristics of their voice, their ability to conform exactly or in an exact way—sometimes start with a smaller voice and build up, coming into the traditional spot of sound; some start right away, very powerfully in that spot. Therefore, it sounds like they may be starting at different tones but it is not really; it just has to do with the particular voice.

DC: Have any women ever learned Tibetan chanting?

Khen Rinpoche: Yes, there are other traditions, not so much in the Tantric Colleges, but in the tantric choirs of some of the other monasteries. There are some traditions of chanting in a higher voice. The Tibetan nuns' choirs have usually cultivated that kind of chanting, even though they do not have this deep resonating kind of chanting. They do have very specific styles and with musical scores and so on as we have. They do have chanting methods, but at a higher register.

DC: Where are those to be found today?

Khen Rinpoche: Any nunnery has this knowledge. They have certain melodies that they know; there are some very important universal ones that everybody practices, such as at the Guru Puja, the worship of the lama rituals. These are very widespread. Then there are these special melodies of offering the mandala which all of the monks and nuns do.

DC: What is the average amount of time used in chanting in your tradition? In the Gregorian tradition there are offices sung nine times a day. What are the similarities?

Khen Rinpoche: We do not do chanting all of the time. Within a month we, as a whole, chant three to six times, depending on the season and on different circumstances. In those times it is more or less depending on the occasion. During times of extensive ceremonies we chant all day long. Sometimes this will go on for two, three, or four days almost without interruption. Then sometimes there will be occasions where we will chant for two or three hours a day for two or three days in a row. This is because in our rites there are extensive or concise versions which we will use on different occasions, in different contexts. When we have very extensive rites, we will sometimes get up at two in the morning and go on until eight or nine at night. There are exceptions to this, when a young monk is in training; they will ask questions and learn certain methods and meditations, and then they will practice alone. They may practice every day for several years. There is a particular exercise of going to the side of a loud waterfall and practicing until a state is reached where they can clearly hear their own voice amidst the roar of the water. This is done in the process of training, which takes place individually, until they reach a certain level of proficiency. Once we have learned this special chanting sound, it must be often used. If we do not chant this way for a couple years, go to another monastery, or do our daily recitations in a thin or conversational voice, then the powerful voice is lost.

DC: In the different sects of Tibetan Buddhism is chanting taught in different ways?

Khen Rinpoche: I do not really know all the systems of the other orders. I think they have their own methods of chanting and their own way of teaching and practicing it. I am quite sure that no others, even in the other monasteries in our own order, are like the Gyuto Tantric monks with this deep, special kind of resonating voice. Even our sister college, the lower Tantric College of the Gyume tradition, uses a much lighter voice than we do. This style of chanting is sort of unique in Tibet and is of the Gelug order founded or renewed by Je Tzong Khapa. This deep voice chant does not originate in India, though there are many chanting methods to be found there. Various lamas who were heading this order and its monasteries had revelations. They had visions of deities like Yamantaka or Mahakala. These visions of deities were like gifts to them and taught them certain ways of making sound. They said that if we chant using this method, it will benefit all human beings. It was through this kind of revelatory composition and not just their own sort of investigations or their own creations or inventions that they would adopt a new kind of chant. By the various heads of the order actually meeting with the deity in a mystical experience these sounds emerged. These were people in the lineage of followers of Je Tzong Khapa in the history of the Gyuto Monastery or the Gelugpa Order from the sixteenth through the eighteenth centuries.

DC: How important is the chanting in relationship to enlightenment? Is it for personal self-growth, or is it for the ability to help simultaneously all sentient beings?

Khen Rinpoche: It is not directly connected to the path of enlighten-ment in the sense that we do not consider it directly a vehicle to enlightenment, nor a direct vehicle of spreading enlightenment. It is directed to the sound as a thing in itself. Indirectly we do it this way (demonstration) for the process of living beings trying to attain en-lightenment, either for ourselves or another.

There are various favorable circumstances and there are unfavora-ble obstacles. We believe that there are certain deities that we call dharma protectors or guardians of the faith, who are powerful beings who can assist in keeping away or clearing away obstacles in our practice to realize or achieve enlightenment—for ourselves and oth-ers. For example, if there were not protective beings, we would have terrible wars. This would interfere with the path and practice of enlightenment, since we would not have time to meditate or think of higher things. Therefore, in order to propitiate these deities [we] request them to protect living beings from misfortunes and to put favorable circumstances in their way for understanding, studying, and the achievement of enlightenment: "Please protect them against obstacles that would [cause] them [to lose] their human minds and allow them to practice the teachings of enlightenment."

In requesting this, we are, in fact, indirectly affecting how other people are able to practice for enlightenment. When we request in a way which pleases the deities, and which is beautiful, this has a certain energy and becomes an ornament for them and something that they would rejoice about. Then, these deities exert themselves more energetically, and it has a stronger effect. It is in that context that our chanting relates to the progress of the enlightenment of all.

This applies to the kind of chants, such as the Mahakala chants, which are offered to these protectors. There are other chants of the bodhisattvas which are concerned with the Buddhic deities, whose sole concern is bringing one to enlightenment, by reciting or visu-alizing the content of the higher treatises. Using chant is a way of showing reverence for the teaching, of showing the greatness of the teaching. Chant makes a powerful impression upon one's mind and in the minds of others of the incredible value and preciousness of the teachings.

The other point is that there are a variety of approaches to this: the discipline, the yoga of chanting, and the yoga of using these rites in the monasteries. It is different for different people who are doing

181

them. In Tibet, for example, there are two midtracks in the Tantric College of the unexcelled practice of yoga tantra. One track is known as the creational stage and the other is the perfectionist stage. The creational stage is for the cultivation of the imagination and visualization. Those who are in this track have a prerequisite understanding, but are mainly concerned with the issues of selflessness, enlightenment, compassion, and so forth, cultivated directly through the tantra visualization practices. Others in the perfectionist stage come from the studies of exoteric meditations of transcendent wisdom. As they enter the tantric monastery, they are considered to already have achieved some level of enlightenment—though not perfect, at least a general understanding and an accomplishment of initial stages. It is considered that at least some members participating in those rituals have attained levels of enlightenment, so they are able to lead the group through the ritual. There have to be both those who are practicing the visualization and those who have achieved certain realizations. Then the chants can become very powerful vehicles for people. Each one enriches the other's particular type and stage of realization and ability. They also become powerful vehicles of expanding an enlightened vibration to others. There is a certain kind of complex mix within the Tantric Colleges in practice.

A final point is that Westerners may not realize that there are advanced practices of tantra. It is almost a prerequisite to have achieved an initial stage of realization of selflessness. A definition of *enlightenment* is "the wisdom that realizes selflessness." It may not be total or all the way through the unconsciousness, but at least in the conscious mind and in some of the unconscious mind, there must be some insight of the selfless life. Due to this insight, there will be a dedication of the will to the enlightenment of body and mind that is a wish to liberate all other beings from suffering. This is kindness, love, and compassion. This special new energy is based on the insight of selflessness. These two things must be there in some form before one can begin to practice tantra. Tantra is not an alternative in the sense that, "Oh, I am going to do tantric chanting instead of studying selflessness or compassion." It does not work like that. Those other studies are prerequisites which directly relate to the proper practice of the original and ancient ways in our tantric tradition. There are many around today, in our orders and even other religious systems, who say they are practicing tantra, who we would consider not to be properly practicing.

DC: How can the Western ear be opened to experience Tibetan chanting?

Khen Rinpoche: In general, in regard to sound, there is what is called agreeable sound and disagreeable sound. It may come out to the same thing, but the way that I would understand the impact of sound on the nervous system in the body is as follows: When an agreeable sound goes into the ear, then it is appropriated by what we call the aural consciousness, and the mind gets involved and takes it over through the hearing faculty. Once the aural faculty in the mind has appropriated the hearing faculty, it generates a pleasant mental faculty, mental consciousness. Mental consciousness is what we call mental delight or mental happiness. When this mental happiness rises in the consciousness, which is a sixfold system of consciousness, the coordination of the five sense consciousness feels a delight, and this creates a secondary relation to reverberation in the physical consciousness, or what we call the body consciousness. When it does that, the body consciousness feels a kind of ecstasy or bliss—a different kind of energy—and it produces a transformation which, if you are reading them as chemical transformations or electrical transformations, would be an intensifying of the immune system or some other kind of positive effect.

The way we would explain how this works is that it happens in the mind first through the aural consciousness and secondarily through the mental consciousness. There is a feeling of a certain kind of delight that stimulates these physical changes. Rather than it being the sound going into the brain or the skull, which is a more mechanical model of explanation, I would explain it through the system of the sixfold consciousness. We understand the body as a secondary effect which corresponds with the state of the mental consciousness. It is something different than the five sense consciousness; it is this sixth element of consciousness which determines the state of the body. So we say that the body corresponds or follows after the state of the mind. In this model we understand sound as a material phenomenon of waves which are propagated in a medium of some sort and result in molecular reactions taking place as energy reactions in the subatomic level of the neurons from the ear to the brain. In this theory of sound, certain kinds of unpleasant sounds, through the energy reactions in the brain, could cause somebody to get angry, to kill someone, or to be frightened. This accounts for people reacting in a negative way.

DC: I am amazed at how similar what you are saying is to the research of the Parisian, Dr. Alfred A. Tomatis, about charged sound and discharged sound. He is testing and measuring sounds that empower the mind and body with strength and clarity.

Khen Rinpoche: That is very good, to admire the subtlety of sound on mind and body. This type of observation in theoretical language in Western science is subtle—looking at these things and especially the level of subtlety in the atomic kinds of things and the neurological kinds of things. Western science has felt limited by its inability to talk about nonmaterial phenomena or mental phenomena. To combine these auditory perceptions would be very excellent, very excellent. I am glad to speak to you.

The following recordings are available of Tibetan Overtone Chanting:
The Gyuto Monks: Tibetan Tantric Choir
Windham Hill Cassette 2001
Box 9388
Stanford, CA 94305

Tantric Harmonics: The Gyume Monks
Spirit Music
Box 2240
Boulder, CO 80306

Donations for the development and availability of tantric chanting as well as support for the Gyuto Tantric University may be sent care of:
The Society for Gyuto Sacred Arts
PO Box 358
San Rafael, CA 94915

IV

Music Therapy and Transformation

What Song did the great fireball sing? What tune accompanied the formation of the galaxies? The music that ushered in the cosmos played on, inside us and around us.

                                                              Brian Swimme

The world of music therapy recently became known throughout the country when in 1991 Grateful Dead drummer Mickey Hart declared to the Senate Special Committee on Aging, "Rhythm is at the very core of our lives." Doctors and patients testified that "music is better than medicine." Stories of rehabilitation, treatment of chronic diseases, and clear directives were given that could save Medicare millions of dollars as music becomes a viable replacement for drugs and other costly therapies. In addition, innovative schools such as Naropa Institute in Boulder, Colorado, are integrating music therapy, toning and imagery into degree programs in creative art and psychology.

In this section, three certified, registered music therapists tell of the impact of imagery and voice in psychotherapy. Sara Jane Stokes of the Mid-Atlantic Institute gives a detailed account of Helen Bonny's technique of playing classical music and allowing images to emerge in the mind. Ken Bruscia of Temple University in Philadelphia expands this technique into current work with people living with AIDS. Laurie Rugenstein, Associate Director of the Institute for Music, Health and Education in Boulder, Colorado, explores the role of voice in working with women's issues.

These are but a few of the dozens of methods music therapists are using throughout the country. For more detailed accounts refer to part 3, "Music as Timeless Therapy" in my book Music: Physician for Times to Come (Quest, 1991), which contains articles by renowned music therapists and researchers.

17
Letting the Sound Depths Arise

SARA JANE STOKES

We want to be fully alive, but there may be blocks in our psyche that deaden and numb us. Forgotten wounds and hurts may lessen our participation in the fullness that life has to offer. Many people are searching for the "missing something" in their lives, hoping to find what is lost. Within a therapy context, the experiential therapies seem to hold much promise in offering an in-depth process of releasing and healing wounds. This is because they directly engage the sensory and feeling levels and help uncover the truth of what is real.

It is a wonderful miracle that the human psyche has the potential to regenerate and heal itself, regardless of how wounded we may be. The psyche (or soul) contains an innate pattern of wholeness, unique to each individual, and is always drawing us to hear its call. Sometimes this comes as a whisper, and at other times we are chased down by the "hounds of heaven." The challenge in any helping process is to be able to access this inner call in a direct participation with the very depths of one's being—to know the truth that will set us free.

Music, especially the great music of the masters, infuses and attunes us with the mystery that resides in our depths. The healing power of music can awaken our patterns of wholeness, while simultaneously evoking the stories that can reflect the blockages to growth. This uncovering process can unleash one's potential for becoming radiantly alive. This too is a miracle.

Music, the language of the soul, is at the very center of the potent approach to therapy called the "Bonny method of Guided Imagery and Music" (GIM). It is helpful to distinguish GIM from other similar techniques which utilize visualization and imagery paired with music, usually referred to as "guided imagery" or "music and imagery." GIM is essentially an uncovering process used as an experiential therapy for individuals and groups. It depends upon the skilled intervention of a trained guide and uses specially designed classical music programs.

A hallmark of this method is that the flow of imagery is spontaneous. It unfolds in its own time and way, much like a conscious dream. This is in direct contrast to imagery techniques which use visualization for a desired outcome or goal, such as relaxing at the beach, or shrinking a cancerous tumor. In GIM, clients are encouraged to be their own healers and to discover their own answers. The GIM guide draws upon such qualities as intuition, "presence," and specialized guiding skills to help with problem-solving and catharsis. The GIM guide artfully leads clients to their own insights and aha's!

Music, the primary healing agent, acts as a catalyst and container of the altered state experience. The music "informs" beyond the rational mind, evokes feelings, stimulates problem-solving, and awakens the healing potential of the body, mind and soul. In GIM, we are "played" by the music and are attuned by it to the miracle of our capacity to heal and be whole.

GIM began in the early 1970s with Helen L. Bonny, Ph.D., a music therapist and Research Fellow. She was invited to participate with a team of renowned researchers in the field of human consciousness who were developing new therapy interventions through the use of psychedelic drugs. Located at the Maryland Psychiatric Institute in Baltimore, the researchers treated such populations as terminal cancer patients, alcoholics, drug addicts, and other psychiatric categories.

The researchers were particularly interested in the human capacity for peak experience (Maslow 1971) and the profound healing that sometimes occurred. Bonny's role was to design special music programs to amplify and complement the action of the mind-expanding drug experience. As a musician and violinist, Bonny was well acquainted with the music of the Western classical tradition, especially the great masses and requiems. These masterpieces were used to help sustain the healing and integration that occurred during the peak state of the therapy session, after conflictual material had been worked through. It was her genius to know which selections to use and how to best sequence them for the desired effect.

In their research Bonny and Panhke (1972) found music to be a powerful catalyst in achieving their objectives. They reported music's effectiveness in the following ways: facilitating the release of intense emotion; directing and structuring the experience; providing a sense of continuity in a state of timelessness; and contributing toward the desired peak experience.

As the research evolved, drugless methods began to be developed for continuing this depth work. Bonny was encouraged by Hanscarl Leuner, a European psychoanalyst well known for his work in imagery techniques. He suggested that she combine music with his method of therapy, called Guided Affective Imagery (GAI). Bonny found that the music she had used with psychedelics, when listened to in a deeply relaxed state, provided a safe yet effective way to access the unconscious. This approach opened the possibility for much wider applications with a variety of subjects and situations.

Following her original tape themes and design, Bonny condensed the listening programs to thirty to forty-five minutes for use in more conventional settings. The names of the tapes reflect the thematic material to be evoked: Nurturing, Grieving, Emotional Expression, Death-Rebirth, and Peak, to name a few. With the spontaneous emergence of imagery, feelings, and insight, the client's psyche was free to heal itself, in its own time and way, by honoring the wisdom of the inner self. The dynamic power of the music, the imagery experiences, and the creative interaction between the GIM guide and the client may combine synergistically to elicit the miracle of transformation.

Currently, GIM is used with individuals and groups by trained GIM facilitators, called GIM Fellows. Trainings are being established in several different countries, and must be approved by the Association for Music and Imagery, the national board for conferring credentials. GIM guides and clients alike develop a profound appreciation for the opportunity to work with this method and are continuing to pioneer a growing number of applications.

The Bottomless Pit

The following case is an example of one woman's healing journey through GIM. Her story is interspersed with comments in brackets which refer to specific psychodynamics of her process, as well as guiding and music interventions. The case is followed by a discussion of music as "cotherapist."

Caught in a web of indecision, Susan felt desperately alone, seeking solace in an addictive affair and secret drinking. Appearance belied her inner turmoil. A thirty-nine-year-old attractive redhead, Susan had a well paying consultant job and what outwardly looked like a happy marriage. One of her hobbies was singing in the community chorus, and she was intrigued by the idea that music could be used as therapy. She had tried traditional talk therapy in the past, but intellectual insights had not led to change. Her affair and the drinking were getting harder to hide. [Many people escape from their loneliness in substance abuse and codependent relationships in order to numb themselves. Without real help they continue down a path of self-destructive behavior.]

Susan and I contracted for a series of ten GIM sessions and planned to meet weekly. Her early key images revealed a sad little girl, a faceless high school cheerleader, a bottomless pit in her stomach, and a foreboding dark cave. The music helped her connect with her feelings by triggering significant memories that had been frozen in her psyche. In her third session we began to see the dynamics that contributed to her aloneness.

As Susan lay relaxed on the mat, she listened to the opening measures of the Mostly Bach tape, well suited for depth exploration. The repeated musical pattern of the fugue form in Bach's *Passacaglia and Fugue in C Minor* evoked a physical sensation of spiraling downward. Though she felt apprehensive, she reported, "The strings seem to say I have to go down to that cave and go in." There in the hidden recesses of the cave, she encountered her brother who had committed suicide. In her imagery, she cried out in anguish, "How could you do this and leave me? You were my best friend!" Selections from the Grieving tape facilitated Susan's fully feeling the pain of abandonment that she had never resolved. [When we do not fully feel the tragedies of our life and experience their pain, the psyche may gradually become frozen and the capacity to give and receive love become impaired.]

As a result of this session, Susan willingly cooperated with her healing process by working with other difficult and painful material from her childhood. She read Bradshaw's classic book on recovery, *Homecoming* (1990), and started a journal. In her sixth session, Susan came into the office depressed. She and her husband Ken had been arguing and she felt, as hard as she tried, she couldn't trust him with her feelings. She felt impelled to keep her secret affair going, though she felt guilt pangs. I used the Nurturing Tape to help Susan again face her emptiness. The music of Britten, Vaughan Williams, and Berlioz allowed her psyche to unfold its trauma in a session we later entitled "The Bottomless Pit."

Sharing her imagery, Susan reported, "The sky is brilliant blue, the scent of fall is in the air. I hear the crowds cheering. I'm sixteen, in my blue and gold cheerleader outfit at the game. I look bubbly on the outside, but I know something is wrong." I suggested that Susan step into her imagery and be that sixteen-year-old once again. [The music was influencing Susan below the level of awareness, evoking a mood of longing, and was working as my cotherapist to trigger feeling and memory.]

Susan continued in subdued tones. "I look happy, but on the inside I feel hollow and split." I asked her, "What do you need to happen?" [This kind of well-timed guiding question enables the psyche to problem solve from its own depths. In GIM, it is important not to rescue people or give advice. The wisdom of the inner self knows exactly what it needs.] "I want to be whole and stop hurting," Susan softly cried. At this point the melancholy yet tender melody of the music was encouraging her to stay with the wounds of the past. "I am slowly sliding down into that black hole in my stomach now," Susan said in a resigned voice. "It's that familiar feeling again—the bottomless pit place." Susan wept, "I have no soul, no heart."

Later in the session as her tears subsided, Susan was able to take the music with her down inside the hole. Lovely voices singing Puccini's "Hummingbird Chorus" from *Madame Butterfly* seemed to caress her, and she felt their gentle harmony as angels of mercy. Susan's face was relaxed now. "They are comforting me," she whispered, ". . . and the darkness is beginning to lift. They are telling me it's going to be alright. . . . I'm going to bring the cheerleader and the little girl in here with me. It's OK now. I'm able to give them love as the angels are loving me. I feel [the angels'] presence. They are singing to us. I feel their light." As the music ended, Susan sighed deeply. "I'm ready to come back now."

Afterwards, as we discussed the significance of the session, it appeared that today had been a pivot point in Susan's therapy. She confronted the emptiness within and was then able to begin a process of reparenting herself from the roots of her childhood. She was amazed at how real the angels were. Although she did not consider herself religious, she accepted them without question. [In GIM, working through core wounds in the psyche often allows the emergence of transcendent or spiritual levels of being. In Susan's case, the angelic "helpers" brought their treasures of love and light to assist in the miracle of deep transformation and reconstruction of the personality.]

In Susan's eighth session, she found herself on a bridge of indecision, still churning about the dilemma of not ending her affair. She was feeling better about herself but still felt stuck. I used the Transitions Tape to facilitate further exploration of her issues. As the music began, Susan found herself on the middle of a bridge, surrounded by a barren landscape. She felt stuck, standing in the middle, unable to choose between going back to her husband Ken or going forward to her secret lover. Neither seemed to feel right. "I can't decide. It feels overwhelming. I don't know what to do," she lamented. I guided Susan to stay with the indecision, really feeling the tension of not being able to act. [This freed stuck energy in the psyche by acknowledging heretofore unconscious patterns. The music acted as cotherapist by "containing" the intensity of the emotional conflict until it began to release.]

As Susan felt her stuckness, breathing techniques were used to assist her in breaking free. The "Adagio" movement of Brahms' *Second Piano Concerto* evoked a spontaneous shift to a totally new scene—an old-fashioned ballroom filled with dancers. To her surprise, she and Ken were dancing, feeling the rhythm of their movements and harmonizing together. "It's natural," she said amazed. "Our steps are in time and in tune without effort. I know we *can* be this way. Maybe I can someday try to trust again." [In this session, the imagery clearly reflected how inner psychological conditions may undergo change. By directly experiencing the stuckness, being on a lonely bridge in a barren landscape, Susan's imagery dramatically shifted to the richness of relating "in tune and in time" with a partner in a beautiful ballroom.]

During the following week, Susan's homework was to use her dance image as a metaphor for exploring some risk-taking with Ken. Could things between them really be different? As her GIM journey of several weeks came to a close, Susan's imagery unveiled new possibilities as her outer choices reflected her inner changes.

In her last session, Susan revisited the dark cave where she had once grieved over the lost brother. This time a curious thing happened. She relayed, "I'm here in the cave, and I see a pool of water. There are ripples on the surface . . . it's the kind you want to get into." She fell silent and then continued, "There is a kind of glow coming up from down under. It is sort of a diffused light. It's coming up inside me and all around me." Then, "Oh, my aura is glowing," she exclaimed. "It's wonderful!" The strains of the Peak Tape provided a beautiful background to this ineffable experience of light. Later, during Wagner's exquisite masterpiece, "Prelude" to *Lohengrin*, Susan closed the session with a memorable reunion. "John, my brother, is here," she declared. "We are holding each other. He is proud of me. I feel so grateful, there are no words . . ."

Today, Susan regards herself as being a different person. She states she is generally much more open emotionally and willing to try new things. She feels more confident and reports she and Ken are getting along much better. They actually signed up for ballroom dancing classes, something they had always talked of doing. To Susan, GIM was a miracle. The dark cave, the bottomless black hole in her stomach, the bridge of indecision no longer plague her with loneliness and self-doubt. She is free to love, to grow and risk—to be fully alive.

GIM as Co-Therapist

In the GIM process, music plays a unique role of "cotherapist" with the GIM guide. Music, with its own special vocabulary of rhythm, melody, harmony, pitch, tone, and timbre, speaks directly to the unconscious. It is a moment-to-moment experience, a sound presence, a palpable and living force. It goes beyond words into the heart and soul. A few examples from Susan's case (in parentheses) describe some of the many possible interventions that music can make:

It dissolves the ego's defenses (". . . the music is relaxing me and helping me to let go . . .").

It stimulates catharsis (". . . how could you leave me!"; "I just can't decide, its overwhelming. . .").

It provides a moment-to-moment continuity (". . . the music is here with me in the black hole").

It becomes a projective screen (". . . the voices are like angels bringing me love and comfort").

It supports moments of healing (". . . we are dancing in rhythm, in tune and in time. . .").

It allows for the transcendent to emerge (". . . the soft diffused light is coming up inside and all around me. . .").

It celebrates moments of integration ("John, my brother, and I are holding each other. . . . I feel so grateful. . .").

The movement and mood of the music contribute to its ability to bring about change. Bonny (1978) fully discusses this in her monograph entitled "The Role of Taped Music Programs in the GIM Process."

The great composers used archetypal motifs such as death-rebirth in an attempt to grapple with or musically solve the great existential questions of life. The powerful influence of music as cotherapist serves to assist clients in their search for answers to questions in their own lives: Who am I? Where am I going? How can I be free? These questions always surface in times of crisis and change. In GIM, it is possible to let the sound depths arise, allowing the deeper self to reveal its innate wisdom and truth.

I would like to share one last example of a transformative event within a GIM session. Doris, a woman in her forties, had been struggling with issues of identity, both personal and professional. She imaged vividly, in the metaphoric and symbolic realm. In this session, Doris's images incorporated the well-known "Adagio for Strings" and the "Offertory and Sanctus" from *St. Cecilia Mass* by Gounod. This music is sequenced as the climactic sections of the Positive Affect Tape. With this music Doris experienced a direct participation with the motifs of union and regeneration contained in one powerful symbol, representing wholeness. In her own words, as she wrote after her session: "I felt I was giving to birth to this very difficultly birthed child. The labor was long and painful. As it was born, a sonorous voice rang out in the distance and announced, 'It's a champion! It is done!'

"As the music held me in its power and strength, I had the feeling of a warm afterbirth pouring out of me, and a penetrating light and euphony of a full-bodied major chord played by a full orchestra surrounding me. When the delivery was over, I discovered I had given birth not to a child, but to myself—a huge brilliant sunmoon. I was alive with ecstasy!"

18

Visits From The Other Side:
Healing Persons with AIDS through Guided Imagery and Music
KENNETH BRUSCIA

Guided Imagery and Music

Guided Imagery and Music (GIM) is a form of individual therapy or healing which involves imaging to music in an altered state of consciousness while dialoguing with a guide. It was originally conceived by Helen Bonny (1978a), and has been used effectively in a variety of settings. Because it is an in-depth method of personal and transpersonal exploration, the use of GIM requires the guide to have intensive training.

Each GIM session begins with the "traveller" and "guide" exploring feelings or concerns pertinent to the traveller at the time. This may be done through verbal discussion or nonverbal techniques such as mandala drawing, musical improvisation, movement. Based on themes or images that emerge through these preliminary explorations, the guide then designs or selects an induction to help the traveller relax and move into an altered state of consciousness. As this occurs, the guide focuses the traveller's imagination, usually with a specific image or scene, and then introduces the taped music program. Several music programs have been specially designed for use in GIM (Bonny, 1978b), each consisting of works from the classical music literature which have been carefully selected and sequenced for specific imaging purposes. While listening to the music and allowing one's imagination to unfold, the traveller may have body sensations, visions, feelings, memories, fantasies, or a variety of internal experiences, all of which are regarded as "images." A dialogue is maintained throughout the imaging, with the traveller describing experiences as they occur and the guide supporting, reflecting and amplifying them. Meanwhile, the guide keeps a transcript of the dialogue for later reference. When the images and music come to an end, the guide helps the traveller bring closure to the experience and return to an alert state of consciousness. The traveller is then encouraged to describe, react to, or elaborate upon the experience, either through verbal or nonverbal means.

The kinds of transformations that take place in the GIM process vary with the traveller, guide, and goal of the series. Depending on one's orientation, the transformations can be described as physical, emotional, or spiritual healing; psychotherapeutic progress; developmental growth; or self-actualization.

Visits from the Other Side

For the last three years, I have used GIM to support gay men living with the AIDS virus. During that time, and based on over two hundred and fifty sessions with twenty men, I have discovered something that, to me, is astonishing. No matter what the personal history, level of maturity, course of the disease or severity of symptoms, and no matter how emotionally or spiritually challenged—for every man the healing process has begun with a "visit from the other side." In a GIM context, such a visit takes place when a deceased loved one appears to the traveller while imaging. Invariably, the visitor comes from the other side for a specific purpose, and does or says something that assists the traveller either in beginning the healing process or preparing for the crossover to the other side.

Persons living with AIDS face many emotional and spiritual challenges. After the initial shock of diagnosis and the need for various forms of denial, the person often struggles with core emotions at a very deep level. Fear, loneliness, anger, guilt, and grief are most common. Although these emotions are closely related to the experience of living with AIDS, they are often derived from earlier wounds in the person's past. Thus, healing nearly always involves a return to earlier times and a search for unconditional love from significant others from the past.

Loved ones from the past can offer many kinds of support and assistance in the emotional healing process, depending upon the role they had taken throughout the person's life. What is important to realize is that when a loved one passes on, there is no replacement—and the specific kind of loving support that a deceased parent, sibling or friend once offered is usually no longer available from anyone else. Thus, it seems most logical that the psyche continues to search and wait for the loved one to return and to resume the same supportive role.

Visits from the other side can therefore be understood as the traveller's attempt to rediscover or reclaim lost love. This is important because it suggests that love is the most essential ingredient of the healing process, and that when finding it is made difficult by AIDS, there is a need to return to those persons who have offered and modelled it unconditionally. For the psyche, it makes no difference whether the loved ones are on this side or the other. When love is needed, the person will seek and find it wherever it was given in the past, regardless of whether the loved one is living or dead. For this reason, the appearance of deceased loved ones in GIM can be as real and life-changing as the actual support and assistance provided by them in the past, or by loved ones in the present.

Case Examples

What follows are examples of how persons living with AIDS have found the love they needed to heal their lives. The examples have been selected to show how the main emotions experienced with AIDS have been the focus of such visits.

Getting Out of Limbo

Being diagnosed "HIV-positive" triggers various forms of denial, and especially when there are no symptoms. Some men deny the diagnosis itself, living life in the fast lane and actively avoiding any reference to the virus. Others deny they have any feelings with regard to the diagnosis, and cut themselves off from it as if they have no emotional reactions. Often these individuals intellectually minimize the impact of AIDS on their lives. Finally, there are others who deny that they still have a life to live. These individuals often give up their careers, dreams, goals, and pleasures, and instead ruminate over the virus, the possibilities of illness, and the "inevitability" of succumbing to the disease.

Tom was thirty-two years old, and had been diagnosed but asymptomatic for two years. He was ensconced in many forms of denial: He lived in the fast lane. He was split off from the grief and anger he felt over the deaths of several loved ones. He had completely given

197

up his career goals. Tom had been working as a waiter, despite impressive academic credentials and an invitation to teach at a prestigious university. Thus, he was living high, but had little hope for the future; and he was filled with emotions, but had dissociated himself almost completely from them. Tom had lost his most dearly beloved sister to suicide; his older brother had recently died of AIDS; and he had buried scores of friends with AIDS. The losses he had sustained seemed overwhelming, yet Tom showed no feelings.

For months, we worked to help Tom "get out of limbo." Nothing seemed to help. We began the sixth session with Strauss's "Ein Heldenleben," as I suggested that Tom let the music bring him whatever he needed at the moment. After a long silence, he said: "I keep seeing my sister. We are exchanging glances, and there are no words for the flood of feelings we are having. She is trying to say something to me: 'Don't be afraid of needing others. It's good to be strong, but you don't have to be alone. That's what my downfall was. You wouldn't be alone if you would allow yourself to be more vulnerable. Real strength is knowing when you need others.' She is embracing me. It feels so good to be close to her again." Tom reported that she continued: "You used to do so many things; then suddenly you withdrew from life. You must go on. Your health will not stop you from taking hold of your life, and doing what you have prepared yourself to do all these years. Everything is there waiting for you. Take it all—now—while you can!"

Tom was moved by his sister's visit. He even shed a tear, though reluctantly. The full impact of his sister's message was yet to be understood. However, one week later, Tom quit his job as a waiter and took a full-time position at the university; more importantly, Tom began a journey into his soul and began to connect with his feelings of grief and anger. Just recently, he told me how glad he was that he had accepted his vulnerability, and that the ability to acknowledge his needs had become a strength for him and a reassurance for his loved ones.

Healing Relationships

People with AIDS often grapple with feelings of isolation and loneliness. There are several reasons. They spend many days at home alone when they are sick; they are not always able to maintain an active social life; and often they are stigmatized, abandoned, or unintentionally neglected by friends and loved ones. One also finds that people with AIDS often discover that the love they so desperately seek during the illness is actually the love that was never given to them in the past, either by family or friends. The following case example is the story of a man who longed for his father's love, and by his own admission, became "sexually addicted" to men after his father's death.

Ray was a thirty-year-old psychotherapist who tested positive to the virus but was asymptomatic. He had been taking *The Course in Miracles,* and experienced altered states of consciousness often, all in the hope of finding himself and healing his life.

Ray had a visit from the other side in his very first GIM session. As he listened to the "Rhosymedre Prelude" by Vaughan-Williams, a very gentle and nurturing orchestral piece, Ray regressed to his first year of college, and recalled that he had drawn a picture of himself in his diary. The picture consisted of concentric circles around a small core. It was entitled "Aloneness." In his image, he began to search through the diary, and remarked that he had done this drawing during an important year in his life—his father had died, and there were many issues left unresolved. As the imaging continued, Ray returned to the drawing of himself and started to erase the outer circles, as if to take down the barriers that had kept him so isolated. Then as the circles disappeared, he noticed that he was being surrounded by many loving people. After a long silence, Ray said, "I have an undescribable feeling that my father is here with me right now." I asked him how he knew this, and he responded, "There's an openness right here [pointing to his heart and crying]. I can see his face . . . he's smiling at me in a boyish way—not like he used to, but more the way I smiled at him when I was a boy. He looks so undefended with me now, just as I was with him then, but now I am the same age as he was when he died, and we are both undefended with each other. It is so nice to be able to love him, and feel it back. There is no fear of him, and he has no fear of me."

Finding Forgiveness

If diseases are manifestations of specific emotions, then AIDS can be considered the disease of guilt and shame. Because many persons have contracted the virus through sexual contact or drug use, they are often "blamed" by society for whatever behaviors led to infection, and then dismissed because they "deserve" to get sick. This is especially true in homophobic or puritanical environments. While this judgmentalism contributes greatly to the stigma attached to the disease, many persons with AIDS also blame themselves. Gay men, for example, frequently blame themselves both for being homosexual and for engaging in specific sexual activities. For them, and for those who disapprove of their sexual orientation, AIDS is seen as a punishment.

One of the most poignant examples of how painful guilt can be is the case of Rob—a very handsome man in his mid-thirties. Rob often expressed disappointment and anger at his parents, who, according to him, rejected both him and his gay lifestyle. Yet, Rob himself was quite homophobic and often tried to "pass" for straight. He expressed his shame over being gay and HIV-infected through images of self-belittlement, martyrdom, and self-mutilation.

A recurring image that disturbed Rob greatly was of himself sitting alone in his living room—almost completed emaciated, wasting away, and looking like "someone starving to death in Bangladesh." As he would sit there crying, Rob would call out for his Granny to come and take care of him, but for some reason, she would not come. Rob had been raised by Granny and was closer to her than to his mother. Unfortunately, Granny had died before learning of Rob's diagnosis, and now as he was developing symptoms and worrying about the course of his disease, Rob needed her desperately. Sadly, no matter how long he waited for her in the images, she did not come. When he would finally give up waiting for her, Rob would sob like a child and lament: "She doesn't love me anymore. Now she knows I am gay and how I got AIDS."

Then in the seventh session, something unexpected happened. In his images, Rob bade his parents good-bye and set off alone by boat for an island. His description of the island reminded me of Molokai, the Hawaiian island formerly reserved for lepers. I had the ominous feeling that Rob was going there to die. Upon his arrival, Rob found throngs of people queuing along the shore and looking up into the heavens. As he joined them, Rob realized that they were all "waiting for redemption." He immediately began to search the heavens for his Granny. This time (with the help of Wagner's "Prelude to Act I" of *Lohengrin*), he was more confident, and even remarked that he felt good because he had finally made peace with his parents. As the music moved him through the heavens, Granny finally appeared. Upon embracing her, Rob cried deeply and expressed his relief that she had not left him to die alone. Granny chastised him "for being so silly," and asked, "How could you think I would not love you—no matter what?" She then explained why she had not come earlier. "It's not my forgiveness you need, it's your own. I have been waiting for you to find forgiveness in yourself."

Putting Anger Aside

Anger is sometimes unleashed when an AIDS victim discovers the virus or suffers the ugly ravages of opportunistic infections, and especially when such feelings have been buried or smoldering within the individual for some time. Persons who have been abused, neglected, unloved, or rejected can easily conclude that contracting the virus is the ultimate "put-down" by God, or the "last straw" in an already rotten life which has brought them nothing but pain. AIDS is a bitter pill to swallow, and one's bitterness makes it even more so.

Bill was a forty-five-year-old millionaire who had as much anger as wealth. He hated his deceased father intensely, referring to him only as "the selfish bastard." Apparently, his father had psychologically abused Bill and his mother, and then left the entire family for another woman.

In this third GIM session, Bill relived his father's funeral. In recalling his own conduct, he began to realize that he had many of his father's traits. As he pounded the floor, screaming and crying, Bill shouted "I am so afraid of turning out that way. I hate him! He only thought of himself!" After the images came to a close, Bill talked about the need to forgive his father, and to look at his own life more closely and honestly. He also acknowledged that his mother, who had died a few years after her husband, did not want him to hold a grudge against his father.

Bill's visit from the other side did not come until the fifth session, four weeks later. As the music began ("Adagio" from Marcello's *C Minor Oboe Concerto*), Bill found himself in his bed, with a picture of the Sacred Heart of Jesus hanging over him. Suddenly, Bill's mother appeared and told him that he needed to be saved. "You still have time to be healed, but you must allow yourself to be washed in the blood of Christ." The slow movement of Rodrigo's *Guitar Concerto* began. Bill found himself at the bottom of the cross, and began wiping the feet of Christ. "I'm rubbing his blood into my hands until it is absorbed. This is my healing and salvation."

In the next and last session, Bill announced that he had made an important decision. In order to forgive his father and to become the person he wanted to be, Bill had offered complete financial support to every member of the AIDS support group he attended. "This will be a demonstration of the generosity that I always wanted from my father, and that I always expected of myself."

Bill died six months later.

Embracing Life and Death

After getting out of limbo and finding the love needed to survive the emotional trials of AIDS, there is one last step in the healing process: to embrace life while dying, and to embrace death while living.

Carl was in his early forties when he began GIM. At the time, he had entered final stages of the disease and was struggling with several problems, including extreme susceptibility to respiratory infection, fever, retinitis (which eventually led to blindness), and bouts of forgetfulness and confusion (which ultimately ended in dementia).

Over the eighteen months that we worked together, Carl was very much like a teacher to me. As my first client with AIDS, he introduced me to the challenges that both of us would face, and as a deeply spiritual person at the doors of death, he invited me to accompany him on his excursions to the other side, always sharing his discoveries and insights with great love and generosity. From the beginning, Carl saw our relationship in reciprocal terms. My role was to bring him the musical and personal support he needed to heal himself; his role was to teach me what he was discovering about the healing process and the "other side."

I am dedicating this chapter to Carl's memory, because it was he who revealed to me the role of "visits from the other side" in the healing process. Though it was one of his most valuable teachings, we never talked about it. Rather than telling me what I needed to learn in my work with AIDS, he led me to discover it through his imagery.

Carl's visits began in his very first GIM session, during Ravel's *Daphnis and Chloe*. Carl had a fleeting image that all his deceased loved ones were gathering as a group to visit him in his home. It was not until later that I realized that each person from this group would come for a separate visit.

The first separate visit came in the third session. Carl had a high fever that day. During the slow introduction to Copland's *Appalachian Springs*, Carl saw a group of dancers moving on stage as if they were legs of a Chinese dragon. The dragon wound around slowly until the tempo quickened. Then the dancers suddenly broke out of formation and began to dance around Carl. The elated dancers created breezes to cool Carl's body, and in the slow sections of the music they dragged vapors of the fever away from him. During Tschaikovsky's "Scherzo" from the *Fourth Symphony,* the dancers did somersaults and ran figure eights around Carl—as fast as subway trains. Carl smiled and said: "It's not so much the breeze they are creating as much as their generosity—their loving hearts are really what is healing me." In the next piece, *The Dove* by Respighi, Carl looked back at the paper dragon lying lifeless on the stage, and at the sight began to cry. "The dragon is lying the same way that Alan used to lie. It was Alan who brought the dancers to heal me." (Alan was a best friend, the brother that Carl never had, who had recently died of AIDS.) As Carl lay beside the dragon, it began to spread out and form a protective blanket. Alan had come back to take care of his friend, not merely by taking away his fever, but by bringing him "spirits" of love and generosity from the other side.

After this experience, Carl's imaging began to take on a basic form. During the first five or ten minutes of music, Carl would allow images of what was happening in various parts of his body to arise. Then, after getting a sense of what his body needed, he would relax and allow the music to present the appropriate "healing" images. As the actual healing took place, Carl would describe it in vivid detail, and I would help him to search for the sources of his healing. Although each healing began with the body, the process always ended either in spiritual healing or in a metaphor for emotional healing.

During the next eight sessions, Carl was visited and healed by each deceased loved one in the group, until finally they all returned together for a final visit to his home. This time, however, it was a reunion for them, and Carl was only an observer. In fact, he was a visitor from this side.

After this session, Carl's images began to center on living loved ones, and in a similar vein, he used body healing and his love for others as a context, or perhaps more accurately, a pretext, for emotional and spiritual healing.

Carl had learned to embrace life and death as one and the same. What made him want to live was the healing love he received from those around him; and what made him comfortable with dying was the love he knew was waiting for him on the other side.

The remaining months were difficult. Carl was in and out of the hospital, and his health declined steadily. Yet he was always loving, and he never stopped joking. In his last session, Carl was blind and very confused. He began the session fearful of closing his eyes: "If I close my eyes, the music might go away; I know this is not true, but I can't take the chance. My eyes need to be open, even if I cannot see. I often picture myself waiting for you—you have often been my eyes—and now I need to look into and through your eyes." As he continued, his images shifted continuously, and the only one that recurred was that of the letter V. After the imaging ended, Carl became lucid for a moment and said: "V is for victory over the virus—but it is clear to me now that it will come through peace, not fighting." Carl died a few months later, very much at peace.

Visits as Miracles

Much has been written about the nature of miracles, and many different criteria have been established throughout the centuries. Not being an expert myself, I started my inquiry with Webster's Dictionary which presents definitions that are quite relevant to the phenomenon I am describing. It says that a miracle is "an extraordinary event manifesting divine intervention in human affairs." It also cites the Christian Science notion that it is "a divinely natural occurrence that must be learned humanly."

In the examples above, the men described their visits as extraordinary events. The presence of the loved one always had a vividness or intensity that was noticeably greater than the ongoing stream of images in which it occurred. In fact, most men described the visits as going beyond mere imaging. They were more than figments of the imagination but rather were experienced as real communications with the loved one. Needless to say, the visits were also extraordinary because the dead do not ordinarily appear to the living with such clarity and purpose. Moreover since the loved one is on the other side (viz., in heaven), the traveller invariably attributes the entire experience to "divine" or spiritual intervention.

It is also interesting to note that these visits have rarely been predictable. The presence of the deceased loved one often occurred without planning, either as a surprise or intrusion within the context or sequence of the ongoing images, or as an unexpected but logical outcome of them. The visits did not seem to occur as the result of efforts by the traveller or manipulation by the guide. The deceased relative cannot be summoned, but rather appears when needed and when the imager is ready. Since the loved one plays a significant role in helping the person to overcome emotional or spiritual obstacles, the visits can also be viewed as types of "divine interventions" in the healing or therapeutic process. Lastly, because the traveller is deeply affected and changed by the visits, it often feels like a divine lesson to be learned by humans.

GIM and Miracles

If these visits are, in fact, miracles, it is unlikely that their occurrence depends entirely upon any one factor, but that a number of circumstances are necessary before they will occur. This suggests to me that they are miracles of synchronicity—that various events and conditions must converge before a visit can take place. From my observations, the most important synchronicities are: (1) the imager (or host) must be ready to receive the visitor; (2) the environment must support interactions between the host and visitor; and (3) the host and visitor must have a mutually loving relationship (even if not fully realized).

As elements of the GIM experience are considered in these terms, specific roles can be discerned for altered states of consciousness, the music, and the guide. The host readied himself for the visitor by entering an altered state, by moving his psyche from one axis of time and space to another, or more accurately, from the here-and-now of natural reality to space and time zones of supernatural reality. These are the zones most amenable to visitors from the other side. Thus, the host was literally placing himself in the right place at the right time. In addition, the altered state prepared him for the visitor by relaxing usual or reality-based boundaries and expectations. This also helped him to be more open to whatever might happen during the visit and to whatever the visitor might bring.

As is well known, music helps to sustain and deepen altered states of consciousness. Thus, music helps in preparing the host as described above. In addition, however, its main contribution is the emotional and spiritual environment that it creates before and during the visit itself. It is the music that seems to actually invite the visitor. Once the host is in an accessible time and space zone, the music seems to call out to the visitor on behalf of the host. (I have often wondered whether the music determined which of the possible visitors actually comes forward. Perhaps each deceased loved one responds to different music!)

Once the visit begins, it is the music that sustains the interaction between the host and visitor, while also setting its general tone. Finally, it is the music that describes, expresses and realizes the mutual love that the host and visitor have for each other.

The role of the guide is quite different. From the very beginning of the work, the guide must insure that the imager feels comfortable exploring supernatural spaces and time zones. Certainly, this requires developing rapport, engendering personal trust, and establishing a safe, holding relationship. Clearly, most of this must be accomplished well in advance of the visit. Then, during the visit itself, the guide must be careful to stay out of the way, while still being a supportive presence. The visit is a moment of intimacy between two loved ones. There is no place for an inquisitive or chatty bystander. Thus, I often step into the imager's identity, and guide him as if I am another part of himself acting as host.

* * * * *

As a music therapist seeking to understand the practicalities of my discipline and as a student of the many gamuts of human experience, I have a nagging curiosity about the miracle of music. In the previous discussion I offered some rational explanations on the role of music in inducing and supporting visits from the other side. The more difficult (and perhaps more meaningful) question is whether this is its most significant role. Is the role of music to make a visit take place? Or is it the music that makes each visit a miracle?

Another haunting idea is that musical compositions might be containers for spirits. Are there spirits of composers and performers living in each piece of music? Are they set free every time the music is brought to life? When we pass on, do our spirits reside in certain pieces of music that we have identified with during our earthly life?

I close with an admission: What I have written is a description of what I have observed happening on this side. I have no idea what is happening on the other!

References

Bonny, H. (1978a). *Facilitating GIM sessions*. Salina, KS: Bonny Foundation.

Bonny, H. (1978b). *The role of taped music programs in the GIM process*. Salina, KS: Bonny Foundation.

19

Becoming a Sound Woman
by Reclaiming the Power Within
LAURIE RUGENSTEIN

We come into the world with the tools we need in our journey toward wholeness of body, mind, and spirit. We often choose to discount our own resources, entrusting our healing and "wholing" to an external authority. These "miracle workers" have taken many forms, from priests and shamans to the drugs and high-tech equipment of modern science. The worst of these have created dependency, stripping us of our personal power, while the best have facilitated the awakening of the healer within.

Sometimes it seems as if our own tools are imperfect or inaccessible due to physical or mental handicaps, childhood abuse, chronic illness, or other life circumstances. However, these seeming limitations may serve as catalysts for growth, challenging our creative resources to transmute lack and pain into wholeness and compassion. Sound, especially our own sound, is one of the tools we have been given to access the inner wisdom that can guide us on the journey toward wholeness.

I have chosen to explore the role of sound in working with women because that has been the basis for most of my personal experience, and because I feel that many of us have relinquished our voices and sounds in a way that is unique to women. I believe that reclaiming our voices can lead to reclaiming the power we have given away.

As young girls we were cautioned to speak softly and never to express anger or other "undesirable" emotions with our voices. Even our expressions of joy were often stifled. We were told that such "outbursts" were unladylike. Many of us were denied the ecstatic pleasure of singing because our tone quality or pitch-matching ability did not measure up to our teacher's or choir master's standards. We began to learn that our spontaneous expression was unacceptable. We learned to lie, not only with our words, but also with our sounds. We learned that there was safety in silence and invisibility. When we no longer voiced our true sounds and feelings, we began to forget them. Parts of us began to wither, and our connection with our personal power began to fade.

Years of unvoiced feelings and self-censorship, often accompanied by a sense of powerlessness, manifest as dissonance and fragmentation in our lives. This dissonance may appear in the form of physical illness, emotional anguish, or a pervasive sense that "something is wrong." Physical and emotional pain are often the catalysts that urge us to break the silence, but many of us have forgotten how to access our own sound.

My personal journey with breaking the silence began with a few timid steps in the late 1960s. I listened for hours to records of two women singers—Janis Joplin and Tracy Nelson. Both were blues singers, but worlds apart in style. It was not the lyrics of their songs that attracted me but the *sound* of their voices. I was awed by the sheer unbridled passion of Janis's voice as it cracked with emotion, ignoring the constraints of melody and making sounds that no lady would dare to make. Tracy Nelson affected me in a different way. Her dark contralto and undulating blues riffs evoked a purely sensuous experience of sound, touching a place deep within me that words could never reach.

I knew I had to sing to get out what was locked inside me, but I was too scared to do it in front of anyone. There were too many self-judgments, fears of not doing it right, or not being "good enough." (I was one of those who was not selected for junior high school choir.) Several years later I overcame my fear enough to begin singing with a local band, but it was still a terrifying experience, with my inner judges definitely holding the upper hand. As I continued singing, the energy and emotion I could access became so important that my fear no longer mattered. I worked as a professional musician for many years and had the opportunity to sing everything from country to jazz. Although I was unable to articulate the fact at the time, music had become my therapist.

Another step in my journey came during my graduate training in music therapy. We were experiencing a technique called toning, which was described to us as free vocalization, making any sound that comes to you. A group of ten of us lay on the floor of a darkened dance studio waiting to make our sounds. This was something very different for me. There were no rules, no melody, not even a pre-determined form to use as a basis for improvisation—nothing but the space to let the sound emerge. I felt naked and exposed. What unexpressed feelings lay within me? Was I ready to release them with other people in the room? I took a deep breath and timidly let a soft sigh escape. The sigh became louder, giving voice to the weariness and stress that were close to the surface. My sound blended with the sounds of others, and I let go of my self-consciousness. The sound evoked images of buzzing bees, roaring jet planes, crying babies, primitive rituals, and angelic choirs. I felt exquisite pleasure in play-ing with the sound, moving in and out of the sonic tapestry we were creating, and sensing my body spinning with the strangely beautiful, spiraling harmonies. The experience was merely an introduction, but it awakened a yearning for more exploration.

I began toning alone. Often I *felt* the vibration of the sound as much as I heard it. I began to experience my entire body as a musical instrument. Like the body of a cello, my own body acted as a resonating chamber for sound, allowing it to reverberate through my head, chest, and pelvis. I learned to direct the sound to different places, bringing awareness to areas of my body that had long been desensitized and ignored.

There were also numinous moments, times when I encountered a part of myself that normally lay hidden, and sensed a connection with a larger reality. One of these moments came during a GIM (Guided Imagery & Music) session. I was well into the session, experiencing an altered state of consciousness, when I began to sense my body taking on the form of a white she-wolf. As wolf's presence filled me, I knew I must give voice to her sound. A high, clear howl came from deep in my body. At first it sounded strange and un-familiar, almost ghost-like. Slowly I began to understand that wolf's message was to voice my truth, and that this sound was releasing my unspoken grief over lost dreams, lost friends, and lost love, the cries of the children I would never carry, my swallowed anger, and the strength of the dreams that still lay within me. As my sound faded, I felt an emotional and spiritual cleansing, as if light had entered the dark corners of my soul.

Since that time, I have had many experiences toning—by myself, with clients, and with groups. Each toning experience was unique.

Some were playful and joyful, evoking the child within. Others were gentle and soothing, inviting deep rest and relief from stress and pain. Still others were wild and exhilarating, as energy blocked by sorrow and anger was released. I have felt wordless bonds form among group members as the sound resonated deep within, touching a common core and assuring us that we are not alone in our pain, our fear, or our joy.

During the past five years, I have had the opportunity to serve as mentor to nearly 300 students and professionals who participated in an independent study program in toning offered through the Institute for Music, Health, and Education. They used their own voices to guide them in exploring their somatic, emotional, mental and spiritual realms. Their tones were often tentative at first, but after several consecutive weeks of toning, richness and resonance began to develop. Their voices became more fully embodied and integrated. One woman described her toning as "a means to Sonic Individuation." As she recognized and claimed the tonal power of her own voice, she experienced greater self-acceptance and a deepening of her connection with others.

As we begin to use our voices to explore the inner landscape, the primitive sound of uncensored emotion rising up from the depths of our bodies can evoke horror of the dark unfamiliar places in ourselves. We might ask: Is this sound really coming from me? Is it a part of me I want to look at? Will I be overwhelmed, consumed by this sound? Do I deserve to express this much joy? Can I accept being this alive? The initial terror can be very real, but, as we continue to release our sounds, we bring light into the darkness and recognize ourselves there. We feel the stirrings of our own power reawakening.

This is not power over others, but the power to be who we truly are. It is the power that comes with the acceptance of our bodies, as the sound resonates deep within our bellies, affirming our sexuality and creativity. It is the power that comes with being able to speak our truth without shame or excuses. It is the power of knowing the true voice of our own sound and awakening the inner healer.

Sara's Story:

I have learned two important lessons from my work as a music therapist. The first is that I do not heal anyone. The second is that whenever I work with another human being, I am entering sacred space. My role is to enter into a private and confidential relationship with each client through sound/music that provides an opportunity for healing to take place. However, the healing comes from within the client.

In choosing to tell Sara's story, I have wrestled with a difficult question: Would this be a violation of the trust and sacred space that existed between us? In our relationship, which lasted slightly over one year, I gained tremendous respect for Sara as she faced the difficult challenges life offered her. It is from this sense of respect that I share the story of our time together.

I have chosen to work with many clients who are dealing with cancer and other life-challenging illnesses because they have been my greatest teachers about living. Sara was one of these clients. She came to see me following treatment for cervical cancer when she was thirty-four years old. It was shortly after Christmas, and it had been four months since her surgery. During that time she had received both radiation and chemotherapy. A medical examination one month before our first session showed that her tumor was gone.

Sara was grateful for her physical healing, but was dealing with residual pain and emotional issues related to her illness. She felt that sound/music could help her healing process in these areas. Her spirit was vibrant as she explained how the last four months had been "a tremendous learning experience about life." But there was a dark side. As grateful as she was to be alive, she had to give up her dream of having children. She was angry with those acquaintances who pointed out how lucky she was, never acknowledging her loss, and those "new age church goers" who asked why she had drawn this illness to herself. Most of all, she was hurt by the friends who stayed away because they did not know what to say.

Sara and her husband were under extreme financial stress as a result of her cancer. Not only had she been unable to work for several months, but they were facing staggering medical bills with no insurance. Sara tried a part-time job, but found she tired too quickly even for that. She felt guilt over having brought about this financial crisis and over her inability to alleviate it. I offered to work with Sara for no fee, but she found that unacceptable. We finally agreed that she could bring me pieces of jewelry, clothing, or small household items and let me select what I wanted as payment for her sessions.

In her first session, Sara chose to work with alleviating some of the residual physical pain from her cancer treatments. I worked with her using a combination of Therapeutic Touch and toning, providing her with energy to be used as her own body's wisdom dictated. Sara indicated that her pain level was significantly reduced during this session and that she experienced a deep state of relaxation. I also showed her how to use her own voice as an internal source of vibration, sending sound into painful areas of her body through bone-conducted humming. The following week she reported that she noticed increased mobility in her hips and had been able to sleep on her left side without pain for the first time in two months.

In subsequent sessions we continued to work with the pain and also focused on the emotional issues raised by Sara's illness. She observed that she had not found ways to express her tremendous anger concerning the cancer. She chose to confront this issue directly, as is frequently the case with those who have faced the reality of death. She pounded out her anger on drums and xylophones until she uncovered the grief that lay behind it. We used our voices together to tone into that grief, acknowledge it, and let it flow. There was no need to pretend that "everything was okay," and sound let her touch her "unacceptable" feelings and make friends with them.

When spring arrived, Sara and her husband decided to give up their apartment and spend several months visiting friends and family across the country. She now had the tools she needed to continue working on her own, and many of her emotional issues seemed to be resolved. We had become very close during the winter and said good-bye with promises that we would be in touch when she returned.

I was excited when I received a call from Sara in mid-summer letting me know she was back in town. She scheduled an appointment and said she had a lot to tell me. She walked in with a cheery greeting and a simple statement— "There's more cancer." Malignancy had been discovered while she was at her parents' home several weeks earlier. It was a very small tumor, and she wanted to avoid medical intervention, based on some of her negative experiences the previous fall. She felt the toning was an important part of the holistic treatment she planned. She was also planning to use Chinese herbs and acupuncture. For a while the treatment seemed to be working, but by later summer she was getting noticeably weaker and experiencing pain. There was also pressure from her family and friends to seek medical help.

Sara finally agreed to have another biopsy. She had a severe limp

213

when she arrived for her next session and related her story of the experience: "When I arrived at the hospital they told me that a different doctor would be performing the biopsy. I overheard him asking questions and learned that he had never done this procedure before. By this time I was really anxious and felt like I didn't have any control over the situation. He stuck this long needle into my pelvic area three times. He missed what he was going for all three times. The fourth time the needle hit a nerve plexus, and I screamed that they had to stop. I guess I made such a big scene that they listened to me. I tried to drive home, but it hurt too much. I just parked beside the road and cried until I felt like I could go on.

"When I got home, I called the hospital and told them how I felt about my treatment. It sounded like they were kind of scared . . . like they were afraid I might sue them."

Sara was elated because she felt she had been able to avoid becoming a victim in a situation in which she would have felt powerless at one time. However, she was still experiencing a great deal of pain. Toning and Therapeutic Touch were effective in alleviating the pain, and, following the session, she noticed an increased range of motion in her hip.

Several days later I received a phone call from Sara. She sounded excited. "My pain was much better for at least twelve hours after our last session. I called the hospital and told them that, and guess what they agreed to do? They'll pay for my music therapy sessions if you'll write up a treatment plan and send it to them!"

I drew up a treatment plan for two sessions a week for six weeks. Sara was delighted. She was finally able to regain some of her pride through being able to pay for her sessions. What neither of us knew then was that she would be in the hospital before the end of those six weeks.

It was a beautiful October day. Sara did not show up for her session. It was unlike her to miss a session or to be late without letting me know. I called her home and got the answering machine and that awful knowing that something was wrong. Later that evening Bob, her husband, called to tell me he had taken Sara to the hospital because she could not keep any food down. He said she would be there a few days until she could eat again.

A week later she was still in the hospital. There were other complications, including a blood clot in her leg. It seemed she might be in the hospital for a while. I decided to go there and have our session.

I did some toning and chanting and played my Native American flute. Sara joined in the toning and chanting some of the time, and eventually drifted off into a peaceful sleep.

Sara never went home from the hospital, and I continued to visit her there throughout the fall. Her fighting spirit always seemed to be present when I saw her. Her family gathered in her room at Thanksgiving to celebrate Christmas, thinking she wouldn't make it till then. Sara confided in me, "They're all here because they think I'm going to kick the bucket." She refused to accept the fact that she was dying, although she once told me that she was frightened at night because she felt as if she had to decide whether she wanted to die or not, and it was just too hard. I knew I had to let go of my own judgments about her decision and support her choice.

When Sara was strong enough, she joined me in the chanting and played a rattle made of a vitamin bottle filled with popcorn. As she became weaker and talking became more difficult, the music became an even more important form of communication. Her family welcomed the toning sessions, though they must have seemed strange at first. One evening two nurses came in and stood by silently to learn what was happening to ease Sara's restlessness and pain. The toning and chanting were becoming familiar sounds in Sara's room.

The last time I saw Sara was just before Valentine's day. She had been moved to a residential hospice and was very happy with her new surroundings. She talked about how much she liked the wallpaper, the pictures, and the tree outside her window. She also liked the fact that "nobody's coming around poking needles in my arm all the time." I played my flute and did some soft toning. We hugged each other, and I found a way to tell her how much I had learned from her, how much I loved her, and how much our time together meant to me. I didn't say good-bye, but we both knew it was good-bye. Several days later when I got home from work, there was a message on the answering machine—"Sara died today."

Some people would say that Sara was not healed. I disagree. I wish things could have been different and her life could have been longer, but I know she found healing and brought it to those around her.

V

Therapeutic Healing with Sound

Getting the Ego Humming: Therapeutic Application of the Auditory Archetype "M"
  Arden Mahlberg
Psyche and Sound: The Use of Music in Jungian Analysis
  Patricia Warming
The Tomatis Method: Auditory Retraining Through Music and Listening
  Judith B. Belk

Unconscious listening is more dependable [than conscious listening]. Carlyle maintained that if you "see deep enough, you see musically; the heart of nature being everywhere musical, if you can only reach it."

In signifying only itself, music becomes a language translatable by the universal awareness latent in everything. This most complex of expressions is also the oldest and so appeals to our most primitive level, inexplicable through reason. At that level we all hear music the same way.

Ned Rorem

Clinical psychologists, anthropologists, foreign language teachers, movement therapists and dozens of other professionals are now using music to enhance their respective fields. Public consciousness is coming to the remarkable awareness that ambient music, attitudinal music and some new age music work significantly to release stress, improve memory and activate attention.

Different kinds of music—classical, religious, shamanic sounds, new emerging styles—have different physiological and educational effects on the mind and body. Part of the response to music and sound is subjective, according to the preference of the client, teacher and therapist. Other parts are universal in the human brain-body system.

Arden Mahlberg's unique and fine research on auditory archetypes relates to the toning experiences I noted in Part III. Jungian analyst-musician Patricia Warming gives significant insight into Jung's late-in-life awareness of music as an essential component to the analysis process. Judith Belk amplifies the importance of sound stimulation through the Tomatis Method in her work as a speech-language pathologist.

In the coming decade, there will be hundreds of therapeutic and educational fields cross-fertilizing to create the miracle of healing with the tools of music and sound. Overly clinical, left-brained schools of thought will be confronted with the effectiveness of the intuitive and improvisational methods. The very intuitive, not yet fully researched fields of imagery, music and shamanic responses will mature with more research in the traditional schools of thought. We do not yet have a full understanding of music's transformational power in many areas. This is a time of new codings when old and new strategies are blending and unfolding for a new era of miracles.

20

Getting the Ego Humming:
Therapeutic Application of the Auditory Archetype "M"

ARDEN MAHLBERG

> She moves like an angel
> And seven evening stars
> Dance through the window
> Of her universal house
> Her voice a crystal echo
> Lies humming in your soul
> So patiently awaiting
> For your ears to behold
> Cat Stevens (1972)

Cat Stevens heard a humming in his soul and it mystified him. Socrates heard it and it gave him comfort and clarity of purpose in the face of death. When Crito visited Socrates in prison while Socrates was facing the possibility of being executed, Crito found him asleep and remarked at how peacefully he was sleeping given the circumstances. Socrates explained that he was hearing a humming or murmuring in his ears that kept him content and focused on what he must do, what his identity called for in the circumstances. The sound made him secure within himself. Inner humming is widely reported and has universal meaning.

As an image, the sound of the phoneme "M" has archetypical significance in the shaping of identity. It provides a connection between the human and the Divine and forms a foundation for the development of ego. The term *ego* is used here to mean the structure

A version of this paper was presented at the Fourth World Conference on Imagery, May 31, 1991, in Minneapolis, Minnesota.

of individual identity from which we operate in the world. In this sense, a strong ego is a positive factor in being effective in the world and does not imply self-centeredness or being egotistical. The "M" sound provides the basis for ego as well as the transcendence of ego in that it connects the human and the Divine. So to hear the sound internally or image the sound can have a formative and therapeutic effect in one's life. It is the sound of self-affirmation.

Kabir heard the sound and was ecstatic. In his poetry he expresses its transformative power:

> This is the Ultimate Word: but can any express its marvelous savour? He who has savoured it once, he knows what joy it can give.

Kabir further says:

> Knowing it, the ignorant man becomes wise, and the wise man
>   becomes speechless and silent,
> The worshipper is utterly inebriated,
> His wisdom and his detachment are made perfect;
> He drinks from the cup of the in-breathings and the
> outbreathings of love.
>
> (Tagore, 1974, pp. 64–65)

Kabir, like other mystics, suggests that we do not need to wait to hear the inner sound. We can experience its transformative benefit by forming the image of the sound in our minds:

> O Sadhu! practice that word!
> The Vedas and the Puranas proclaim it,
> The world is established in it,
> The Rishis and devotees speak of it.
> But none knows the mystery of the word.
>
> The householder leaves his house when he hears it,
> The ascetic comes back to love when he hears it,
> The Six Philosophies expound it,
> The Spirit of Renunciation points to that Word,
> From that Word the world-form has sprung,
> That Word reveals all.
> But who know whence the Word cometh?
>
> (Tagore, pp. 102–103)

The transformations Kabir describes as coming from practicing the inner sound are changes toward completion or wholeness that go beyond the established personal identity. The householder leaves his house; the ascetic comes back to love. As I explain later, I think this happens because the inner humming sound, as an archetypal image, evokes the foundation from which the self and the ego are formed. The foundation provides the security from which personal change can occur.

In my psychotherapy practice I have for several years used the humming sound as an image for meditation with clients who are working to establish a stronger sense of identity from which to make personal changes. One such example was a thirty-five-year-old man whose life had been controlled by feelings of inadequacy, even though he was very intelligent and broadly talented. He was dominated by his wife, who had affairs, and he felt trapped in an electronics trade that made little use of his talent resources. He had chosen the trade because it was safe from risk of failure. When he dreamed of personal and professional change, he felt inadequate to make any decisive moves and was gripped by fear of failure.

For many years he had suffered from fairly continuous mild depression and was occasionally suicidal. He had been engaged in quite a bit of psychotherapy and personal growth work in the past, with modest results. When he began regularly meditating on the humming image, a very clear change began to occur. It started with his experiencing the image as providing a comforting sense of security, perhaps similar to what allowed Socrates to sleep so restfully. He then began to experience his fear of failure as being outside himself, as "not me," though it had been a feature of his self-image for as long as he could remember. This shift in his identity perspective relative to the fear of failure and feelings of inadequacy made it possible for him to resolve those feelings and change his line of work to one that better utilized his abilities.

Part of the conceptual change was that he no longer saw things in terms of categories of failure or success. He came to view these categories as repressive final judgments on past actions that served to inhibit future action. Instead, what emerged was a sense that judgment precedes action: if he decided that something was worth doing, it was worth doing regardless of the outcome. This supplanted the retrospective judgment that had helped paralyze his action in the past. From this change in perspective, he began to venture into new activities and social relationships that led him into a variety of business experiences. This also changed his marriage relationship to one of greater equality.

In general, the therapeutic benefit that I have seen from the use of the "M" sound as an auditory image has been that it helps deepen the sense of self and strengthen the ego as an operator in the world. "M" is the sound of self-affirmation. We discover this by noticing how we use the "M" sound. "Hum . . . " is an expression of wondering and consulting one's self to find one's real thoughts. "Mmm" means good and "Um hum" is an affirmation. When I told a colleague about my hypothesis that the "M" sound is an auditory archetype, he made the affirming sound, "Um hum," and then offered "Oh, the Carl Rogers archetype!" (Rogers encouraged expression by such confirmatory responses.) Actually, in a study done many years ago, "Hm" was found to be one of the sounds most frequently uttered by psychiatrists (Jaffe in Ostwald, 1961).

While the use of mental imagery has become popular in this country, auditory imagery remains rather neglected in favor of other forms of imagery, especially visual imagery. In the collective psyche, however, the power of sound is widely acknowledged. Words such as "abracadabra" or "hocus pocus," as well as the names of God, are thought to have magical powers.

In the East, sound images are considered to have enormous and precise power. There is a strong tradition behind using auditory images or mantras for focus in meditation and for a wide variety of problems. A yogi could choose from thousands of mantras to help someone with problems from everyday financial concerns to character flaws to spiritual aspirations. Even imagining sounds is considered to have power or utility.

Carl Jung (1973) discovered that sound is a powerful basis for associations. When he asked people to report whatever came to their minds in response to a particular word, he found that they usually gave another word that was associated conceptually or by meaning. However, the more the attention weakened, e.g., the more unconscious subjects were, the more they associated words phonetically rather than by meaning—bed, bad, bread. Such clang associations are an example of psychotic thought process. Paul Kugler has suggested that phonetic associations are "precisely where the archetypal presents itself," which is to say that sound carries meaning in some universal way (Kugler, 1982).

In many mystical traditions, such as Nada Yoga, Shabda Yoga, Tantra, Sufism and Eckankar, it is believed that creation occurred and is occurring through sound. In most major creation myths, sound is the means of creation. "In the beginning was the Word."

As Joseph Campbell (1972, p. 112) explains this inner sound:

[It] is of that primal energy of which the universe itself is a manifestation. It is thus antecedent to things. One might think of it as comparable to the great humming sound of an electric power station; or as the normally unheard humming of the protons and neutrons of an atom: the interior sound, that is to say, of the primal energy, vibrating, of which ourselves and all that we know and see are aspirations. And when heard, they say, the sound that it most resembles is OM.

Oddly enough, radio astronomers detect a constant sound, the same sound, everywhere in the universe and speculate that it comes from the sound of the Big Bang. Sound may have an association with creation.

As a fetus, the human individual develops within an ocean of sound; the darkness and the fluid of the womb form a kind of sensory deprivation chamber. But as recordings taken near the head of the fetus reveal, it hears both the surging sound of the blood pulsing in the mother's arteries and a more constant background humming sound (Murooka, 1974).

The humming sound also seems to be universally associated with comfort and sleep. Mothers hum their children to sleep, just as Socrates was lulled to sleep by the inner humming sound.

In Eastern meditative traditions, the "M" sound is associated with the deep sleep state (Govinda, 1972; Radhakrishnan, 1953). Deep sleep, as we know it, is dominated by delta waves, which are the slowest brain waves. It is a dreamless state, the closest thing to no brain activity at all. Delta waves are the first brain waves to be detected in the fetus and may provide a foundation for other brain wave activity. The "M" sound as it is associated with deep sleep may be in a sense the womb of consciousness.

The deep sleep state, associated with the "M" sound, is the most serene state in sleep, as Socrates experienced. Of this state, it has been said, "As a falcon or any other [swift] bird having flown around in the sky becomes weary, folds it wings and is borne down to its nest, even so this person hastens to that state [of self] where he desires no desires and sees no dream" (Radhakrishnan, p. 261).

Another interesting connection between the "M" sound and sleep is that according to Hupa Indian tradition, when you wake up feeling not yourself or out of sorts, humming will help the spirit that you lost in your sleep come back to you so you are whole again (Hobday, 1981).

Delta wave sleep has priority over REM (dreaming) sleep in recovery from sleep loss. Deficits in the deep sleep cycle accompany emotional and mental disturbance. It is known that sounds such as traffic and airplane noises can disrupt deep sleep. It may be that we feel we should wake up to find out what is going on instead of being able to let go and totally relax. That same inability to let go may be involved with emotional disturbances, though in this case it may be mental traffic noise that interferes with deep sleep. If the "M" sound is associated with the deep sleep state, it may be that imagining the "M" sound could help strengthen slow wave sleep.

In the Mandukya Upanishad, the "M" sound, as the deep sleep state, is described as providing the fundamental distinction between thinker and thought. It is the foundation for the distinction between me and not me, self and other, and inner and outer. Without that foundation, there are disturbances in the sense of self, in ego boundaries or in the ability to operate in the world.

Put even more strongly, the Mandukya Upanishad says of the "M" state of deep sleep, *"This is the self:* it is the deepest essence of the Soul, the image of Godhead," (Radhakrishnan, p. 669). And so, the resting place is the Self. "Even as birds, O dear, resort to a tree for resting-place, so does everything here resort to the Supreme Self. They all find their rest in the Supreme Self" (Radhakrishnan, p. 662).

In mantra traditions the "M" sound, again associated with deep sleep, provides the foundation for ego or a sense of individuality or separateness that can operate in the world. The "M" sound is a connector; it provides the link between the Unmanifest or the Divine and the manifest, or between the formless and that which has form. The traditional mantra OM is thought to move one from the objective world to the link with the Divine or formless; while moving in the other direction, the sound HUM links the formless HU, with the world. "M" provides the link in both cases.

In the East, the sacred sound AUM is said to have first been used as a closure for the recitation of religious verses. It was used as a response to the verse as an affirmation, a "yes, so be it." Christians similarly use Amen, which also has the "M" as the core. Khan (1972) claims that AUM and Amen are of the same origin. They do have similar functions. Using Amen in prayer is an act of connecting with God. The term AUM was used in ancient Egypt in a similar manner. In India AUM was also used before every recitation of the Vedas to help the listener attain one-pointedness of attention on the Divine in order to connect and hear the Word.

While OM, AUM and Amen move consciousness from objective reality to the Divine, the tone of HUM makes the link in the other direction, with HU as the sound of the Unmanifest and "M" providing the link to the manifest. The sound HUM is symbolized in the Buddha's gesture of touching the earth. "This word in Hindustani expresses limitation. *HUM* means I or We, both of which signify ego" (Khan, 1972, 1990, p. 90). Similarly, the Sanskrit term for the feeling of mineness is *mamata*. "M" in both Sanskrit and Tibetan is visually imaged as a dot, a drop or a small circle. Relating this to the meaning I or ego, it provides the center around which personality forms and operates in the world, as well as linking the person to the Divine. This is visually portrayed in the mandala where the bindu, or point at the center of the mandala, is the sound "M." This is the case with *Sricakra*, which is the ultimate of mandalas, giving a geometric projection of the relationship of the One to the many. "M" is the center.

Frazer (1975) reports that among many tribes in Australia and New Guinea the initiation of boys into manhood involves the use of a device that produces a loud humming noise that is associated with a spirit who devours the boy and then restores him to life as a man. Again, the "M" sound is a tonal link or transition point in developing a separate self, in this case, separate from one's parents.

In a more mundane way the "M" sound has archetypal significance as the connection that supports the development of the separate person. As Lewis has observed (in Talbot, 1967), when the infant phonates while sucking, it automatically makes the "M" or "N" sound. When this movement is made with nothing in the mouth, the resultant sound is "mama," which globally is the most common first word that a child speaks. Ostwald (1961) also notes that in many languages the word for *mother* emphasizes the "M" sound.

Greenson (1954) and Ostwald (1961) have published the observation that some mentally disturbed people hum in order to reex-
that was lacking or deficient. They apparently regard this as a nega-

perience the connection of the mother or to experience a connection tively regressive activity. However, from the point of view that the "M" sound is related to the foundation of Self or ego, one might expect that humming and toning could have a beneficial effect. While I do not advocate the use of meditation for people with schizophrenia, it is notable that Green and Kinsbourne (1990) found that very quietly humming a single note resulted in 59 percent reduction in auditory hallucinations for people hospitalized with schizophrenia.

One of the interesting things about the Green and Kinsbourne study is that they minimized the mechanical effect of voicing the "M" sound, such as its effect on masking other sounds, by having people hum as quietly as possible. The mantra traditions suggest that a specific kind of beneficial effect will result from simply imagining the sound. Based on its archetypal meaning, imagining the "M" sound should have a beneficial effect on the sense of Self or ego strength. This idea has not been empirically tested.

Some subjective effects have been reported from imagining language sounds. Morse and Furst (1982) had people imagine a variety of complete words, and they reported differences in the subjective effects of the words. Moltz and Carrington (reported in Carrington, 1977) used nonsense syllables as objects of meditation and also found subjective differences. However, I know of no study using the image of phonemes nor of any other research with direct bearing on the notion presented here.

There is now a scientific theory that relates to this matter. Sheldrake's hypothesis of formative causation (1981) supports the prediction that the influence of an image on a particular individual would tend to be similar to the archetypal meaning of that image. Some aspects of Sheldrake's theory of formative causation have empirical support, including my own test of his theory (Mahlberg, 1987).

Sheldrake suggests that there is a dimension outside of space and time that contains resonance patterns that correspond to the forms that things take within space and time. Basically, we could say that this dimension contains collective or archetypal forms. He hypothesizes a two-way interaction between a form that exists in space and time and the corresponding archetypal form. As a result, an individual's concentrated experience with imagining the "M" sound would tend to be consistent with the archetypal meaning of the sound, unless personal associations interfere.

Knowing the archetypal meaning of the "M" sound, I have used it in my adult psychotherapy practice with clients in situations where I might otherwise have used techniques with an auditory focus, such as Benson's Relaxation Response technique, which uses the word "One," or Carrington's Clinically Standardized Meditation, which allows the person to choose an image. Focusing on "M" would not seem to pose any obvious risks beyond those of other techniques. I have not used procedures with "M" with people who have psychotic conditions. In other conditions, in which clients are having trouble with boundaries or sense of self, I have them imagine the "M" sound rather than using other relaxation procedures. Subjectively, such people tend to experience a greater solidity or sense of identity within themselves that allows them to be more assertive and more confident in setting boundaries with other people.

The procedure is quite simple. I have clients sit with their backs supported, feet on the floor and heads erect. I have them take a couple of deep, even breaths and close their eyes if that is comfortable. Then I suggest that they imagine the "M" sound, then extend the sound a bit and gently and easily repeat the sound. I briefly vocalize the sound as an example and then have them continue it silently, spending some time searching for the pitch and rhythm that feels strongest to them. I encourage clients to enjoy the feeling of the sound. After a few minutes, I end by having them bring their attention back to their breath, to their feet on the floor, and to the room around them by slowly opening their eyes. I recommend doing this once or twice a day for five to twenty minutes, depending on what is comfortable for the client. This procedure is, of course, to be done in a setting without distractions or interruptions.

This procedure is only a small part of the work I do with a client, of course. In addition to an imagery exercise once or twice a day, "M" can be used as a cue in real-life situations to help people keep a sense of their boundaries when they feel a threat. For example, I worked with a woman with depression and dependency features who had a history of codependent relationships. After her second divorce from an alcoholic, she was able to develop a fairly autonomous, positive self-image. After she again married, she began to feel absorbed into her husband with a loss of her new-found sense of identity. As in previous marriages, she had a tendency to lose herself and become an extension of her husband, doing whatever he wished. The humming exercise helped her experience a stronger sense of self. When she was interacting with her husband and felt herself giving control over to him, she would remember the humming sound. It helped her act from consideration of her own self-interest and dignity, as well as her husband's. Remembering the sound acts as a cue to evoke a stronger sense of self.

In general, in my experience the "M" image has been a useful aid in the process of strengthening the sense of self. Archetypally, the sound provides the connection and foundation from which the individual can develop. It is a universal inner companion, the sound of affirmation, the sound affirming the Self. "Thus the divine Word is uttered in the temple that is us" (Meister Eckhart, p. 457).

References

Campbell, J. *Myths to live by*. Toronto: Bantam, 1972.

Carrington, P. *Freedom in meditation*. Garden City, NY: Anchor/Doubleday, 1977.

Eckhart, M. *Breakthrough: Meister Eckhart's creation spirituality in new translation*. Garden City, NY: Image Books, 1980.

Frazer, S. J. G. *The golden bough: A study in magic and religion,* Vol. 1, abridged ed. New York: Macmillan, 1975.

Govinda, L. A. *Foundations of Tibetan mysticism*. New York: Samuel Weiser, 1972.

Green, M. F. and Kinsbourne, M. Subvocal activity and auditory hallucinations: Clues for behavioral treatments? *Schizophrenia Bulletin,* 1990, *16,* 617–625.

Greenson, R. R. About the "MM. . . . " *Psychoanalysis Quarterly,* 1954, *23,* 234–239.

Hobday, S. M. J. Humming home your shadow. *Parabola,* 1981, *4,* 23.

Jung, C. *Experimental researches, Vol. 2 of the collected works of C. G. Jung*. Princeton, NJ: Princeton Univ. Press, 1973.

Khan, I. *The mysticism of sound*. Mokelumme Hill, Cal: Health Research, 1972.

Kugler, P. *The alchemy of discourse: An archetypal approach to language*. Lewisburg: Bucknell Univ. Press, 1982.

Mahlberg, A. Evidence of collective memory: A test of Sheldrake's theory. *J. of Analytical Psychology,* 1987, *32,* 23–34.

Morse, D. R. and Furst, M. L. Meditation: An in-depth study. *J. of the Amer. Society of Psychosomatic Dentistry and Medicine,* 1982, *29,* 4–96.

Murooka, H. *Lullaby from the womb*. Hollywood: Capital Records, 1974.

Ostwald, P. F. Humming, sound and symbol. *J. of Auditory Research*, 1961, *1*, 225–232.

Radhakrishnan, S., ed. *The principal upanishads*. London: Allen and Unwin, 1953.

Sheldrake, R. *A new science of life: The hypothesis of formative causation*. London: Blond and Briggs, 1981.

Stevens, C. Angelsea. Catch bull at four. Beverly Hills: A & M Records, 1972.

Tagore, R., trans. *Songs of Kabir*. New York: Samuel Weiser, 1974.

Talbot, T., ed. *The world of the child*. Garden City, NY: Doubleday, 1967.

Tucci, G. *The theory and practice of the mandala*. New York: Samuel Weiser, 1973.

21

Psyche and Sound:
The Use of Music in Jungian Analysis
PATRICIA WARMING

> We are the music-makers,
> And we are the dreamers of dreams,
> Wandering by lone sea breakers,
> And sitting by desolate streams.
> > A. O'Shaughnessy,
> > "The Music Maker"

My recent studies and experiences of the power of sound and music have brought me the sense of having come full circle in finding an underlying link embracing my interests in religion, depth psychology and music. I feel the same spark of enthusiasm that I felt many years ago when I discovered that Jungian psychology was the natural bridge between my interests in religion and psychology. I am only now discovering how music also "fits" with these interests. I was, in fact, a voice major in college, and I have always known that music is very therapeutic to me. As the years slipped by, however, my "instrument" got relegated to the closet. About the most I did was to bring it out on occasion, tune it up and join with a chorale in singing a major work of music that I knew moved my soul. What I did not know was how to use music in my therapy practice or that it even fit there.

During the course of my studies at the Jung Institute in Zurich, I do not remember anything ever being said about Jung's relationship with music. I do recall one of my control analysts, who was formerly a musician, saying that he could hear the "animus" in a woman's voice. I have a vivid recollection of one of my first clients, a woman who was cut off from her emotions. She occasionally cited instances of weeping during symphony concerts. It was obvious that music made the connection with her deeply buried feelings and emotions. Music reached the deeper layers of her psyche, which were cut off from her normal state of consciousness. Emma Jung's reference to music in her writing on the nature of the animus in 1931 speaks to this:

Music . . . gives sensuous representation to our deepest associations and most immutable laws. In this sense, music is spirit, spirit leading into obscure distances beyond the reach of consciousness; its content can hardly be grasped with words—but strange to say, more easily with numbers—although simultaneously, and before all else, with feeling and sensation. Apparently paradoxical facts like these show that music admits us to the depths where spirit and nature are still one—or have again become one. For this reason, music constitutes one of the most important and primordial forms in which woman ever experiences spirit. [1]

Jung's Relationship to Music

Some time after I left Zurich I read an article titled "The Therapy of Music," in which concert pianist and music therapist Margaret Tilly of San Francisco (1900–1969) told of her personal encounter with Carl Jung. Jung had read some of her writings and invited her to his home in Kusnacht to meet with him while she was on a trip to Switzerland in 1956. On this occasion, she asked him about his own relationship to music and was surprised at his reply. "My mother was a fine singer, so was her sister, and my daughter is a fine pianist. I know the whole literature. I have heard everything and all the great performers, but I never listen to music any more. It exhausts and irritates me." [2] When she asked why, he replied, "Because music is dealing with such deep archetypal material and those who play don't realize this." [3] She concluded from this that the idea Jung was not particularly sympathetic to music came from the fact that he cared too much about music, not too little.

In the course of her visit with him, Jung requested that she demonstrate just how she would use music with various patients. He was deeply moved by the work and at the end burst out with: "This opens up whole new avenues of research I'd never even dreamed of. Because of what you've shown me this afternoon—not just what you've said, but what I have actually felt and experienced—I feel

231

that from now on music should be an essential part of every analysis. This reaches the deep archetypal material that we can only sometimes reach in our analytical work with patients. This is most remarkable."[4]

Jung recognized the unconscious levels of the psyche as a special sphere of experience with laws of its own. It was, for Jung, the eternally living, creative, germinal layer in each of us: Not only did the unconscious contain the sources of instinct and the whole prehistoric nature of humans, but also the roots of all creativity. This background and substratum of the psychophysical world is forever bringing forth spontaneous forms in a manner analogous to nature. The collective unconscious is the source of all psychic creation: religion and ritual, social organization, consciousness, and finally art and music. The archetypes of the collective unconscious are compelling tendencies toward specific experiences. They are intrinsically formless psychic structures which become visible in dreams, visions and body states, as well as in music and art.

In Jung's view, the suffering of normal as well as neurotic individuals stems from a dissociation between the conscious and unconscious levels of psychic life. The task is to reestablish this lost connection. The growth of consciousness is therefore not limited to awareness of an "outside" world, but recognizes in equal measure our dependence on intrapsychic forces. Traditionally Jungian analysis works to bridge this gap through dream and imaginal work. The process can be likened to an artistic endeavor as we seek to unravel the symbolic language of the unconscious. It is analogous to any act one engages in with a religious devotion. Working with the unconscious necessitates a life-long dedication to following the labyrinthine paths of one's dreams and fantasies. In this way one sees the unfolding movements, developments, conflicts and interactions of that vast cast of characters and motifs that play themselves out in our individual psyches, mirroring the unfolding of our individual destinies as well as those of the human race. We have the gift of being able to convert the invisible realm into visible form, so that it can be contemplated and experienced in its transformative power. Dreams mirror the life of the soul and connect us to forces that are superpersonal and transcendent. Here we confront the religious function of the psyche—that inborn demand for meaning and inner experience.

Throughout his lifework, Jung gave primacy to the psyche and its manifestation in dreams and imagination. In a letter to Serge Moreux in 1950 he added that music expresses this same reality in sounds:

Music certainly has to do with the collective unconscious. . . . this is evident in Wagner, for example. Music expresses, in some way, the movement of the feelings (or emotional values) that cling to the unconscious processes. The nature of what happens in the collective unconscious is archetypal, and archetypes always have a numinous quality that expresses itself in emotional stress. *Music expresses in sounds what fantasies and visions express in visual images.* I am not a musician and would not be able to develop these ideas in detail. I can only draw your attention to the fact that music represents the movement, development, and transformation of motifs of the collective unconscious. In Wagner this is very clear and also in Beethoven, but one finds it equally in Bach's 'Kunst der Fuge.' The circular character of the unconscious processes is expressed in the musical form; as for example in the sonata's four movements, or the perfect circular arrangement of the 'Kunst der Fuge,' [Art of the Fugue] etc.[5]

Jung acknowledged that music penetrates to the archetypal transcendence that is the inner life of the world. What speaks to us in Bach's *Art of Fugue,* a late Beethoven quartet, or Mozart's *Requiem* is a breakthrough of what Rudolf Otto aptly termed the *numinosum.* Jung referred to it as: "a dynamic agency or effect not caused by an arbitrary act of will. On the contrary, it seizes and controls the human subject, who is always rather its victim than its creator. The *numinosum*—whatever its cause may be—is an experience of the subject independent of his will."[6] Rudolf Otto gave a new direction to religious studies in 1923 with his book *The Idea of the Holy,*[7] in which he focused on the irrational as the factor all religions have in common. Jung saw religion as designating the peculiar attitude of a consciousness that has been changed by an experience of the numinosum. Religious experience is something that happens to the individual.

We know that the creative power of the unconscious seizes an artist or musician with the autonomous force of an instinctual drive. It often takes possession of the person without the least consideration for his or her life, health or happiness. Such an individual is an instrument of the transpersonal. Great musicians such as Mozart and Beethoven knew that the spirit blows where it will. When the archetypes which are striving to be born in the light of the world take form in these masters, their work expresses and gives form to the future. Creative artists and musicians are the heroes and heroines who make possible the dawn of a new era. In this sense the musician is close to the seer, the prophet and the mystic.

Berlioz revealed that dream and reverie states allowed him access to a mysterious world of musical forms: "Last night I dreamt of music, this morning I recalled it all and fell into one of those supernal ecstasies. . . . All the tears of my soul poured forth as I listened to those divinely sonorous smiles that radiate from the angels alone. Believe me . . . the being who could write such miracles of transcendent melody would be more than mortal."[8]

Finding Our Own Music

Few attain the level of such truly great musicians. However, that in no way negates the possibility of finding within ourselves the music or sounds expressive of our own deeper selves or of our emotions. Jung related that during times of upheaval he managed to translate his emotions into images. Through this process he was inwardly calmed and reassured. He learned how helpful it is from a therapeutic point of view to find the particular images which lie behind the emotions.

In the same vein, I have learned how helpful it is to turn the emotions into sound. Using the voice helps to discharge emotion physiologically. Holding different vowels (whichever is most expressive of the emotion) at varying pitches for an elongated period of time (ten minutes, for example), as in the process of "toning," is a very good way of working through an emotion. Yelling, for example, may be cathartic, but toning is more helpful in grounding the emotion in the body and moving through it in a way that is really therapeutic. Also, staying with the sound allows it to shift or change, so that one begins to sense what it is in the background that wants to happen. It is vitally important to note what happens in the body and what images occur simultaneously, and to follow these processes also. Arnold Mindell offers helpful suggestions for doing this in his book *Working on Yourself Alone*.[9]

Another way of working with sound is a form of what Jung called active imagination, a process of assimilating unconscious contents through some form of self-expression. The aim is to give voice to parts of the personality normally not heard, thus creating a mode of communication between consciousness and the unconscious. In some ways the process is like dreaming, except that you are fully awake.

Active imagination can take place spontaneously or can be induced by concentration. One way is to personify a content of the unconscious. You focus on a figure from a dream, for example, until the process of concentration begins to animate it. Then you carefully observe any changes in the image. These reflect the psychic processes in the background.

Conscious participation in the process is the next step. It may be in the form of a dialogue in which you talk and interact with the figure. In turn, you listen carefully to its response. You are often startled by a point of view different from your conscious one. This stage includes an honest evaluation of what you have learned about yourself and a commitment to act on the insights. Participation also may include giving another dimension to the unconscious content through drawing, painting, sculpting or movement. Something goes on here between creator and creation that contributes to a transformation of consciousness.

I experienced a similar process with sound during a tone and breath intensive workshop sponsored by the Institute for Music, Health and Education. Don Campbell asked me to do a vocal scan. As the sounds in the scan began to become animated, he coached me to turn them into a song (without words). He took me by the hand and led me around the room. My eyes were closed, so I did not know where I was until he asked me to sit down. I felt a piano bench under me. He then accompanied on the piano the sound that came out of me. Afterwards I knew that what came up from my own depths was a song that I never would have guessed was there or could be expressed by me. Feedback from the group reinforced the experience.

That night I dreamt that I was at the ocean where I was staying in a cabin similar to one I had been to recently where I had to bring my own kitchen/cooking utensils. There had been a minor earthquake and something happened to my cooking utensils so that I could not get them back. I felt the dream showed me that something had shifted and that my psychological processes could no longer cook in the same vessels.

I could not forget this experience and go on as if it had not happened. I had to continue using sound as a form of expression. I felt somewhat inhibited in making sound in my apartment. However, I discovered a fairly uninhabited beach where I can sink my feet into the sand and give myself full range of self-expression. I go there often. I have a song which I feel to be a true expression of my soul, which isn't present to me in my normal state of consciousness. I can easily tap into the song after some moments of toning. I have been experimenting with the spontaneous expression of tones, sounds and melodies. Movement often follows automatically.

Instrumentalists know the art of improvisation, but they may fear it because they have invested so much of their time in playing the music of others. Yet instrumentalists have their *own* songs waiting to be found. We need to turn inward, trusting our innate ability to break into that soul world which is the background of both personal and universal music. The purpose is to claim our own innate music, our own musical birthright.

I am now aware of how important it is to keep my voice "tuned" and "toned" for the sake of expressing my own soul, *not* for the sake of a performance. Pir Hazrat Inayat Khan wrote: "The body is an instrument, the most sacred instrument, an instrument that God Himself has made for His divine purpose. If it is kept in tune and the strings are not allowed to become loose, then this instrument becomes the means of that harmony for which God created man."[10]

Analysts need to be much more attuned to their own voices, as well as to those of their clients, and to develop the capacity to hear all that the voice communicates about our overall physical, emotional, mental and spiritual states. We may in fact get a more accurate picture of individuals by listening to the tone of their voices rather than to their words. This necessitates developing a listening awareness in relation to the vibrational energies within the space of the body.

We can accomplish this awareness only by becoming involved in experiential work with sound and tone. We also need to listen to the best music from other cultures, recognizing that the condition of the soul and the richest values of each culture are reflected in the music. The physiological effects of sound should be studied as well as the spiritual. For example, the singing of Gregorian or Tibetan chants is a form of respiratory yoga, producing sound frequencies that charge the cortex and result in pronounced physiological effects that contribute to the health of both the singers and the listeners.

In the Beginning . . .

I have often quoted James Hillman as saying "In the beginning was the Word, and the Word was image" and Don Campbell as saying "In the beginning was the Word and the Word was sound." Are these not two sides of the same coin coming together today in the search for a new paradigm by some of the "new scientists"? The idea of morphogenetic fields, as proposed by biologist Rupert Sheldrake,[11] for example, regards organisms as instances of undivided wholeness. Sheldrake does not differentiate between physiological and psychological structures. An organism is complete within itself and maintains its form amid changing circumstances, with its characteristic internal structure and vibrational frequencies. Jung put forth the idea of the psychoid unconscious in 1946, referring to a level of the unconscious that is completely inaccessible to consciousness. It suggests archetypal imprinting of the physical and inorganic world, and by the cosmos itself. Previously Jung had been concerned with archetypal configurations in the realm of human thoughts and emotions and of instinctive and organic life. Here Jung proposed the bridge to matter in general and the possibility of an underlying unity between psyche and matter.

This unity is evident in Cymatics, the acoustic field where the archetypal nature of sound can be clearly seen. In Cymatics experiments with vibrational effects and wave phenomena reveal typical structural patterns and dynamics. A musical tone becomes a "visible" figure in a concrete material (matter). Experiments have been performed with various materials such as water, alcohol, various oils, paraffin, powder, viscous pastes and iron filings. The material is "excited" by a tone, and a pattern emerges, which can be observed. These formations are created by sound. At the same time they are the creation of the natural vibrations in the liquid itself and are seen flowing and pulsating while simultaneously fitting into a pattern of symmetry. The formations always display uniform characteristics and are extremely regular with regard to number, proportion and symmetry. The results depend upon the properties of the liquid or substance, its quantity, and the frequency and amplitude of the tone. It makes no difference whether the substance is vibrated as free drops, in shaped vessels or as a film. Changes in amplitude abruptly produce different patterns.

The details of these formations can be observed as they appear, and the experiments can be repeated. The phenomena are subject to definite laws. Nature produces this form only and no other. These vibrational effects, which are so comprehensively ordered, are called *harmonic*. From a Jungian perspective, we would see this as archetypal patterning inherent in nature.

Hans Jenny, in his detailed studies of Cymatics, concludes that sound is primordial; it is the creative principle. Sounds can be seen as forces which can shape the world. A comprehension of the wholeness of vibration or oscillation gives us an instrument for bringing clarity to our view of the physical nature of the world. Jenny suggests the procedure for pursuing these mysteries: "By letting sounds, noises, musical tones elicit their effects we have discovered perfect systems of order comprising numbers, proportions and symmetries. These systems are not rigid figures but pulsate, flow and undergo transformation; they weave textures out of their polarities and metamorphoses. They grow in intensity to become phenomena manifesting 'everything' in patterns where orderliness prevails in spite of all the kinetics."[12] Jenny asks, "Where does a Beethoven Appassionate or a Mozart Jupiter symphony come from?" He states: "It is not aesthetic descriptions, explanations and cultural commentaries that are required here. Indeed, in our view, when an Appassionate is written, the systems of order, the proportions of the melodies, the symmetrical variations, dynamics and configurations all belong to one and the same cosmos. . . . The work must take us back to its *Urgrund* . . . to the generative, creative, ever-active primal cause."[13]

Vibrational energy is an analogue of Jung's concept of libido as psychic energy. Jung dealt with human drives as manifestations of energic processes that have measures of intensity. He wanted to provide as thorough a view for psychology as he saw in the physical sciences' theory of energetics. Accordingly, he observed that the psyche has a natural tendency to maintain a balance, just as the body is a self-regulating system that maintains its equilibrium. If one watches the meandering design of his or her dream life over a period of time, a sort of hidden regulating or directing tendency becomes apparent. A long series of dreams begins to mirror successive steps in a planned and orderly process of development—what Jung called the individuation process. Here he observed the natural drive within the psyche to restore the balance and provide material necessary to produce wholeness in the personality.

The organizing center, from which this regulatory effect stems, Jung called the Self. It is the inventor, organizer and source of dream images and creative inspiration. Whenever an encounter with the Self takes place, the ego is encompassed by the nonego, and a change in the personality takes place. Jung knew these experiences to be numinous or divine and to carry the feeling of timelessness, eternity or immortality. For Jung, the *immanent* God made itself known directly through the symbols of the Self in the form of images and sounds. Thus Jung demonstrated the capacity for self-transformation of the human personality.

In the musical world, Beethoven exemplifies this potentiality. At the end of his life when he was deaf and almost completely solitary, he wrote music that expresses the most profound depths of the human soul that any artist has as yet conveyed. In his last quartets he communicates a higher state of consciousness. The movements radiate, as it were, from a dominating, central experience characteristic of the mystic vision, and they present to us a vision of life. Here is surely an expression of the Self in sound.

The Therapeutic Use of Sound

Analysts involved in the care of souls are engaged in a prolonged encounter with what is broken and hurts, that is, with psychopathology. *Psyche* means *soul, pathos* means *suffering,* and *logos* has been interpreted as *image* or *sound.* Therefore, one may say that psychopathology is finding the images or sounds of the suffering of the soul. Therapeutic practices necessitate giving full attention to pathologies. In 1945 Jung wrote in a letter, "But the fact is that the approach to the numinous is the real therapy and inasmuch as you attain to numinous experiences you are released from the curse of pathology."[14]

My initial experiences with elongated vowel toning and breath brought me face to face with my own pathology. Something was slightly awry, for I was not quite getting to the deepest levels of the work. It was not until I admitted to taking a sleeping medication that the mystery was unraveled. I felt secretly guilty about this because I have a bias against medication if it can be avoided. I had confessed my use of it in analysis for a long time, but no suggestions or work seemed to help me overcome this. I don't recall receiving any suggestions from my mentor as I became involved with tone. Something was simply working! On my own, I went cold turkey on the medication and have never taken it since. It seemed miraculous that my addiction was suddenly ended. I surmised that the experience of toning helped me to plumb those boundaries to the unconscious on a more cellular level. I have always been a night person trying to live in a day world. I feel that the use of tone helps me to be more flexible in adjusting my rhythms to a schedule that is not natural to me.

In order to facilitate further my own therapeutic work, in 1989 I arranged to do some sessions with the staff at the Institute for Music, Health and Education in Boulder, Colorado, on their sound or vibratory table. The table resembles a massage table, but speakers are built into the entire table so that what one experiences is a sonic massage. The design of this particular table was developed by Don Campbell. It is a very unusual and profound experience to hear music through skin conduction and bone conduction, as well as auditorily. Through the therapeutic use of sound in this way, it was possible for me to connect more readily with my own body, to move through very deep emotions and to work with spontaneous imagery that occurs during this process.

I now have a sound table in my own therapy practice. I use it whenever it is appropriate in the ongoing analytic work of a client. It has helped clients to move through deep experiences of grief, to access memories including those of abuse, to experience spontaneous images arising from the unconscious and to assimilate dream work into their bodies. Often it is helpful simply to experience letting go and allowing whatever wants to come up to do so. There is no set expectation so clients are free to follow their own inner processes. In many cases it is extremely important for people to be in touch with their bodies in this way. In addition, I am able to observe where blocks are in their bodies. Sometimes parts are so deadened that one does not even feel the vibrations there.

I have, for the most part, used the recordings suggested by the Institute which are helpful in inducing general and deep relaxation and visualization. Ethnic music is also helpful. I try to use sounds with which my clients are not familiar, so as to minimize their personal associations connected to a piece of music.

These experiences with sound occur at a deep level, both psychically and physiologically, so this work initially needs to be processed in a nonverbal way. I usually request that a client go for a walk following the session and connect in some way with nature. Then it is helpful to discuss the experience during the next analytic hour.

Full Circle

I feel that my work with sound has helped to revitalize me as well as to deepen the dimensions of my work. It is still seminal. I look forward to continued experiences and study that will take it further. The recognition of music as an essential arena in which the numinosum breaks through has challenged me to give it attention equal to that which I have given to dreams and visions. It also provides the bridge to matter—it is a way of helping us become *embodied,* through experiencing the vibrational energies as well as the psychic energies necessary for wholeness of body, mind and spirit. Hence we truly come *full circle.*

Endnotes

1. Jung, Emma, *Anima and Animus,* Spring Publications, Zurich, 1972, p. 36.
2. McGuire, William and R. F. C. Hull, eds., *C. G. Jung Speaking: Interviews and Encounters,* Bollingen Series XCVII, Princeton University Press, 1977, pp. 273–275.
3. Ibid.
4. Ibid.
5. Adler, Gerhard, Ed., *C. G. Jung Letters* 1: 1906–1950, Princeton University Press, 1973, p. 542.
6. Jung, C. G., *Psychology and Religion: East and West, Collected Works* 11, Bollingen Series XX, Princeton University Press, 1958, p. 7.
7. Otto, Rudolf, *The Idea of the Holy,* Oxford University Press, 1923.
8. Drury, Nevill, *Music for Inner Space,* Prism Press, 1985, p. 33–34.
9. Mindell, Arnold, *Working on Yourself Alone,* Arkana, 1990.
10. Campbell, Don, *Music, Physician for Times to Come,* Quest Books, 1991, p. 320.
11. Sheldrake, Rupert, *A New Science of Life,* Shambhala, Boulder and London, 1981.
12. Jenny, Hans, *Cymatics, Volume 2,* Basilius Presse AG, Basel, 1974, p. 184.
13. Ibid.
14. Adler, *C. G. Jung Letters,* p. 377.

22

The Tomatis Method:
Auditory Retraining Through Music and Listening

JUDITH B. BELK

Listening is the ability to be fully present, to tune in selectively to desired sounds while putting other sounds into the background. Listening is different from hearing. Hearing relates to the auditory system's acuity for passively received sound. Listening is an active information processing skill which may be a foundation for academic, social and vocational success. Listening is a voluntary perceptual operation which encompasses focusing on specific details while simultaneously suppressing effects of distractors.

Clinicians who work with individuals who have communication or learning disorders traditionally use cognitive or tutorial methods to reduce speech, language, oral motor or learning problems. That is, the client's intellect and ability to imitate are called upon to upgrade skills in these areas. However, some clinicians, frustrated by the slowness and inefficiency of conventional methods with some clients, have begun to turn to other approaches which rely on nonverbal, sensory-based procedures.

Tomatis's Contributions

Alfred A. Tomatis, a French ear, nose and throat physician, began developing his method in 1947, based on observation and studies in audiology, phonology and psychology. The name "audio-psychophonology" (A.P.P.) describes basic principles inherent in the method. His techniques aim at understanding and structuring the control circuits of voice, speech, language, social-emotional functioning and behavior via listening.

The Tomatis Method is particularly concerned with the process of language integration based on the relationship between *audition* (hearing) and *phonation* (producing sounds or speech). The latter is directed by the auditory system, which is limited to the reactions of the brain/mind as the center of thought, feeling and behavior. The interaction between audition and phonation that he discovered is called the "Tomatis Effect," for which he was honored in 1960 by the Academies of Science and Medicine in Paris.

The Tomatis approach aims at heightening the client's "engagement" abilities. It provides an "auditory tune up" or "earobics," a term (coined by Paul Madaule, director of The Listening Centre, Toronto) to move clients beyond their listening-related difficulties. The Tomatis program integrates music into a unique treatment format to link these five components that make up the Chinese verb "to listen"—ear, eyes, heart, you and undivided attention.

One of Tomatis's fundamental contributions to psycholinguistics states that any modification occurring in the auditory system leads to a modification of verbal output. That is, better listening can improve speech. Tomatis has shown that enchancing auditory functioning by means of the "Electronic Ear," a device which filters sound, improves an individual's listening ability. Enhanced vocal and verbal output follows.

Such training also modifies attitude and improves motivation. Tomatis also clarified the mechanisms of cybernetics that govern the audio-vocal system. The cybernetic loop is the circle that guides all operations occurring in the course of laryngeal function. This circuit, which involves both hearing and speech, constitutes the basis of training processes. By modifying audition—that is, by acting upon the cybernetic circuit—a self-monitoring mechanism is immediately started that allows an individual to readjust the quality of voice, speech flow, rate, rhythm, clarity, intonation, loudness, as well as choice of words, word sequence and sentence structure.

In traditional speech-language therapy, teaching self-monitoring has been challenging to client and clinician, although less so lately because of the use of computer software programs that provide visual and auditory feedback to the client. In the Tomatis program, self-monitoring is enhanced for the client through use of a microphone, earphones and visual input. Training with these devices follows a period of passive listening to awaken the ear's alertness and awareness, as well as its fine-tuning abilities.

Tomatis detected that the right ear circuits have specialized action, and he gave a new orientation to the term *laterality*. Starting with considerations about cerebral dominance, Tomatis hypothesized that cortical mechanisms influence the entire nervous system. He introduced the revolutionary idea that the initial potential of the human ear is to charge the cortex. He holds that the ear transforms auditory stimuli it receives into neural energy and passes this energy to the cortex. This is the basis of his auditory training method.

Listening

For Tomatis, "When hearing gives way to listening, one's awareness increases, the will is aroused and all aspects of our being are involved at the same time. Listening is intimately tied to ability to actively attune the ear to a particular sound signal, with both intention and desire to communicate."

Aspects of listening may be characterized as follows:

(1) Listening which focuses outside, on what another is saying or on what is going on at home, at school or at work.

(2) Listening which focuses inside, checking, monitoring and reproducing correctly what one hears, especially one's own speech and voice.

(3) Listening to the body, skills related to the vestibular system of the ear, affecting balance, coordination, body image and spatial orientation.

Listening-related difficulties may develop well before school age, such as during a mother's stressful pregnancy, in a difficult birth, from a mother's depression or as a result of early separation from the mother because of adoption or foster care. Other causes may include emotional trauma and loss, recurring ear infections, congestion from colds and allergies, other health problems or a physical disability. A public school music teacher claims to recognize which students had been rocked as infants and which not. The latter lack a sense of rhythm, she notes. All of these situations may prevent the ear from becoming an effective channel of sensory stimulation to the brain.

Tomatis has learned that certain types of music, primarily many of Mozart's compositions, inherently offer an invitation to reexperience the development of listening, a process which should begin in utero. Tomatis's auditory training methods create opportunities for the client to make sense out of sounds heard and instill motivation to enhance communication and learning skills.

Two phases, each consisting of thirty hours of special listening experiences, comprise the basic Tomatis program, with the second phase provided in two blocks of fifteen hours each. The first treatment phase consists of passive listening to Mozart and perhaps to a filtered recording of the client's mother's voice. Phase two experiences provide the client with opportunities to actively experience the sound of his or her own voice. The latter supports development of self-monitoring, the cybernetic loop mentioned previously.

"Listening to Mozart is like a kiss from my mom," enthused a six-year-old youngster to her teacher. "Music—it's my lifeline," exclaimed a teenager floundering through high school but uplifted by music. A musician pictures Mozart reaching through the heavens to create his lofty music and to invite and escort the listener on similar journeys. Another listening skills client, an architect, noticed for the first time that within music there is frequently a conversation—a pattern of utterance followed by response. This client described the effect of listening to Mozart as follows: "It makes you want to listen carefully so you don't miss anything said. Now I know where learning to take turns comes from!"

All types of music may induce mood and energy changes, some positive and some not. Some music contains patterns which are unhealthy for the body. Steve Halpern (1985) warns against certain rock and pop music. The standard rhythm in such music is a "stopped-anapestic rhythm—short-short-long-pause pattern." Halpern notes that this rhythm "tends to confuse the body and weaken the muscles. . . . The rhythm of much rock music may tend to override the more subtle signals of the body's own communication system. The end result is that the body's system is confused, the heart's response is irregular, and the body gets weakened. Electronically filtered music, on the other hand, may induce positive changes in an individual's engagement or entrainment with the others and with the environment.

Case Histories

What are outcomes of the Tomatis program?

"Mom, remember when I used to tell you that I always felt empty and never even had a container for my emptiness? Since the listening program, I've been growing a container!" A twenty-three-year-old young man with severe language, learning and behavior issues, reported this recently, after he had completed a second phase of the

Tomatis listening development program. His difficulty relating to others and to verbal information was in keeping with his difficulty connecting with himself. His family had tried a number of conventional educational and therapeutic modalities. None had yielded the gains of Alfred Tomatis's gentle invitation to listening, which relies on music and voice filtered through an electronic device to stimulate more efficient functioning of the hearing system. His treatment outcome is common among Tomatis clients.

Another case history illustrates the notion of music reaching to the core. A teenager finishing a phase of the Tomatis program began to be aware of conflicting feelings. On the one hand, the filtered sounds of his adoptive mother's voice brought up early memories of a time when he was young, memories which for survival he needed to bury. On the other hand, he was keenly aware of the message portrayed in a class he was taking to redirect teens who had been arrested for stealing. He had learned that people come in two categories: those who do not steal and those who are criminals. His difficulty juxtaposing the sweet, innocent child within himself with the teenaged criminal caused him to become despondent and confused. Finally, he was ready to go beyond the foundation of inner speculation encouraged by his Tomatis consultant.

For several days after his last few Tomatis program sessions, this young man worked with a music therapist who understood the dynamics of the Tomatis program. With her help, the teen composed two songs, weaving into the lyrics key issues in his life. He learned that he was being fully listened to and that he was empowered to deal actively with major issues rather than to deny their existence or to harm himself physically. He took great joy in presenting the following song to his listening therapist and family:

I try to think of things I've done and how to stop the beating of the drum. But it just won't stop. Boom! Boom! Got to stop the beating of the drum. Boom! Boom! The beating of the drum. Boom! I sneak into rooms and take what I want. I run and stash it in hopes I won't get caught. But that same day or later on, I always hear the beating of the drum. Boom!

As I look ahead to what the future has to offer, it scares me to think of the possibilities. But I know that my friends are there to help. They may not be many but they're enough. I like my friends. I can tell them my secrets and my problems. They don't put me down or make me frown. They always are glad to have me around. If I want to keep them I must change the beating of the drum.

His parents, incredulously observing the transition their son was making, insisted that all the conventional counseling sessions the family participated in for years had never cut through to the heart of this young man's dysfunction. However, as a result of his music therapy, the teen was functioning in a more facilitated state, and more issues had risen to the surface. In the future, he may have a very productive experience in conventional counseling dealing actively with critical issues. Combining the Tomatis listening program with music therapy assisted this client greatly.

Reviewing three-hundred and fifty files of individuals seen over the past five years at the centers for Communication and Learning Skills in Tucson, Arizona and Oswego, Oregon, led to the compilation of a composite list of positive changes to similar kinds of music therapy reported by clients and/or their families. Generally these clients had been treated for learning disabilities, auditory processing problems, attention deficit, attachment discord, dyslexia or autism. Positive changes reported include the following:

greater "presence"
increased interest in verbal/nonverbal communication
longer attention span
wider range of interests
increased curiosity
increased compliance
expanded utterance length, type and complexity
increased alertness and awareness
improved concentration and on-task behavior
increased initiation of contact with others
spontaneous expression of sincere affection
generally appears happier, less irritable
decreased seizure activity
improved sleep patterns
normalization of appetite
decreased incidence and severity of headaches
improved language comprehension
increased independence
improved sequencing ability
improved ability to deal with abstract vs. concrete
improved speech clarity
improved self-modulation of vocal quality, loudness and pitch

improved recognition and consideration of others' feelings
improved posture
improved motor coordination and balance
improved orientation in space
less sensitivity to bothersome sounds
improved ability to tune in to desired sounds and dismiss others
increased tolerance level
improved ability to represent concepts through art forms
improved turn-taking abilities
willingness to taste a wider array of foods

A particular client may achieve some—or occasionally none—of these changes.

Other Brain-Ear Approaches

HemiSync, a sound technology introduced by The Monroe Institute, facilitates synchronization of electrical wave patterns in the brain's left and right hemispheres. According to Monroe's research, to accomplish the optimal condition for improving human performance, HemiSync uses "blended and sequenced sound patterns which can gently lead one into focused, whole-brain states of consciousness." (Monroe, 1989)

Suzanne Evans Morris, Ph.D., a speech-language pathologist who specializes in oral-motor and feeding issues in children with handicaps, uses HemiSync music tapes to "create a more sustained focus of attention for learning, facilitate a more balanced activation of the information processing capabilities of both the right and left hemispheres of the brain, reduce fearfulness and negativity which interfere with the learning of new skills, increase focus of attention, and reduce tactile defensiveness and sensory overload."

In addition to incorporating HemiSync tapes into her therapy, Evans Morris also uses a variety of audio tapes for quiet, centering music and uses folk music with simple melodies and clear rhythms. According to Evans Morris, "Folk music is a bridge between childhood and adulthood. Both traditional songs and those composed in the folk style contain elements which are attractive to both children and adults." The choice of music used in therapy is very important, Evans Morris says. "Specific types of music are highly effective in creating a special background that maximizes learning within therapy programs or in the classroom. When music is appropriately selected, it can increase the effectiveness of whatever we do with a child." Evans Morris has noted increased effectiveness of her therapy since adding specific types of music. In general, Evans Morris concludes, "Music creates a bond, a special envelope of sound enfolding the child and clinician, which brings them together in a shared journey of learning." (Evans Morris, 1991).

Miracles?

Should results achieved by music-based programs be considered miracles, or are they predictable on the basis of what is reported about music's energizing and organizing effect on the brain?[1] The thought that something might be miraculous generally makes scientifically-oriented professionals uncomfortable. *Miracles* comes from *mirari* (to wonder at) and from *mirus* (wonderful). In theology, a miracle is an event or effect which apparently contradicts known scientific laws and is, therefore, thought to be due to supernatural causes. Miracles are beyond the ordinary, beyond anything within the usual framework of cause and effect. Tomatis clients generally develop greater ease in connecting with others and in refining communication and learning skills. Do these positive changes noted in clients in music-based therapy programs reflect "miracles," or have we learned some critical factors about music which allow us to expect remarkable changes?

Experience with music as a medium which reaches to the core of the human being suggests that music serving as a lifeline may be predictable. With additional rigorous research we may understand more about the dynamics of music-based listening programs which permit or prevent change. One study being designed will look at pre- and post-treatment functioning of the brain as measured by brain mapping. Known more technically as neurometrics, this quantitative method of attaining, analyzing and interpreting brain electrical activity produces evidence of the extent of the anatomical and functional integrity of the brain. Data from this proposed study may assist in correlating observable behavioral change with brain activity.

Predictability will be increased when results obtained from statistical analysis of research data provide a basis for developing a profile of clients well-matched to specific treatment programs for listening-related problems. Researchers are coming closer to achieving such a tool.

Research may also reveal what it is about music that provokes such change for a young client with autism to prompt him to say at the end of treatment, "This is very better!" Another autistic child, when asked how his ears were after Tomatis treatment, answered, "Surprised!" We are getting closer to understanding such seemingly miraculous changes.

Endnotes

1. See Tomatis's interpretation of the neurophysiology which underlies his system in "Overview of the Tomatis Method," in Gilmore, T., Madaule, P., and Thompson, B., *About the Tomatis Method*, Toronto: The Listening Centre Press, 1989.

VI

Sound As World Healer

There are different ways of listening to music. There is a technical state when a person who is developed in a technique and has learned to appreciate better music, feels disturbed by a lower grade of music. But here is a spiritual way, which has nothing to do with technique. It is simply to tune oneself to the music; therefore helpful it is to a spiritual person; but at the same time one must not forget there are lamas in Tibet who do their concentrations and meditations while moving a kind of rattle, the sound of which is not specially melodious. They cultivate thereby that sense which raises a person by the help of vibrations to the higher planes. There is nothing better than music as a means for the upliftment of the soul.

Hazarat Inayat Khan

There are really no words for music. All the writings, viewpoints and debates on music do not have the power of beauty and inspiration of a simple lullaby, a Mozart symphony, "Amazing Grace" or "The Rose" sung by Bette Midler. The highest aspirations toward the universal tone, or the simple heart of the love and the joy of expression, can never be measured by a logical device. It is the soul inspiriting the body—through the intangible energy of sound beyond the senses—that calls us to genuine awareness of "essence," "principle," "source," or the "fiery monad."

This last series of articles come from the inspired, heart-written stories of futurist Barbara Marx Hubbard, concert pianist Loren Hollander, and composer Kitaro. They weave the knowledge of sound with the miracle of hope through the medium of art.

23

Will You Join the Dance?

Music, Vision and the Future

LORIN HOLLANDER

Music. Music . . . there are simply no words! Words cannot adequately convey what music can express. Music deals with the highest reaches of the human soul. It touches the most exquisite, elegant crystalline structures of creative vision and is imbued with the glory of human emotion. Every area of human experience is touched and expressed most beautifully and wondrously by music: the yearning, the searching, the joys and sorrows, hopes, dreams and visions, the emotions, the symbolic mythology of the unconscious. Yet music is more.

In the realm of the body, music undulates with the sense of pulse, dance, rhythmic movement. In doing so it becomes a metaphor for all life. Much of nature manifests rhythmic movement: the seasons, the ebb and flow of the tides guided by the cycles of the moon, the heartbeat, the breathing, the life cycle of plants, the beat of wings, life and death itself—all are rhythms, cycles, pulses. Our sense of well-being is intimately entwined with our sense of rhythmic pulses.

And vibrations! In the universe itself, the spiraling of galaxies, the birth and death of stars, the planetary movements, light—all these are manifestations of waves, vibrations, cycles. Indeed, the creation and explosion of the cosmic egg at the Big Bang, its expansion through unfathomable distances and speeds—falling back eventually to its original primordial state, only to explode again—appears more like a Big Twang! Our scientists are finding that the ultimate ground of being appears, in fact, to be vibration. We are discovering at every turn what Pythagoras sensed: there is a Music of the Spheres. The universe is shaped the way it would sound. Interestingly, at both the microcosmic level explored by quantum physics and the realm illuminated by astrophysics and cosmology, our most poetic scientists use music as the metaphor to best describe what they are discovering.

Music is a profound mystical science. The musical keys and the twelve tones—like the twelve disciples of Christ, the twelve tribes of Israel, the twelve astrological signs, the twelve gates of New Jerusalem—are deeply intuitive ways of knowing oneself. Profound mysteries are unlocked in music. Herman Hesse in *Steppenwolf* speaks of Mozart as one of the "Immortals," masters who in their creative process poked their heads out and glimpsed what Hesse termed the "Icy Ether"—a transcendent, ineffable vision of absolute beauty and truth, the ultimate reality spoken about so often in mystical traditions as to be what Huxley termed the "perennial philosophy." This is a vision of reality that C. S. Lewis says in *Perelandra* is too definite (precise and exact) for words, being the very structure and implicate order of the universe. It is what was experienced by Mozart, Bach, Goethe, Jesus, Gautama Buddha, as well as countless gifted children, people awakening from sleep, and those making the transition from this life to the beyond. It is the "Eternal Golden Braid" that Hofstatter speaks about in *Godel, Escher, Bach,* the glorious patterns and topological foldings of crystalline perfection upon which the great mathematical concepts, graphic tessellations, and fluid musical structures of those giants are shaped. The great cathedrals are built upon the reflection of its laws, and the mosques are decorated with its intricate designs.

Music can have very personal meaning. When I was a boy of five I used to play for my grandmother the last movement of Beethoven's *Tempest Sonata,* quite slowly, as almost a fatal lullaby. She used to hold me in her arms and sing it to me if I awoke frightened at night. Years later, while she was already entering the next world, in the state we call on this side a coma, no one and nothing could make contact with her. So it was for many weeks. But when I visited her, I would sit on her bed, hold her in my arms and sing the *Tempest* lullaby in "our tempo." She would always open her eyes, make unmistakable contact, and smile. It is remarkable that if I sang too quickly, it missed her entirely. There does not seem to be a tempo too slow.

In my travels I often visit the hospital wards for the dying. In playing or singing certain of the most touching and powerful works of Bach, Schubert, and Mozart, I have experienced scenes similar to those depicted in the remarkable film *Awakenings*. Their apparently unreachable dying souls were suddenly transformed into a room full of undulating, humming, and singing angelic beings. Hospital staff members where I visit continually tell me that these scenes when I play are some of the most powerful of the rare moments when they see living spirit in the bodies of those who are at the place we will all be too quickly.

It has happened so often that I have ceased finding it remarkable. While I am practicing at the piano, the personality of a friend or family member will suddenly be vividly present in my consciousness, seemingly pressed against my face. At that moment the phone will ring and the caller will be the person I envisioned. One night I was performing the Schubert *Sonata in B-Flat Major,* opus posthumous, a work Schubert wrote several weeks before his death, ostensibly with full knowledge that he was dying. In the slow movement, the personality of one of my closest friends, a very great young composer named Richard Danielpour, felt present to me for a few moments on the stage. The following day Richard told me that at approximately the same time as the concert experience, he had a similar awareness of my being in his room. That night he dreamt that Schubert visited him, though *dreamt* does not capture the correct experience, since Richard felt vibrantly awake at the time. Richard and I have had so many experiences in which we have both been in the presence of Spirit within moments of each other that we no longer find it unusual. We take these mutually shared visions as miracles with a half-hidden purpose.

Gustav Mahler on his deathbed, when he appeared to be sinking into a final state of shallow breathing, suddenly and with intense, almost superhuman energy, as the legend goes, sat up with eyes wide open and pointed, wildly excited, to a place in the distance. He said with a sense of wonder, "Mozart!"

My own father, while a wonderful musician, never believed in such possibilities. Five years ago when he died, at the point where the life monitors were barely indicating any activity, my mother described that he tore out the tubes and monitoring needles and suddenly sat up, almost stood, eyes staring wildly, and pointed "out there," before his body fell limply back on the bed.

255

Rumi, thirteenth century Islamic master, wrote:

> We have heard these melodies in Paradise;
> But while we are thus shrouded by gross earthly veils,
> How can the tones of the dancing spheres reach us?

If we can learn anything from the linking of the ancient magic of the shaman and the recent confirmation of this reality in music psychology, it is that the forces of rhythm, the power of song, and the fluid infrastructure of music conceptions verify the truth of the shamanic experience and illuminate a world of great power and mystery. Since experience of this is the key to the creative process, it is perhaps the most important area of scientific study for new age humanity. Our very survival depends on our grasping the fundamentals of this visionary realm. Through it we may nurture the creativity of our children through education and demonstrate to those still unconvinced that the study of music is as necessary to life as fresh air, fresh water, and abiding love.

Music expresses the divine, yet music may be most important because, as John Blacking pointed out in *How Musical Is Man?*, it prepares us for the task of learning how to love.

But there is a curious and tragic paradox. The importance of music (as well as the other arts) in education has been questioned. The concept of "back to basics" does not include music and art as "basic." Music is not recognized in our society, as it was in classical antiquity and in numerous other societies, as the center of education from which all else flows, the basic among basics. Music programs are being removed from many schools throughout the United States. They are seen as frills and are considered expendable. Obviously the profound psychological and spiritual importance of music is not generally understood. The paradox lies in the fact that there is a growing body of worldwide psychological and cognitive research that confirms beyond question the psychological importance of music and art experience for children. This information is not filtering down to the local level where many decisions on the content of school curriculum are made. (Much of my own work presently involves bringing this information to the communities that I visit in my concert travels and sharing it with those who have the power to effect a change.)

The current crisis in education and the growing realization that we may be damaging the creativity and emotional well-being of our children offers an unprecedented opportunity for music education to reestablish a central position in education. The relevant psychological research demonstrates how, specifically, musical experience is related to the creative and emotional processes on the deepest somatic psychological levels and how music can help heal the neurotic distortion of these processes.

The hope for the future of humanity rests on the ability of the next generations creatively, brilliantly and with vision to lead us into the future, solving the seemingly insurmountable problems and glimpsing the next steps in the unfolding of consciousness. Without creative solutions there is no hope. We are at that turning point; we could head towards either extreme of Fullers' "Utopia or Oblivion," or embrace either of Teilard de Chardin's "adoration or annihilation." To quote Peter Russell once again:

If we are to avert a collective catastrophe some fundamental changes will be necessary . . . in our awareness and appreciation of the world. A new world view is needed, one that is holistic, nonexploitative, ecologically sound, long-term, global, peaceful, humane and cooperative.

What is needed are humane leaders, humane professionals, humane educators, humane artists, humane scientists. Where are such transformed, creative people to come from? What has the power to effect such a change? What will nurture the creative vision necessary to turn around a world possibly heading towards its own destruction?

Music. Music can be the key. Music changes us. Music allows us to discover parts of ourselves we had not discovered before. Music, perhaps alone, can transform us. Listen to Bach's *St. Matthew Passion* or the *B Minor Mass;* such gentle beauty, wonder, and awed acceptance changes one's experience of being!

Equally important is the power that music can have in education. A child who hears and plays great music can discover and keep alive many aspects of the creative process and is in the position to learn firsthand about the nature of emotion, as well as about the creative blocks and fears that will plague him throughout the years of school.

This is where the fields of music therapy (and the other art therapies, especially dance therapy) and ethnomusicology teach us something very valuable about all creativity. When a person feels unfairly criticized, frightened, or resentful, the body tenses and clutches. One also begins to withhold communication and ceases to share emotions positively with others. One can remain in this state of creative deadness for a lifetime. Remarkably, as it turns out, that which IS the experience of the clutching in the body—what has in fact tightened or becomes stuck in this state (as many musicians have discovered and as music psychology is confirming)—is the sense of pulse, rhythm, and dance, a human experience nearly as basic as the heartbeat and breathing. When we also consider the withholding of communication and emotional expression that accompanies this, we realize that the creative and emotionally stifled person has stopped dancing, singing, and expressing. The golden opportunity for music education lies in the discovery that the path back to creative wholeness involves learning again to dance, sing, and express. (Harry Haller had to learn to dance to approach enlightenment in *Steppenwolf*.) It appears that at the deepest psychological levels, stifled creative fluidity in any area of human endeavor, as well as much emotional suffering, can be healed through the depths of the musical experience.

What does this mean for musicians and music educators at this time in history, when the very survival of humankind depends on nurturing the creativity and humanity of our children? Music has the power to accomplish this! How basic can you get! "Will you, won't you, will you, won't you, will you join the dance?"

We are in complicated territory because music education itself is sometimes as guilty as areas of other education in inadvertently stifling creativity in young people. We must be careful because children are perhaps most deeply sensitive to criticism when expressing themselves through art. There has also been much concern recently about the education of our most gifted young musicians. Many suffer bitterly from stress and competition. Somehow in the conservatory or music school they become overly concerned with the speed and accuracy of their playing and the skills to win competitions and form careers. They lose sight in their playing of the warmth, humanity, emotional expression, and joy of making music. How to nurture the future poets and visionaries among our young artists is a major challenge.

An opportunity lies in the fact that, as musicians and music teachers discover how to break through their own blocks and fears, they may become able to lead others in this process. The enlightened music teacher has the potential to heal creative ills and nurture humane values and emotions in children. They also could nourish the love of music in the young people they touch, who are our future audiences. Music education can equip our future teachers and performers with the necessary insight and psychological wisdom to carry out this important work.

So here we are in a world with awesome possibility that is drowning in mediocrity and destroying itself with violence, greed, and stupidity. Our system of education is removing the study and experience of the very art form that could nurture the creativity to transform the situation. The study of that art itself is suffering from the same imbalances that so much else in life suffers from. There are no easy answers. What we do know is that we must depend on our children to guide us safely home. How will we prepare them for this work? What will we share with them to give them the vision? It is like the lullaby in Bach's *Christmas Oratorio* where Mary sings to the baby Jesus:

> Sleep my dearest, enjoy your slumber
> And wake again to save us all!

Music. We hold the key. Bringing music to children and children to music is as important a task as can be found in our world today. Symphony orchestras employ musicians who can be of tremendous value to education in the community. Music programs for children must become a top priority for our symphony orchestras. Often performers get frustrated and feel that educational programs are expendable or are at least subordinate to the complicated work of putting on subscription concerts, but that is like a farmer neglecting to plant the seed. Nurturing a love of music in children, while developing a future audience, should be our most burning concern, not only for the music business but for a society starving for meaning, greatness, and beauty. With the recognition of the crisis in education and the growing understanding of the importance of music to the creative and emotional life of a child, there is opportunity as never before for the articulation of the importance of great music in our communities, our families, our hearts and souls.

24

Music for the Birth of Planet Earth

BARBARA MARX HUBBARD

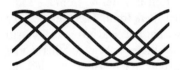

Music is the most direct, universal and immediate mode of lifting us into higher awareness. Through vibration, harmony, tone, melody and meaning, music stimulates within us direct experience of expanded reality.

Two experiences with music, sound and tone deeply influenced my life and gave me a clue to their miraculous power, especially in the realm of spiritual awakening.

I have never been "musical." I could not carry a tune and could hardly keep a beat. Yet my first profound spiritual experience held within it a tone which literally connected me to all Earth-life and still reverberates in my inner ear, beckoning me onward to reexperience it again and again.

This experience occurred in February, 1966. I was taking a walk in Lakeville, Connecticut, on a fiercely cold day, so bitter that the air froze in my throat and it hurt to breathe. I bundled up and headed out upon the windy path around an isolated hill.

I had been reading Reinhold Neibuhr on the subject of community. He quoted St. Paul's famous phrase, "All men are members of one body." I thought about the birth of Christ . . . it was one story that changed the world. I realized that we are one planet. We must have one story. I asked the universe a question: What in our age is comparable to the birth of Christ? What is our story?

With that question my mind's eye pierced the blue cocoon of Earth. I was witnessing ourselves—all life on planet Earth—as a living organism. We were gasping for breath as pollution clogged our planetary lungs. We were in pain as children died of hunger and weapons exploded in our body.

The planet and we were one. We felt the pain of the whole body of earth as our own. Then suddenly the movie sped up. I saw something new—a flash of extraordinary light, more radiant than the sun, gleaming in outer space. And with that light I heard a tone, a low, resonant vibration that seemed to be the sound of the Earth itself. It entrained the human breath and held all of us in a single field of consciousness.

With this sound and light, in one instant, we were aligned. We saw the light together; we heard the tone together. Love began to pulse in waves of irresistible attraction through the nervous systems of the members of the one body of Earth. The tone grew louder. We began to chant and sing. A planetary beat arose; the mass media picked it up as news. Mass healings occurred. We were transfigured.

All at once, billions of people aligned in the magnetic vibratory field of light and sound. We opened our collective eyes and together saw the light.

I heard the words, "Our story is a birth. What Christ came to Earth to reveal is true. You are all members of one body which is now being born to universal life. GO TELL THE STORY, BARBARA!"

I was kinesthetically imprinted with this experience. I have been "telling the story," for all these years. I believe we are, as a planetary body, actually approaching such a birth experience. It will be a real event in real time, perhaps in the lifetime of the generation living now. For as the crisis could destroy us in this time frame, so a collective shift of consciousness to oneness could evolve us.

Carol Rosin and I have invented a small musical instrument called an "Attuner." It is a little pitchpipe tuned to D♭ embellished with a heart-shaped Earth. D♭ is a tone is resonant with the vibrations of the Earth. Perhaps if one percent of the human race "attunes" with the same vibrational frequency and the same thought of world peace and love to all beings, the collective consciousness of the Earth will change definitively. I sense this is true. To have fifty million people sound their Attuners simultaneously, in a "birthday party for planet Earth," thereby helping to induce a "natural childbirth," would create a mindful, metaphoric transition from our separated to our unitive state.

My second mind-altering musical experience occurred during a

261

large stadium concert in Montreal. A symphony orchestra was behind a transparent screen. William Shatner from *Star Trek* was reading excepts from Arthur Clarke's *2001: Space Odyssey*. The orchestra was playing the music from the film. Ron Hays, the video artist, was projecting extraordinarily beautiful images on the screen. Violet, gold, silver undulated in sensuous mandalas in rhythm to the space music, pulling us inward to the infinitesimal and outward to the infinite.

The words, images and music began to activate the collective psyche of the audience. Gradually we were in resonance together. My heart felt as though it were beating in unison with the thousands of people. We began to sway, to move as one body. I lost consciousness of myself as a separate being.

As the concert was ending, something began to rise up. First it was clapping, then it was shouting, then it was roaring, then it was all-out, uninhibited rejoicing with ecstacy.

The audience was in "ec-stacy," standing outside themselves in a transcendent experience. For that instant we all were consciously members of one body being born toward universal consciousness. The combined stimulus was awakening us to the experience that we are connected within one living system.

The sounding continued. We did not want to separate, to go back to our former condition. We wanted to stay connected continuously.

Having had the planetary birth experience many years before, I felt this event, and many others like it, are calling us to an actual Great Awakening, collectively, on a global scale, that will communicate via mass media—the nervous system of the planetary body—a set of events that will in fact change the world.

These expanded reality experiences, often induced through music, have been shared in a variety of ways by millions of people in "flashes" of unitive experience. It is my belief that they are in fact planetary intuitions of an actual birth process that is happening in Russia, Asia and throughout the world.

Let's track recent events like "planetary LeBoyers," midwives of a peaceful birth, imagining that our planet may be one of billions of life systems in the universe, undergoing a natural transition from its terrestrial to its universal phase of life. Our labor started, perhaps, in 1945 with the explosion of the atomic bomb. A still self-centered, womb-oriented, geocentric species had gained the power to destroy the world—or to build new worlds.

In 1957 we launched Sputnik and in 1969 landed on a new world and saw from the moon that in fact we are one body. What the mystics had revealed to us is actually and pragmatically so. Then came the first Earth Day in 1970. We were the first generation to be responsible for the future of our world as a whole. The environmental movement began.

Then in 1985 the television special "Live-Aid" music linked two billion people for eighteen hours as one global heart/mind/body on the subject of hunger. The planetary child "awoke" in response to the needs of its body. Great popular musicians came together and sang a song that united the world in compassion: "We are the world . . . we are the children."

In 1986 John Randolph Price initiated the first World Healing Meditation. In his book *The Planetary Commission* he called for fifty million people to meditate, pray and contemplate on one single thought of peace simultaneously at noon Greenwich time, December 31. (Remember the Attuner!) He said this alignment would shift the collective consciousness.

In 1987 music returned to the scene. The Harmonic Convergence was the largest spontaneous grassroots demonstration the world had ever experienced. Countless millions set out to meet at sacred sites around the world to "harmonize" with the Earth, to "resonate" with one another, to attune with spirit.

The mass media was mystified. "Why," news people asked, "are all these people humming?"

It seemed there was a natural impulse to sound the same tone, to hear the same sound, to speak with one voice, saying/singing/breathing as one body—We are one. We are whole. We are good. We are universal. The people of the Earth, despite the current leadership, sounded the tone of the coming planetary "birth."

In 1988–1990 totally unpredicted events began in communist Eastern Europe and in the Soviet Union. Perestroika. Glasnost. The grip of totalitarian dictatorship crumbled. Gorbachev, a genuine world leader, and the people together changed the world. The irresistible evolutionary impulse for human rights and freedom triumphed over the tanks and the bureaucrats.

Now we are approaching the year 2000. The environmental crisis has become our obvious birth crisis. We can no longer continue overpopulating, polluting, starving, over consuming, and defending at the expense of life itself. We must recognize that we are all members of one body, and that our future as one is infinitely greater than as separate and warring peoples. We are at the very threshold of our birth, either by violence and disease, or through a shared experience of oneness.

I believe that music, sound and auditory vibration make up a critical factor in the graceful path to the next stage of evolution. I hope we will all deepen our process of attuning with one another, with nature and with the creative spirit of the universe, however we understand it. I hope that we will work together for world events in which music, words and images can in deed and in fact join us together as one body in our lifetime.

(To learn more about attunement, write Barbara Marx Hubbard, P.O. Box 813, Larkspur, CA 94977-0813.)

25

The Beat of Heartsongs:
An Interview by Don G. Campbell
KITARO

I remember flying into Virginia Beach, Virginia, ten years ago to speak at a national conference. A friend had just given me a cassette, prescribed to be excellent for relieving the stress of air travel, O'Hare airport and sitting in seat 47F. I truly glided into town on "Silk Road," a beautiful soundscape of easy listening, heart-centered melodies. Since that time, the music of Kitaro has always insured me a warm and spacious experience.

Recently I was invited to spend the Fourth of July evening with Kitaro and his friends near Rocky Mountain National Park in Colorado. In a wonderful Alpine setting overlooking a lake, his collection of ancient and modern instruments was ready to release "spirit." As we spoke, Kitaro shared many stories and ideas about music. Here is part of our conversation:

Don Campbell: Here I am, surrounded by a hundred ethnic percussion instruments and some huge Japanese ritual drums. What can you tell me about them?

Kitaro: They are very, very old, over five hundred years old and made of very hard wood the Japanese call *kaocki*. I think it is harder than redwood. Originally a Shinto drum, this one could as well have been used by the Buddhists. I think this one [pointing to another drum] weighs over two hundred kilos.

Don: Magic, miracles and mystery are three things that are the power of music. Did you feel there was a mystery or a magic in sound and music when you were a child?

Kitaro

K.: I didn't know about music's power when I was very young. In high school it was my dream to be a professional tennis player.

D.: So when did the magic of music begin to touch your heart?

K.: The first experience was after high school. I started performing rock music for fun. In the beginning it was not so deep, but as I listened and played, music came as a "strange" feeling. Not "strange" as weird, for it was a good feeling for me. It was not the imaginary world, but the actual world, actual sound. Music's power was a surprise.

I was seventeen when I started my musical life, and in my twenties I changed my style. Between seventeen and twenty I was playing many different kinds of commercial music. I changed my music life—changed my style, changed my equipment—and suddenly I came to a new step. I can't explain it but it felt like fantasy or a kind of dream. In my music my feelings would sometimes get elevated.

In my twenties, I changed my life and my music because I started to meditate and to practice yoga. Before my twenties I was doing *tai chi* and similar things. I still do *tai chi* as dynamic and musical meditation. As I sit here, this is meditation. As I move, this is meditation for me—a higher state, elevated and extended.

Music is magic. Music can make what people call a miracle. But it is not a miracle. There is a reason! Music has a power, but it's not only the music. *Sound* owns the power.

D.: Sound has the power, and it has a reason?

K.: Yes. It is like these large *taiko* drums. They have low end sounds, low, deep frequencies. It is hard to play these drums for very long. Physiologically it is stressful. I have to put some spirit into these drums, because if I "just" play sounds nothing happens. If we can put some spirit into these drums, we can make it happen—a magic, a miracle, a reason happens. When you are behind these *taiko* drums, you can feel the air when I hit the front side. There is spirit!

D.: How do you prepare so that spirit can come to you in performance?

266

K.: Through meditation. To take a walk, this is meditation. To take a bus, this is meditation also. To eat is a meditation. To sleep is meditation.

D.: So you feel the spirit is always there?

K.: Always! When I started these meditations I could feel a fire or light inside of me. I go into this fire and this light. I am doing this today.

D.: In a concert have you ever experienced a special miracle or suddenly a grand spirit?

K.: Before I started the world tours I did concerts in Japan. Many years ago at the holy mountain of *Ontake,* the mayor of the village was worried about rain. He asked me, "So, what about the rain?" He thought I was a kind of rain man. Then I said to him, "You don't have to worry about the weather if our energy is going to the right spot." There were over ten thousand people in the audience, and there was a heavy rain before the show. I said, "Don't worry about it." Thirty minutes before I started the show, the rain stopped. During the show there were clear skies with no clouds, a shooting star and a full moon! Five minutes after the encore the heavy rain started again with a big thunderstorm.

The next year they were worrying about the weather again. I said, "Don't worry about it." It was almost the same situation. This mayor was so surprised. "What happened? What happened?" He had experienced the power.

For eight years, I have been doing a ceremony at Mt. Fuji near Kamikuishiki, annually in August. It is at the second level of Mt. Fuji where there is still forest and farmland at a 3500 foot elevation. I was trying to play the *taiko* drums from sunset to sunrise at the full moon. The first year I did this alone. I played eleven hours and didn't stop. It was as if my mind stopped working and there was a feeling of an altered state. My hands were bleeding with many sores, and I finally decided to tie the sticks on my hands. People said, "You're crazy!" I said, "Thank you." I was just saying thanks to Mt. Fuji and this Mother Earth.

When I lived at Mt. Fuji almost fifteen years ago, in 1974 or 1975,

267

I would experience strange and mysterious feelings. I could see Mount Fuji through a window of my house. I spent a whole day and a whole night watching the mountain as if it were a big picture. I watched the fall colors change. It was very beautiful.

At night there was a big rain and thunder storm, and a large mud slide moved the house. When I felt the big rain and heard the thunder, I just closed my eyes, yet I could still see the image of Mt. Fuji perfectly! I stayed sitting in the same place. In the morning the window was facing the opposite direction!

I was afraid that I was going to die, but I sat in the same place day and night in meditation. That was the first major spiritual experience for me.

D.: In an experience like that in meditation, do you hear melodies or music?

K.: Sometimes I hear melodies, but I don't always know how to get the melody through my body into my fingers. My body has to move to translate it. I have experienced, in a trance-like state, my fingers automatically moving to create music.

D.: So, many times when you compose, you feel the music just coming through you?

K.: Yes, but I don't think about music because I just want to get into the inner state of beauty and play. And after that we just listened to the sound and said, "Oh, this is nice!"

D.: Have you received letters or heard stories about experiences people had when they heard your music?

K.: Yes. Mostly Japanese people have written to me about their experiences listening to my music. Once a high school girl was trying to kill herself by cutting her wrists, but did not do it perfectly. She came to my house to visit, and I talked to her about many things. We listened to my music as we talked. She changed her life at that time. Her depression and distress left her as she listened.

D.: Do you know stories about using your music in hospitals?

K.: Yes, in San Francisco, at the AIDS clinic. A friend told me that people who were there liked my music because it allowed them to relax. People can find some lights through music when they are near death. Until people die, they continue to search, and the music helps. I think spiritually they are looking for a life after death—the next step.

D.: So it gives them the power to heal spiritually in the process of dying and transformation?

K.: Yes. But I am also afraid to die. I have experienced the death of friends. One musician was driving my car as I walked behind. He fell into the canyon in Japan as I watched. That experience caused me to question many things and resulted in a big change for me. After he died I decided it is not my human life, it is the spirit life.

D.: Have you ever worked with an instrumentalist?

K.: I am thinking about Mr. Kojima who was a fiddler, a violinist. He worked with me for almost five years. He was handicapped and was trying to develop his strength. Before I met him he was living reclusively trying to escape from people. I said, "Come on to the mountains," and we composed a couple of songs. He composed a song for the planetarium. When he started to work with me, his life was changed.

D.: So, by being around you, with your music, one enters a kind of music therapy or music healing.

K.: I need the music. The music is for me. Sometimes my mind is crazy and speeding. Then I decide to listen to music. I cool down and think more simply and deeply about things.

D.: How did you develop your music ability?

K.: I never learned music. Today I am composing music for films. I can do the orchestration, but it is not normal composition for me. I have a good friend who is a great composer and conducts an orchestra. I can't do that. I can do my own sound process and style, even though I do not know musical language.

D.: But you compose from the heart and you orchestrate with your ears. Is it more like painting?

K.: It is like painting, constructing sound with chords. I am like a sound carpenter. I like making many things, though now I am making a jacuzzi house with friends.

D.: You have a natural genius that is developing. It takes magic of heart and simplicity and knowledge. You are giving us many gifts. Do you think everyone is musical?

K.: Yes, I think all people can make music and make sounds. We could all feel the sounds, the kinds of vibrations in people, animals, trees and grasses. When most humans do feel these good sounds, then this world will be in peace and be healed.

Today we have many kinds of music for entertainment. Some of it is too violent and excites people to be violent and to make war. I think composers and musicians have to learn responsibility, because the music's power is incredible. The musicians have to know this.

D.: Which of your albums or your music do you like to listen to?

K.: I like the music from my beginnings, "Astral Voyage," the first one. I have a tape that I did before I released "Astral Voyage." There are a couple of songs that I like from the early times. Sometimes I go in a different direction and am searching. By listening to the beginnings I come back to the same spirit, and then I can find the right way.

When I changed to the music life, the power of music changed my life. Music is a huge power which struck my brain.

D.: Like the *taiko* drum?

K.: Yes, and because of it I have dedicated my life to music. I think that people can change their lives. The way most people live today is not enough. Life is too fast. People want to change. It is the small things that make the difference, communication between people. If we can change these small things in society we can be free.

I like people and I like to talk with people. It is easy for me to talk with music. With the sound, even if we don't understand, we can feel. Talking with words is sometimes confusing.

D.: That is beautifully said.

K.: This is one of the very, very important things! For example, Don, I can't speak English very well. My vocabulary is small. But you and I can feel the spirit. Even if we don't say anything, we can feel. This is the music we can feel. I like books, but I think music is more direct. With words we sometimes misunderstand, but with the sound we can know. I think we can combine words, visuals and sounds, and that would be the best situation for the future.

D.: What will you compose next?

K.: I am trying to write an opera for next season based on the theme of Kojiki. The Lyon Opera Company in France is going to do this. My friend, Kent Nagano, is a conductor there. It is a seventh century story about the creation of the earth, from the beginning of this planet. It is basically from Shinto.

Shintoism is not a religion; it is, I think, a way of life. Buddhism came to Japan through Shinto. It is very old. In the beginning when Buddhism came to Japan they made the Shinto and Buddhist temples in the same place. They lived together and split the money offerings. It is the same today.

Many years ago people asked me, "Shintoism or Buddhism?" I don't know. Both! When I was born my parents already had Shintoism and Buddhism. I feel that Shintoism is not a religion, it is just life. *Shintoism* means naturalism, the Path. It is very close to Taoism and Buddhism.

D.: Is there anything else you would like to say to your American listeners?

K.: I like to talk to the people with music. I think it is my mission to talk to people and be one who helps connect people—different cultures and societies. I am so happy to be here. I have many friends in America. I am working with many people to make new music for all of the world, for the trees, for everything!

D.: Alleluia!

K.: Alleluia!

Postlude

The miracle of music, the energy of creation and transformation, was expressed in a spontaneous lecture on eternal being by composer-philosopher, Kenneth G. Mills. *Music and Miracles* closes with these ideas to consider:

When you finish finding the soundness of you, YOU will find that it is only a tone that is relevant to the Principle Tone of the eternal diapason of being that is without *any* conduit. It has to be from the full experience of the unimagined and its unlimited nature.

As long as the mind is trying to define a tone that accompanies itself, it is indeed being disciplined to realize its limitations.

The Tone that you will discover will allow you to find the Root and the System from which I AM launched. In That Rejoice.

Index

Index